ART OF REPORTING

ART OF REPORTING

Monita Singh

CENTRUM PRESS
NEW DELHI-110002 (INDIA)

CENTRUM PRESS
H.O.: 4360/4, Ansari Road, Daryaganj,
New Delhi-110002 (India)
Tel: 23278000, 23261597, 23255577, 23286875
B.O.: No. 1015, Ist Main Road, BSK IIIrd Stage,
IIIrd Phase, IIIrd Block, Bangalore-560085 (INDIA)
Tel: 080-41723429
Email: centrumpress@gmail.com
Visit us at: www.centrumpress.com

Art of Reporting

First Edition, 2010

ISBN 978-93-80836-20-1

PRINTED IN INDIA

Printed at Mehra Offset Press, Delhi

Contents

Preface

Most large cities had morning and afternoon newspapers. As the media evolved and news outlets increased to the point of near over-saturation, afternoon newspapers were shut down except for relatively few.

Morning newspapers have been gradually losing circulation, according to reports advanced by the papers themselves.

Commonly, news content should contain the "Five Ws" (who, what, when, where, why, and also how) of an event. There should be no questions remaining. Newspapers normally write hard news stories, such as those pertaining to murders, fires, wars, etc. in inverted pyramid style so the most important information is at the beginning. Busy readers can read as little or as much as they desire. Local stations and networks with a set format must take news stories and break them down into the most important aspects due to time constraints.

Even in those situations where objectivity is expected, it is difficult to achieve, and individual journalists may fall foul of their own personal bias, or succumb to commercial or political pressure.

Similarly, the objectivity of news organizations owned by conglomerated corporations fairly may be questioned, in light of the natural incentive for such groups to report news in a manner intended to advance the conglomerate's financial interests.

Printed news had to be phoned in to a newsroom or brought there by a reporter, where it was typed and either transmitted over wire services or edited and manually set in type along with other news stories for a specific edition. Today, the term "breaking news" has become trite as broadcast and cable news services use live satellite technology to bring current events into consumers' homes live as they happen. Events that used to take hours or days to become common knowledge in towns or in nations are fed instantaneously to consumers via radio, television, mobile phone, and the Internet.

Chapter 1

The Changing Reporting Environment

Advertisements for jobs in journalism sometimes indicate that familiarity with a particular software package would be of advantage to applicants. In general this applies more to positions in broadcast newsrooms, online work or sub-editing positions than to other journalistic jobs. But it's a reminder of the growing importance of computer skills in the newsroom.

Broadcast newsrooms use automation systems—including Avstar, ENPS, Newsboss and Newsroom—to manage different aspects of newsroom administration. These systems handle wire copy, format scripts and bulletin run-downs, archive stories, and compile rosters.

In print-based newsrooms, the dominant production system is CyberGraphics, with software packages such as Photoshop, QuarkXpress, and Photostation also in widespread use.

But these computer systems and packages are just one of the ways in which digital technologies are changing the news.

Others include:

- Advances in the quality of lightweight, non-professional, digital, video cameras.
- The availability of small, lightweight, digital audio recorders.
- The ability to dock audio, still camera and video recording devices with computer terminals.

- The ability to edit, on screen, audio and video, either for broadcast or compression and transmission over the Web.

The Sydney Morning Herald, Stephen Hutcheon, notes that his paper makes "no distinction between how you write for the paper and how you write for online" and that the audience seems to be quite comfortable with newspaper stories on the Web.

And where once he would have said that HTML skills were important, new content management systems that newspapers use have dumbed down the interface used by journalists, though he still believes "some basic understanding of HTML does come in handy". At the same time, other skills have become more important. Stephen says that to work online "you have to be a jack of all trades" and that includes being able to use graphic and multimedia software programs.

REPORTERS' CHANGING ROLES

The changes that technological advances have the potential to make can be put into two broad categories. On the one hand, they make it easier for newsrooms to report for more than one delivery system and, on the other, they can be used by journalists to undertake more of the technical functions of reporting.

The first of these two categories allows the horizontal integration of traditional print and broadcast plus the newer online delivery systems. The second might be considered the vertical integration of reporting functions and its most obvious applications are videojournalism and photojournalism.

Photojournalists have been common for a long time among the ranks of foreign correspondents. Within Australia they are most likely to be found in regional and small suburban newspapers, and some magazines. But even journalists who don't take pictures as a rule may find they are asked to take one from time to time, and being able to provide an entire story package (text plus pictures) is a considerable advantage for freelancers. So there are plenty of reasons why aspiring journalists should be acquainted with the basics of photography.

Videojournalism has been relatively common in the smaller US markets for many years where it predates the introduction of small, high-quality digital cameras. Reporters who shoot their own pictures in those newsrooms do so because it's cheaper than the conventional reporter and camera operator team and the style they employ is no different.

In 1998 an Australian news service, Central GTS/BKN, which broadcasts across South Australia's Spencer Gulf region and to Broken Hill in New South Wales, began using video-journalism for daily news production. Its reporters worked with pocket-sized cameras and edited their stories using desktop software. The stories didn't always look as polished as those on other regional services, but, since the station was the only one in its market, it could afford to take that risk. Text versions of its stories were posted on its website.

By 2001 the metropolitan and regional networks had made their own, tentative moves towards using videojournalism, especially for covering outlying areas. There were reporters using video cameras in northern Tasmania, and on Queensland's Surf and Sunshine coasts. The reportercum-camera-operator had also established a toehold in current-affairs reporting, particularly with the SBS international-affairs programme *Dateline* and in some of the foreign coverage on the ABC.

In 1999, *The Sydney Morning Herald* appointed a videojournalist to provide video reports for its websites. The following year *The Age* did the same. There has also been a slowly developing trend towards reporters working for both television and radio or text and audio and so on.

Over the period 2000 to 2002, the ABC combined its formerly separate radio and television newsrooms in a process of "co-location". ABC reporters can now be assigned to either radio or television stories or can be asked to produce the same story for both media. The radio copy is sent through to the corporation's online newsroom, located in Brisbane. While the ABC's broadcast reporters don't have to write the online editions of their stories, the mere fact that their reports form the basis of the online versions has forced them to pay attention to issues that once didn't concern broadcast journalists, such as accurate spelling and grammar.

Knowing that their material will be fed to an online site creates other pressures on reporters too. For example, broadcast news reporters have traditionally conducted interviews assuming they need only the audio or video for a couple of soundbites. But where the entire interview may be fed to an online section, reporters have to pay more attention to the structure of their interviews.

At the time of writing, most Australian commercial broadcast journalists still worked for either radio or television. Like newspapers, most broadcast stations maintained websites to augment their traditional services. But few commercial services drew on their newsrooms for content other than stories already broadcast.

Instead, some ran AAP material while others used their site as a portal to other news providers or simply posted Journalists in textbased newsrooms can now find themselves working with digital audio and images as well. Reporters at AAP use MiniDisc recorders and audio editing software.

From 2000, AAP reporters began using MiniDisc recorders and desktop editing software to record and edit audio bites for radio clients and for syndicated online news services.

AAP reporters also snap digital still photographs from time to time, though this is most likely to be if they are on remote assignment or working in a remote bureau rather than in one of the metropolitan ones and, as of 2002, there were no plans to have the agency's reporters take video pictures as well.

The AAP experience is instructive because agency news production is, by nature, high speed and broadcast scripts on their website. As a result, few Australian commercial radio or television reporters were expected to write for online delivery.

NEWS AGENCIES

On the other hand, the distinction between working with text or sound and pictures had begun to blur at the news agencies. The skills required of journalists in a multiple media newsroom can be seen at Bloomberg where reporters work with combinations of text, audio and video. The financial news service, Bloomberg, is another news organisation that has embraced multimedia reporting.

At Bloomberg, reporters writing for the text-based service also record audio for use on the organisation's radio arm. The same journalists can be expected to conduct interviews for Bloomberg television. But writing for moving pictures and producing stories high rotation compared to the pace in metropolitan print newsrooms.

The priority for reporters is to generate text stories for subscribers as quickly as possible. As one staffer noted, the "more bells and whistles" are added to a reporter's job, the more it slows down their primary function, which rather defeats the purpose. Like agency work, the online news environment demands high speed, which is not always compatible with multiple-media reporting for television is considered a separate skill from writing text, and is handled by a different group of people.

So how technically savvy will reporters of the future have to be? AAP's Editor in Chief, Tony Vermeer, says it just expects its journalists to keep up with the times and that means they need familiarity with PCs— an ability to store, manage and manipulate files including text, audio and pictures. He says journalism has to adapt to changes in the media at any given time.

We often say to people here that the story is the story. Obviously, the most important thing to do is to tell the story. And now there are different ways of telling. The story can be better told sometimes if it's not just a text story but has a digital audio element and a picture element and, one day, a video element. But I often wonder about the resources needed to produce video. It's almost an extra layer of skills that you can't really integrate with the day-to-day jobs that we're doing at the moment.

Photographs are often described as the "windows" to a page, and this is definitely the case with newspapers, online sites and magazines. Journalists working on regional or suburban newspapers, small magazines, or websites, may have to take their own photographs, as well as write news stories. Even journalists working on larger regional/ metropolitan newspapers, and magazines, should have a good knowledge of photography so that they can offer suggestions about shots to go with their stories.

This section is aimed primarily at those who will be taking their own photographs. As a journalist, or photojournalist, your primary concern should be on the content of the photograph—on the "story" that you are trying to tell with the image. Of course, good technique is also important, though a picture can be technically perfect but still not newsworthy.

According to Deputy Photo Editor for The Herald & Weekly Times, Ian Baker, a photograph should first and foremost be relevant to the news angle of the story. Obviously the pictures have to match the story—that's the first thing. The photograph should also have power, should have currency, and capture the emotive moments or the action of an event. Of course, like the words, it's even better if it's an exclusive.

Any sort of protest was hot on the police agenda at the time. I got an anonymous phone call about the protest from the Friends of the Earth to say they were staging a sit-in outside the office of the Minister for Natural Resources. This was within days of the demonstration at Richmond Secondary College where police made a baton charge on demonstrators. So Peter went up there and the police moved in and used these pressure points. Even though television had the same action, they didn't "freeze the moment" the way Peter did in his powerful photograph.

They said, "If they don't know what they're doing, they can cause long term black-outs and even psychiatric problems. " The next day the police held a press conference to announce that they had to outlaw the tactic on the strength of that medical expert advice. So the power of the picture brought a directive that changed their whole operational procedure. Ian says getting a Walkley Award-winning photograph was a combination of a lot of factors.

Certainly it was a credit to Peter Ward's tenacity. Obviously, there's also a certain amount of luck to it. But having the nous to set yourself up, to be in the right position and have the right lens on, and then ultimately your skill as a photographer—all counts. Now that's just something that comes from years and years of experience.

There are, of course, many other technical and content guidelines to keep in mind—but these are the most important. Editor of *The Courier*, Stuart Howie, says it would be extremely unusual for them to use a "pretty picture" with no news value. He says, "We want the photograph to tell a story."

The characteristics that apply to news stories should also be used to judge news photographs. First and foremost, they must be of something *new* and have currency. Some newsrooms do keep some photographs on file that are timeless, in case an assigned photograph doesn't come through and there is a hole to fill.

These are generally human interest or softernews photos which have a longer life. But news photographer Lachlan Bence says he prefers to take photographs as they are required and that "fresh is best". He says a news photographer has a unique style compared to that of a studio photographer. "You don't have the luxury of time. You have to walk in, sum it up in 30 seconds—the lighting, the mood the subject is in—and then get the shot."

While photographs of prominent people such as the Prime Minister or a celebrity will always be newsworthy, it's important to include different faces whenever possible. For instance, a common complaint from readers of regional and rural newspapers is that the Mayor and the local Member for Parliament appear too regularly.

People are also generally more interested in what is happening in their own street or town, than in national or international stories, and are keen to see pictures of people they know or with whom they can identify. Photographs should also have "character" or "animation". This can be as simple as capturing the smile on someone's face, or the speed of a racing car.

COMPENSATING FOR ERRORS

Despite rapid technological advances, there is *nothing* that can be done with a blurry photograph. Many newsrooms now have auto-focus SLR (Single Lens Reflex) cameras to avoid focusing errors. If you want to focus manually, turn the focus ring until you have a sharp image, turn past this point to ensure it is the sharpest focus possible, and then return to that point. If you have a straight line in the shot, use this to focus. If you are taking a photo of a person, animal or bird, focus on their eyes.

On the other hand, wide shots (i.e. shots that take in too much and have too little detail of the subject of the shot) can be cropped and enlarged. And digital photography does allow a certain degree of correction of underor over-exposed shots—that is, images that are not exposed to enough light and are too dark (under-exposed), or are too bright or have been exposed to too much light (over-exposed).

SHOTS TO BE AVOIDED

Many newspapers have understandably banned certain photographs. These are the ones they consider to be boring and unappealing. Among these are "hand shaking", "cheque passing" and "award giving" photographs.

Another type of photograph also best avoided is the kind described by Tim Harrower as the "execution at dawn". This is when a "clump of victims" is lined up in a row, looking suitably grim and uncomfortable, "to be shot" for a photograph. Such pictures usually include "club members, sports teams and award winners". Harrower also recommends avoiding the "Grip & Grin" photograph (groups of people holding medals, trophies, cheques). He suggests photographers "move out into the real world, where these people actually *do* what makes them interesting".

"Grip and grin" pictures (left) can become repetitive and boring.

Instead, capture the subject doing what makes them newsworthy.

Less is generally more when it comes to photographs. In other words, don't overcrowd the shot. If the local team has just won the regional soccer competition, don't try and crowd the whole team into the photo. All you will have is 11 small blurry faces that you can't see very well. It will have much more impact and appeal if you choose a couple of key figures (the captain and the number-one goal kicker) holding the trophy aloft.

It's like the introduction to the news story—you just can't fit in all the five Ws and H. You need to pick the most interesting point. There are, of course, exceptions here. For example, you might want to show the size of the crowd at a match and thus need to take a wide shot that shows little detail, but takes in the scale of the event.

Photographer Donna Edwards says you must use charm to be the one who is in control of the shot. She says it's all about diplomacy and that you walk a very thin line. I'd never take a photo that I knew I couldn't use. Quite often you'll go to what is supposed to be a group shot of three and all of sudden there are 20.

You need to ask "Why are we doing this?" or "Why have we gone from three people to 20?" And, if there's no logic to it, a lot of the time you can explain there are ways to make a better photo.

You know what you need and you have to remember the photograph will probably only be used as a six-by-four in the newspaper—it's very rare for it to be bigger than that, so if there are more than three heads they are going to be very small when the photo is published.

CAMERAS AND LENSES

Single Lens Reflex (SLR) cameras are still widely used today despite shifts to digital technology. SLRs, as they are commonly known, are those cameras where there is no difference between what the photographer sees through the viewfinder and the image being captured by the camera lens. Different cameras are characterised by the size of their film—from the common 35mm film used by SLRs to medium formats and large formats of up to 120mm.

At its most basic, a photograph is the exposure of film to light, so the better the lens or the more light-sensitive the lens, generally the better the photograph. Whether you're using digital or 35mm technology, your camera relies heavily on the quality of the lenses you use with it.

The ability of the lens to "collect" light is expressed in terms of f-stops (aperture stops) and the smaller the number or f-stop (usually indicated on the inside of the lens ring), the better the quality of the lens. For instance, an f2.8 lens would be of a higher quality than an f5.6 lens.

Many 35mm cameras are now sold with a standard 50mm lens, which is the lens width which most closely resembles the view seen by the lenses of the human eye. To obtain a wider shot, you might use a 28mm or 35mm lens. Or conversely you could go even closer to your subject using a telephoto lens of 100mm or more. You can use the larger lens to cut out any distracting background—as below.

180mm 100mm 35mm

The 180mm lens (left) allows you to cut out distractions and to get closer to your subject than the 100mm (centre) or the 35mm (right).

The telephoto lens can be very useful for a photographer who wants to take a portrait without getting too close—for example, in a dangerous situation such as a war zone or at the scene of an accident.

Sports photographers shooting from the sidelines will also use a telephoto lens.

Zoom or variable-focus lenses give you great flexibility, with a single lens offering views from a wide angle to a close-up (e.g. 30mm to 150mm) without moving the camera or the subject.

COMPOSITION

While you should be concentrating on the content of your photograph, it's important that the composition makes the most of your subject. The key point, or focal point—whether a person, animal, car or fire—should not be obscured. Look at your background. Donna Edwards says if you haven't got a good background then don't include it.

If you have a white-painted wall with venetian blinds, use your depth of field (the amount of the shot, or the depth into the photo, that is in focus) to get rid of it. In other words, blur your background by focusing on the face or the eyes. If you sharpen the face and blur the background, you will have a much more interesting shot.

As with the news story, the main point or angle should be emphasised and should be immediately obvious when you look at the photograph. Try to avoid including more than one key point or centre of interest in a photograph. Fill the frame with the subject (commonly called a close-up) unless you need to show the area around it.

For instance, if you were taking a picture of a runner who had just won a race, you could easily just take a close-up of the person's jubilant face. But if the person had won the race metres in front of everyone else, you might take a wide shot to show the large distance between the runners at the finish line.

These shots can be achieved by using two different lenses (as indicated) or one zoom lens which offers variable focal lengths. The other way to take these photographs would be simply to move closer or further away from the action.

There are two main formats for newspaper and online photographs: the vertical or portrait shot, and the horizontal or landscape shot (above).

Sometimes newspapers will also use a panoramic shot (a very wide horizontal) but that is more common in magazines, particularly where a photograph might be run across two pages (as a centrespread). Photographer Lachlan Bence says many tabloid format newspapers tend to use horizontal photographs, though unfortunately these are sometimes cropped to a square which is "a very boring format".

Many photographers believe a photograph should be composed in thirds. For instance, in a landscape shot, one third would be the ground, one third the ocean, and the final third the sky.

The four points where these lines intersect are the optimum positions for the subject of your shot—the places to which people's eyes are naturally drawn.

Try to avoid placing your subject exactly in the centre of the shot—it's not a focal point and it's just plain boring. But there are always exceptions to every rule. If you have a very strong subject—such as an extreme closeup of an interesting weather-beaten face—this may be best placed in the centre of the photograph. If a person is looking in a certain direction, or running in a certain direction, leave space in front of the subject in the direction they are looking or running, so that they are looking or moving towards the space in the picture.

When you are taking a photograph, there are key points at which to place your subject. To find these key points divide your photo—whether horizontal or vertical—across the width and down the length.

ANGLES

Donna Edwards says it becomes second nature to take a photograph from several different angles. "It's as simple as moving one metre to one side. Stand up on something to get height and to make it more interesting. Nice clean shots with a slight angle on them or something a little bit quirky about them are common in newspapers."

Donna says each newspaper has a different style and it's important to watch what others are doing. It's also common that the photographer won't know what the story angle is going to be so they need to capture a few interpretations of the story. There are always a couple of ways to take it:

It can all depend on the person. Assess the situation when you get there. You don't ever get told details like "this person is old and doesn't like their wrinkles" in advance. You go in cold each time and usually don't have personal details. So you have to make these decisions on the spot. If I had a dollar for every person who has said to me they don't like being photographed, I'd be very rich today.

Lachlan Bence says sometimes there's an angle that hits you in the face as soon as you walk in. "You'll do it and it'll be right the first time. You know within yourself that the one you originally took was *the* one, but you tend to take a few different angles, just to be sure."

How to avoid mistakes:

- *Take more than one photograph:* The professionals do! This particularly applies to photographs of people, as they may have closed their eyes or have a less than flattering expression on their face. Take several photos with different exposures and shutter speeds—commonly known as bracketing. Most newspaper photographers will use one roll (or its digital equivalent) for each shot required. Editors generally like to have a selection to choose from. Bracketing can be difficult with action shots, but most photographers (such as those covering sports) will use a motor drive and simply hold the shutter button down, or put their cameras on "Programme" and "Continuous", to ensure they don't miss the action. Remember also that, while a newspaper or magazine might use just one or two pictures, there's the potential for many more to be used on any related website.
- *Write down the details from each job while you are there:* This is essential and will save you a lot of chasing around afterwards. Don't forget to check you have the correct spelling of names and titles. It is amazing how quickly you forget what is on the shot if you

don't take down the details immediately. It is equally important to ensure you write the caption clearly and with all details. To avoid errors, Lachlan asks the subject to print their own name and details and then pins this information to the photograph and his own typed caption for cross-checking.

- *Avoid defamation:* It's permissible to take pictures of people in public places, but you need to ensure that any publication of the images does not defame anyone in them. For instance, one very serious example occurred when a man was photographed outside a courthouse at lunchtime and incorrectly identified as someone who was later found guilty of stabbing his wife. Journalists should also be aware of any privacy regulations in their state that might affect the use of photos. There are some occasions on which it's common courtesy to ask someone permission to photograph them for publication if it's possible.
- *Check the background:* Make sure the background doesn't intrude or distract. For instance, does it look as though a tree is growing out of your subject's head, or an aeroplane flying out of their ear? Also check the shot for other potential problems. If you are taking a picture of a woman who is sitting down in a short skirt or bending over in a low top, or of a man in short shorts, ensure there are no potentially embarrassing exposures.
- What film should you use? Where is the photo going to be taken? Is it an indoor or outdoor shot? This will dictate the type of film you use. Many photographers use faster film, such as ISO800, so they don't have to use flash. (Films have an ISO rating from very slow, such as ISO25—which needs a lot of light and a tripod—to very fast, such as ISO2400, which can handle very low light conditions.) You used to get a lot of grain with faster film but these days the technology is better, and you

can "push" the film. "Pushing film" means tricking the camera to make the film more flexible. For example, you may have ISO800 film but you set the camera film speed at ISO1600. This is only possible because film today offers a great deal of latitude. This is not possible if you have an automatic camera that reads the ISO rating for you.

- *Use a tripod:* If you have low light conditions and slow film, use a tripod whenever possible to stop the camera from shaking, particularly with long exposures (photographs taken in dark conditions using natural light can take several seconds before the shutter closes). Most people can only hold a camera steady for 1/90th of a second, or 1/60th of a second at best. Tripods are also useful if you have to take a group shot, as you can leave the camera in place while you move the group around.
- Should you use flash? Donna Edwards says she takes portraits and indoor shots using ISO800 film rather than a flash.

Flash is such a harsh light. I'd rather use daylight. It gives the photo more character with shadows. If you're using flash, it's a very flat light. It's like your party snaps when using flash leaves everyone looking like stunned rabbits. There's no shadow detail. I would prefer to use daylight. Bounce your flash off white walls or ceilings so it's not as harsh as straight flash, though this will drain your flash.

If you don't have a reflector you can improvise. Try using two pieces of white cardboard or even car sun shades. Sometimes flash, or fill flash, can be useful to light up a face and take away shadows if the person is wearing a hat, or has very dark skin tones. (Interview with Donna Edwards.)

- Do you have to travel for the shot? Always carry back-up equipment when you're travelling. Donna says she usually takes three cameras— a digital, a 35mm and a medium-format camera—when she's travelling for work. "Never put yourself in the situation of only having one camera which may fail.

Even with flash units—take more than one. Always take too much film or too many memory cards. You can always push film, particularly if you take 800. But you need spare batteries, spare cameras and spare memory cards."

- *Look after your film:* Never leave your film in the car or anywhere else it may be exposed to heat. Heat is light and light is heat. Store film in the fridge before it has been exposed, and even more importantly after it has been exposed but before it has been processed, when it is even more light/heat sensitive.
- Do not introduce the photographer from your newspaper/magazine as "my photographer". Make sure you introduce them as either "our photographer" or "the newspaper's photographer".
- Don't bring out your camera and start shooting as soon as you arrive— it can be very off-putting. Lachlan Bence says it's important for the photographer to talk to the journalist on the way to the job to understand the story, and then to chat with the subject when you arrive to build a rapport. If you are working as a photojournalist, you would be aware that most people are nervous about doing interviews, and about having their photographs taken, so initial care is important.
- *Stay out of the way:* Lachlan also says it's important to stay out of people's way—especially in the case of emergency services. For instance, firefighters at the scene of a fire obviously haven't got time to pose for a photograph. This is where a zoom lens (telephoto) can be very useful. It gets you close to the action without you getting in the way.
- Don't panic! Often you have to go in and set up and take a photo in ten minutes and people new to this tend to panic. Slow down and do all your mental checks. Make sure your camera is on the right setting. Donna says no one is in that big a hurry— they just think they are. It doesn't matter if they

have to wait two or three minutes, but it does matter if you don't get the shot. Check everything before you start.

- If you're shooting for the Web, try to avoid taking pictures that include a large amount of detail. The size of images displayed online can be quite small and since the screen resolution is just 72 dots per inch (dpi), any fine detail may be lost.

One of the results of technological innovation is that it is very rare today for a newspaper to have its own darkroom. Even if the publication is not using digital cameras (which input directly onto computer disks or cards), most newsrooms now have computers which are able to scan both negatives and photographs directly into the system (and later, straight onto the page onscreen).

So, press photographers using film often get local developers (photographic stores or even chemists in some regional areas) to develop the negatives.

DIGITAL TECHNOLOGY

Most newspapers in Australia now use digital photographic technology, and some only have digital cameras. Photographer of 16 years, Lachlan Bence, has seen *The Courier* move from large-format cameras, to 35mm SLR cameras, and now to exclusive use of digital technology.

Most newsrooms will ensure they purchase digital cameras that are the same brand, or of a compatible make, as their SLR cameras, so the lenses and attachments are interchangeable.

Ian Baker of The Herald & Weekly Times says their photographers have laptops and can set up landlines back to the office, so they can be out and about and send the "raw" images from the digital cameras back to the newsroom.

We've outfitted every digital camera with a mobile phone and Photoshop software on the laptop so the photographers can play with the image out in the field. But, if they're up against a deadline like a night football or cricket match, what they tend to do is get the raw images back to the office, and we can work on them back here. They have to compress them into a JPEG file to send to us. Freelance photographers can send in JPEG or TIF files to us. Most email servers have a limit of about two megabytes as an attachment, but we have a large filter here in the office, and you can adjust the image quality and reduce the amount of information in the picture to send it.

Chapter 2

Digital Alteration in Photojournalism

lmost all of the images that we see in our daily newspapers and news magazines today are digitized. As a new industry standard, digital-imaging technology is widely used by media in the United States. A 1998 study demonstrated that digital imaging was nearly universal in U.S. dailies whose circulations exceeded 7,500. The study found that "only 5 papers out of 225 indicated no digital imaging use, 78.7% were 100% digital, and 94.7% used digital imaging for at least 90% of their images". An earlier study showed that no newspapers had discontinued use of digital imaging once they had adopted it.

The trend of embracing digital-imaging technology by the media industry can be traced back to the late 1970s. This trend has the potential to reshape readers' conceptions of what is real. The credibility of photographs used in documentary contexts such as news stories, feature stories, the covers of news magazines, and documentary photographic books has been endangered because digital-imaging technology has provided convenient tools for media professionals to alter images. In the last twenty years, more and more examples of such digital-imaging alterations have been exposed to the public.

However, no scholars have asked readers what they think about the appropriateness of digitally altering images even though digital-imaging technology has been used in the print news media for approximately twenty years. Some studies have been published on newspaper or magazine photo editors' attitudes and their tolerance toward digital-imaging manipulation. Are readers concerned about such alterations? Are they welcoming, opposed to, or apathetic about them? As Kelly pointed out, "the full impact of digital-imaging technology on photography and on audience interpretation of photographic news reports is still in a state of flux." This is still the case today. Most of the time when readers are discussed, researchers only guess at their opinions.

To date, no industry-wide standards have been accepted regarding what level of digital-imaging alteration is acceptable. Since digital alteration mainly involves craftsmanship, a new type of worker is evolving who may not have training or exposure to traditional values of documentary photography. How the media use this new technology can greatly affect readers' understanding of the world.

This study asked readers to confront issues about the digital revolution in the mass media. The central questions addressed by the study are how accepting are readers of digital-imaging alterations and how much they trusted digital photographs used in documentary contexts such as news stories, feature stories, and news magazine covers. The purpose of this study was to provide an empirically based set of newsroom guidelines and principles for digitally altered photographs.

Studies concerning the standards, consequences, and ethics of traditional "wet" photographic manipulation are plentiful. The discussions of the ethics and standards of digital-image manipulation are nothing new either. More than sixty articles about digital imaging were found, but no study addressed how readers react to digital imaging.

In the articles directly related to digital-imaging manipulation, some contained questions about readers' perceptions and about media professionals' perceptions. Terry and Lasorsa asked: "To what extent do members of the public believe the photographs they see published? Is the majority of the populace aware that advertising photographs are routinely modified?" Similarly, Reaves asked: "Do readers make the distinctions between publications (when they read photographs)?"

The subjects in all of Reaves's digital-imaging studies were photo editors. In one study, Reaves surveyed 511 editors from daily newspapers of ranging circulation sizes. Her research questions asked specifically: "What do visual editors at daily newspapers think about specific kinds of computer-editing changes? How much manipulation will visual editors tolerate? Is there any kind of national consensus"?

Reaves found that these photographic editors were very critical of most kinds of digital alteration such as dropping out backgrounds, flipping images in a photograph, using airbrushes to remove or add objects, or cutting and pasting photographs although they generally accepted as standard practice such techniques as cropping, dodging (lightening), and burning in the print. Reaves also found some disturbing facts that this study would test on readers. She wrote:

Among the editors who did show more tolerance toward computer alterations of photographs, there are some discernable characteristics. Among these attributes were: having less familiarity with the technology; ... having no background in photojournalism; participating in less professional development activity; not having a college degree; being older than 35; .... Since there was no research focused on readers, these findings would later help form the hypotheses of this study.

In a later study, Reaves used models from semiotics to explain a number of questions. Specifically, why computer technology was sharpening preexisting attitudes among editors toward photojournalism, the question of creating ethical dilemmas with digital photography, and why newspaper editors would seldom permit the digital alteration of photographs they perceived to be news photographs, but would allow extensive digital alteration of photographs assume to be illustrations.

Based on a semiotic continuum of photographic

categories of newspaper editors, Reaves found that for all nine questions a continuum emerged showing editors being the least tolerant of a particular computer alteration in a "spot-news photo," more tolerant of the same alteration in a "feature photo," and the most tolerant of the same alteration in a "photographic illustration."

In another study, Reeves examined some of the same ethical considerations in magazine editing. Here, she began a dialogue where editors from a variety of consumer magazines could start to confront their beliefs about how, when, and why they might allow the digital altering of photographs.

The study examined consumer magazines, which, Reaves thought, had incentives to use such technology. Reaves found that some editors were concerned about reader reaction to this new technology, and that, although the editorial philosophy of a magazine might dictate how far a magazine can manipulate photographs, many readers still take photographs literally. The question that the study left unanswered - "Do readers make the distinctions between publications?"-is precisely the question this study examined.

Gladney and Ehrlich's 1996 study provides survey data for a cross-media comparison of the ethical responses of newspaper photo editors and television news directors to digital-image processing and enhancement technology. A majority of the respondents disagreed that digital manipulation technology negatively affects news content and damages credibility.

However, photo editors were significantly less likely than broadcast news directors to say such technology has a negative effect. Photo editors were also more likely to agree that digital manipulation technology increases the temptation to manipulate images unethically.

The two groups did not significantly disagree about more subtle uses of manipulation (to achieve a desired hue, correct shadows, or match sizes to scale). Given that almost seven out of eight respondents in both groups said they opposed digital alteration that in any way deceived the public, the authors found it reasonable to speculate that these respondents saw the more subtle manipulations as merely a technical concern.

The exceptionally large percentage of respondents who were neutral about digital alteration suggests that this is an area of considerable ethical confusion.

This reader-response research used a survey method partially built upon existing studies of media professionals. This study examined three major issues: how readers understand (1) different types of alteration (technical and content) in (2) different types of photographs (hard news, feature, and illustration) (3) in different media (newspapers and news magazines, "infotainment" magazines, and tabloids).

By exposing readers to various digital alterations of photographs, this study intended to find out how readers reacted to alterations in a variety of contexts.

In her 1993 exploratory study, Reaves established correlations between editors' acceptance of such manipulations and their age, education, and media experience. Her findings helped to form some of the hypotheses of this study. Apart from those independent variables she used, digital imaging experience, computer literacy, media-exposure frequency, and breadth were added as independent variables that might influence readers' attitudes toward alterations.

Specific research questions included:

1. Are readers aware that most of today's photographs in print news media are digitally processed?
2. How accepting are readers of different kinds of computerediting changes in the content and the technical aspects of a photograph?
3. Do readers distinguish among three types of photographs: hard news photograph, feature photograph, and photographic illustration in terms of digital image uses?
4. Do readers distinguish among the three categories of digitalimaging alterations: technical alterations, content alterations, and composite images?

5. Do readers feel the need to be informed of a digital alteration?
6. What types of readers tend to accept digital-imaging alterations?

Since the first five specific research questions were descriptive and explorative, no research hypotheses were proposed. In order to answer the sixth question, which was correlational in nature and addressed the relationship between readers' demographic background and their acceptance of digital-imaging alterations, six research hypotheses were formulated. These hypotheses were partially based on Reaves's 1993 study:

1. Readers' education will be negatively correlated with their acceptance of digital-imaging alterations.
2. Readers' media-exposure frequency and breadth will be negatively correlated with their acceptance of digital-imaging alterations.
3. According to the logic of hypotheses 1 and 2, readers' photography and digital imaging experiences will be negatively correlated with their acceptance of digital-imaging alterations.
4. Readers' computer literacy will be positively correlated with their acceptance of digital-imaging alterations.
5. Readers' age will be positively correlated with their acceptance of digital-imaging alterations.
6. Since some readers were found in pilot tests to base their acceptance of digital-imaging alterations on their exposure to this new technology, it was hypothesized that the readers who are aware of the use of digital imaging in print news media tend to accept digital-imaging alterations.

The alpha value that determined the size of the region of rejection was set at 0.05.

A typical question in the questionnaire read:

In the right image, a distracting car was eliminated. In which of the following situations would you accept this computer editing change? Circle all that apply.

A = Hard news photo.
B = Feature photo.
C = Photographic illustration.
D = Not acceptable under any of these circumstances.

Survey participants saw a brief explanation to each of these concepts on the front page of the questionnaire. Each concept was also accompanied by an illustrative image. In total, there were seventeen examples of alteration in seventeen questions.

These seventeen questions contained three categories of alterations: technical alteration such as adjusting tonality, blurring, or eliminating background and reverse cropping (Questions 1-5); content alteration such as shifting the position of a subject in an image to fit a layout, eliminating or adding still objects or human beings and digital cosmetology (Questions 6-13); and composite images in which different elements from different photographs are combined into a single image (Questions 14-17). Four statistical measures were created:

- Overall acceptance rate

The percentage of the respondents who accepted an alteration regardless of types of photographs. For instance, if 30% of the respondents circled D (Not acceptable under any of these circumstances) in a question, the overall acceptance rate for that particular alteration was 70%.

- Photo-type acceptance rata

The percentage of the respondents who accepted an alteration in a particular type of photograph such as a hard-news photographs, a feature photograph, or a photographic illustration;

- Alteration-acceptability index

An index showing the degree that a particular alteration was acceptable to the respondents. For instance, did most respondents accept a specific alteration in the context of photographic illustrations only?

Or could they accept it in feature photographs, and/or hard-news photographs, too? An alteration-acceptability index summarizes the three photo-type acceptance rates in a question and gives us a general picture of the extent of acceptance for an alteration.

- Respondent acceptance index

An index showing to what extent an individual respondent was able to accept alterations in general. It is the sum of all A's (hard-news photos), B's (feature photos) and C's (photographic illustrations) that the respondent circled through the 17 questions divided by the number of questions answered. (If there is no missing data, this "number of questions answered" is supposed to be 17.) The maximum respondent acceptance index score is 3 and the minimum 0. This index was later associated with the respondents' demographic information.

Observing the overall acceptance rate enables comparisons among different kinds of digital-imaging alterations. However, overall acceptance rate does not reflect the variance of acceptability of an alteration among the three contexts. Did most respondents circle C only, B only, or A, B, and C together?

Alteration-acceptability index does. Alteration-acceptability index was defined as the average number of responses (i.e., items circled) to each question. If a respondent circled C only, for instance, the alterationacceptability index of this question was 1. If she or he circled A, B, and C, the alteration-acceptability index was 3. If none was circled, then the alterationacceptability index was 0. Therefore, alteration-acceptability indices ranged from 0 to 3.

As noted above, this study intended to find out if the respondents' acceptance of digital-imaging alterations varied among types of photographs and if so, how. And if the respondents' acceptance of digital-imaging alterations varied among the three categories of alterations and if so, how. The study also explored whether respondents accepted digital alterations of photos of human beings the same way they did objects, and if they accepted alterations involving adding elements the same way as they did alterations involving removing elements.

The remaining sixteen close-ended questions concerned

readers' background related to digital imaging. Three optional open-ended questions solicited readers for guidelines they might propose to editors for using digitally altered photographs.

A systematic probability sample of 700 participants was drawn from the city directory of a small Midwestern town.

FINDINGS

The response rate was 33%. As Singletary (1994) noted, mail surveys returns of 30-40% are common. Since the response rate was comparatively low, a response bias was potentially present. Accordingly, the data showed that 47% female and 53% male participated in the survey. The ages of the respondents also showed a fairly normal curve. Therefore, the respondents adequately represented the sampled population in terms of age and gender in spite of a low response rate.

The respondents' ability to distinguish hard news photographs and photographic illustrations (58%) was much higher than their ability to distinguish between hard news photographs and feature photographs (37%) and their ability to distinguish between feature photographs and photographic illustrations (36%). One third of the respondents claimed that they could not distinguish between photographic categories.

Sixty per cent of the respondents surveyed said that they were aware that most photographs published in newspapers and news magazines were digitally processed though not necessarily altered. However, equally significant was that 40% were unaware that digital-imaging technology has been used by the media industry for approximately twenty years.

When asked if they agreed with the opinion that a photograph on the cover of a news magazine like Mme or a documentary photograph book like A Dayin the Life of America is an artistic and promotional presentation, thus legitimating digital retouching, over half of the respondents (57%) circled "Strongly agree" or "Somewhat agree," and about one third of the respondents (31%) circled either

"Strongly disagree" or "Somewhat disagree." Obviously, most respondents would likely give media professionals greater artistic to alter cover photographs, which are often composite images.

Binomial Z-tests on the frequencies of accepting alterations in hardnews photographs, feature photographs, and photographic illustrations showed that respondents most willingly accepted digital-imaging alterations in photographic illustrations, less so in feature photographs, and least so in hard news photographs. This finding supports Reaves's 1995 study of editors.

A respondent made a comment on this relationship that might serve as a footnote to this finding: "I think my standard [for alteration] may be at its highest for hard news, and not quite so high for feature photograph, perhaps not high at all for illustrative purposes." She expected hard-news photographs to be factual without any bias and took it for granted that feature photographs and photographic illustrations would come with some sort of slant.

After correlating the alteration-acceptability indices and the overall acceptance rates of digital-imaging alterations across the seventeen examples, it was found that these two variables were positively correlated with each other (Pearson r=0.92). This high correlation provided evidence of the convergent validity of measuring the overall acceptance rates and alterationacceptability indices.

TECHNICAL ALTERATIONS

A technical alteration does not change the internal structure of a photograph. What is changed is the way of presenting certain information. One exception is that sometimes a certain element, usually the subject of a photograph, is cut out of the background to be presented solely by itself because the editor wants to emphasize the element.

Traditionally, a darkroom technician oversaw technical matters such as changing tonality, adjusting colour balance, cropping, and removing dust or a defect from a photograph.

With digital technology, new possibilities were introduced such as reverse cropping (extending the border of a photograph by copying and pasting elements to make the photograph look either wider and/or taller) and changing the depth of field (making either the background or the foreground, or both, blurrier or clearer). These do not change the internal relationship between or among the elements in a photograph.

Except for dropping out the background, one would still see what she or he saw in the unaltered photograph; the distance between element X and element Y, for instance, is unchanged, though the tonality of element X might be slightly brighter or element Y might look a bit blurrier.

The five examples included in this group contained both traditional alterations and alterations made possible by digital technology.

Technical Example described its alteration by stating:

In the right image, the tones of the background and the subject were adjusted to make the picture more printable in the newspaper. In which of the following photograph types would you accept this computer editing change? Circle all that apply.

A = Hard news photograph. 62.7%

B = Feature photograph. 79.7%

C = Photographic illustration. 72.2%

Overall acceptance rate 89.9%

Alteration-acceptability index 2.15

Adjusting the tonality of a photograph is intended to improve the printing quality of the photograph. Reaves's 1993 study showed that 86.3% of the surveyed editors accepted this kind of computer alteration. In this study, 62.7% of the respondents accepted the alteration for a hard news photograph, and 89.9% of the respondents said that they could accept it for all types of photographs. This represented the highest percentage for all the seventeen questions. Reaves's findings and the findings from this study both suggest that respondents were not simply rejecting editing techniques because they were done on a computer.

The alteration-acceptability index in this example (2.15) indicates that almost all respondents accepted this alteration at least in photographic illustrations and in feature photographs. A small percentage of them even thought that it was all right to do this alteration in hard news photographs.

Changing the tonality of an image for better printing quality is a relatively minor alteration. However, many respondents would prefer that no further alterations be done although they could accept some other kinds of alterations. Respondent, for example, said in his answer to an openended question: "It is OK to adjust the colors [tonality] for print in a mag [magazine], newspaper, etc. but only if they will appear close to what the original image was."

Technical Example described its alteration by stating:

In the right image, both the background and the foreground were blurred to emphasize the teacher. In which of the following photograph types would you accept this computer editing change? Circle all that apply.

A = Hard news photograph. 31.6%

B = Feature photograph. 68.4%

C = Photographic illustration. 69.6%

Overall acceptance rate 83.5%

Alteration-acceptability index 1.7

By decreasing the existing depth of field, the subject of a photograph can either be put in context or emphasized. In traditional photography, the selection of depth of field has to be made before a picture is taken. Digital technology enables such selections to be made after the picture was taken.

The vast majority, 83.5%, said such an alteration was acceptable. One respondent said that this did not seem to have changed the content of the picture. However, only 31.6% of the respondents allowed this kind of alteration to be applied to hard-news photographs.

Most (68-70%) tolerated it in feature photographs and photographic illustrations, and did not treat these two types of photographs in a much different way because of the alteration. In terms of alteration-acceptability index (1.7), almost all respondents could at least accept this alteration in photographic illustrations and the majority of them could even accept it in feature photographs but not hardnews photographs.

Technical Example described its alteration by stating:

In the right image, the right border of the image was extended by copying and duplicating part of the same image to fit the required size. In which of the following photograph types would you accept this computer editing change? Circle all that apply.

A = Hard news photograph. 23.4%

B = Feature photograph. 53.8%

C = Photographic illustration. 63.3%

Overall acceptance rate 76.6%

Alteration-acceptability index 1.41

Thanks to the stamp tool, often called the cloning tool, in Photoshop, editors today can lengthen a photograph either horizontally or vertically by reverse cropping it. As a result, the editor does not need to stretch the photograph. What is added is usually supplementary elements of the existing photograph such as a section of a cloud, sky, or a road. The extension of a border usually involves no substantial increase of information.

More than three-quarters (76.6%) of the respondents approved of this type of alteration. Still, we see a big difference in the acceptance rate between hard-news photographs (23.4%) and the other two groups of photographs (53.8% and 63.3%).

Respondent 56 objected to this alteration "because on the outside it doesn't seem to really alter the intent, the content of the picture, but I think it lends itself to abuse in very much the same way as No. 4. For hard news, I think it should just be, `this is the way it is.'"

Technical Example described its alteration by stating:

In the right image, the distracting background was eliminated for graphic effect. In which of the following photograph types would you accept this computer editing change? Circle all that apply.

A = Hard news photograph. 13.9%
B = Feature photograph. 48.7%
C = Photographic illustration. 64.6%
Overall acceptance rate 76.6%
Alteration-acceptability index 1.27

Eliminating the background of a photograph is another common practice used by editors who may want to show the subject as if the picture were taken in a studio with a neutral background. In other instances, an editor may want to montage subjects from multiple photographs with different backgrounds. Removing backgrounds could make the combining work faster and easier.

For this kind of alteration, 76.6% of the respondents still accepted it since. As one respondent said, "it doesn't seem so sinister to remove it [background]." However, they seemed to tolerate this kind of alteration mostly in photographic illustrations (64.6%), much less so in feature photographs (48.7%), and hardly at all in hard news photographs (13.9%).

This difference between the photo-type acceptance rates explains why the alteration-acceptability index was lower than that in Technical Example though the overall acceptance rates were the same.

Reaves's 1993 study found that 13.5% of the editors surveyed tolerated this kind of alteration. This is nearly the same acceptance rate as for hard news photographs (13.9%) in this study.

Technical Example described its alteration by stating:

In the right image, the subject's face was darkened and the background was lightened for dramatic effect. In which of the following photograph types would you accept this computer editing change? Circle all that apply.

A = Hard news photograph. 7.6%
B = Feature photograph. 15.2%
C = Photographic illustration. 29.1%
Overall acceptance rate 35.4%
Alteration-acceptability index 0.52

Technical Example is similar to Technical Example. Both

involve the change of tonality of the subject and the background, but the tonality in the former case was made darker while the tonality in the latter was made brighter. As a familiar real-life example, the alteration in this photograph published on the cover of Time magazine when O.J. Simpson had just been arrested on murder charges. The photograph could be interpreted as having an ill intent motive and actually was in fact by many respondents.

About a third of the respondents (35.4%) said that they approved of this alteration - a percentage much lower than those for the other technical alteration examples. It is worth noting that the acceptance rates in all the three types of photographs were very low (7.6% to 29.1%).

A two-related-samples t-test on the means of alteration-acceptability index in Technical Example (0=2.15) and that in Technical Example (0=0.52) showed a significant difference.

Simpson's image was one of the most controversial images in these seventeen examples of alteration. By adopting an empathic approach, a respondent commented:

They [editors] need to keep in mind how would they [would] feel if this was them-their mother, sister, father, brother. Alteration is fine for some purposes, but not anything like the O.J. picture. They wanted him to look dark & like a criminal-b4 [before] the court even tried him.

CONTENT ALTERATIONS

A content alteration moves, removes, adds, replaces, or distorts certain element(s), usually minor elements) in a photograph. As a result, the internal structure of the altered photograph is changed. For instance, a telephone pole that appears to be growing out of the head of a subject can be removed. A technical alteration presents the same content in a different way while a content alteration presents a different content in the same way.

Content alterations may or may not substantially affect the meaning of a photograph. A big difference between traditional darkroom alteration of content and digital alteration of content is that the former could almost always be detected while the latter is undetectable if done professionally.

Eight examples were used for this category. In the right image, the man and the tree were moved closer together to fit the image to a required size. In which of the following photograph types would you accept this computer editing change? Circle all that apply.

A = Hard news photograph. 22.2%
B = Feature photograph. 60.8%
C = Photographic illustration. 78.5%
Overall acceptance rate 89.2%
Alteration-acceptability index 1.61

This type of alteration is based on an assumption that the altered representation is credible. In spite of the fact that this alteration involved content, the information loss or distortion did not seem significant to the respondents. A respondent said that she agreed with this alteration because it "didn't really detract from the content." At the same time, she believed that the alteration should not be applied to hard news photographs.

This example received a very high overall acceptance rate (89.2%) as well as a high alteration-acceptability index (1.61). Over 60% of the respondents approved of such an alteration in the contents of feature photographs and photographic illustrations.

Content Example described its alteration by stating:

In the right image, a distracting car was eliminated. In which of the following photograph types would you accept this computer editing change? Circle all that apply.

A = Hard news photograph. 18.4%
B = Feature photograph. 59.5%
C = Photographic illustration. 68.4%
Overall acceptance rate 81.0%
Alteration-acceptability index 1.46

Removing dust, telephone wires, lamp poles, or even a car was practiced before digital-imaging technology came into being. Now, by duplicating the surrounding elements on a computer screen with the stamp tool, such alterations can be executed with much greater ease and without being detected.

Obviously, removing a car did not mean much to the respondents; 81% of them approved of the modification, though the majority disapproved of such modification in hard news photographs.

Content Example described its alteration by stating:

In the right image, the flag in the background was enlarged, slanted, and moved to make the composition look more pleasing. In which of the following photograph types would you accept this computer editing change?

Circle all that apply.

A = Hard news photograph. 18.4%

B = Feature photograph. 50.6%

C = Photographic illustration. 63.3%

Overall acceptance rate 81.0%

Alteration-acceptability index 1.32

This is a typical example of multiple alterations. The flag in the background was not only moved, but also enlarged and distorted. Most respondents (81%) accepted multiple alterations, though the alteration— acceptability index was much lower. One respondent sensed from this example the potential of using altered images to serve a political agenda. This respondent wrote:

It should be refrained from if additions or omissions could in any way serve a political agenda, regardless of whether the editor intends to promote such an agenda. The erasure of unwanted people and the manipulation of the flag made me the most uncomfortable.

Content Example described its alteration by stating:

In the left image, the lower right corner seems empty, so some balloons from another photograph were added. In which of the following photograph types would you accept this computer editing change? Circle all that apply.

A = Hard news photograph. 13.9%

B = Feature photograph. 41.8%

C = Photographic illustration. 58.2%

Overall acceptance rate 69.6%

Alteration-acceptability index 1.14

The opposite of removing elements from a photograph is adding minor elements such as flowers, clouds, animals, or people who are not regarded as the subjects of the photograph to fill in empty space, decorate the photograph, or add something that the photographer or editor thought should have been there but wasn't.

Adding elements is a different type of content alteration because it creates a scene - a combination of elements that did not exist previously. Many respondents rejected such practices especially for hard news photographs. Both the overall acceptance rate (69.6%) and the alteration-acceptability index (1.14) were lower.

Content Example described its alteration by stating:

In the right image, two distracting persons in the background were eliminated. In which of the following photograph types would you accept this computer editing change? Circle all that apply.

A = Hard news photograph. 8.90

B = Feature photograph. 38.0%

C Photographic illustration. 58.2%

Overall acceptance rate 68.4%

In the past, the process of removing a person from a photograph required great care and precision plus a great deal of time, but now, it has become simple and easy on a computer.

Compared to the computer editing change in Content Example, in which a car in the background was removed, this alteration, which involved a human being, received lower acceptance rates for all categories. Also, the general acceptance rate dropped from 81% to 68.4% and the alteration-acceptability index from 1.46 to 1.05.

A two— related-samples t-test on the means of alteration-acceptability index in Content Example showed a significant difference. It is reasonable to argue that the respondents' tolerance for digitally removing objects depended, to a certain extent, on what was removed. As respondent 121 put it clearly: "If an alteration happens to elements like building or places, that's fine, but when it comes to people, I don't like alterations."

Content Example described its alteration by stating:

In the right image, digital dental work was performed on a news figure. In which of the following photograph types would you accept this computer editing change? Circle all that apply.

A = Hard news photograph. 10.8%

B = Feature photograph. 46.8%

C = Photographic illustration. 53.2%

Overall acceptance rate 67.1%

Cosmetic alteration, such as the example above, is another kind of often— practiced content alteration, especially in advertising. In recent years, such alterations have also been used in documentary photographs. For instance, when someone's eyes were accidentally closed at the time when a picture was taken, the editor can digitally open them. In the above example, digital dental work was done to this news figure.

The respondents' attitudes toward such an alteration were mixed. Around 50% of them acknowledged that they would accept it if it occurred in a feature photograph or as a photographic illustration. However, the alteration-acceptability index was comparatively low.

This medium acceptance rate was probably best explained by a respondent's dilemma when answering this question. By putting herself in the shoes of this mother of the famous sextuplets, this female respondent wrote: "I could not decide what to answer to 'dental alteration' (in) picture 11.

On the one hand 'I really look good in the alteration.' On the other hand 'It's NOT ME!!' I don't know how I would react". From a different perspective, Respondent 75 found it "very wrong" to do this digital dental work because, he argued, this picture showed a particular news figure as opposed to just a picture of a generic woman in America. "If it's a particular person, she should be represented appropriately, even in caricature," he said.

Content Example described its alteration by stating:

In the left image, the lower right corner seems empty, so children from some other photos were added. In which of the following photograph types would you accept this computer editing change? Circle all that apply.

A = Hard news photograph. 6.3%

B = Feature photograph. 17.7%

C = Photographic illustration. 42.4%

Overall acceptance rate 51.3%

Alteration-acceptability index 0.66

This alteration is very similar to the one in Content Example. The only difference is that objects - balloons- were added in Content Example while human beings were added in this example.

The alteration-acceptability index was only 0.66. Around half of the respondents found this kind of alteration inappropriate. A two-related-samples t-test on the two means of alteration-acceptability index in Content Example (0=1.14) and 7 (0=0.66) showed a significant difference. This difference, again, tells us that the respondents could accept alterations involving objects much more than alterations involving human beings.

Comparing the averaged means of alteration-acceptability indices for Content Examples - both of which removed either objects or human beings (0=1.26) - and the averaged means of Content Examples — both of which added objects or human beings (0=0.9) - a two-relatedsamples t-test showed a significant difference. The respondents were more open to removing elements than to adding elements to pictures.

Content Example described its alteration by stating:

In the right image, the boom box and the girl on the right were eliminated. One of the dancers was copied, flipped, and pasted to where the girl once stood. In which of the following photograph types would you accept this computer editing change? Circle all that apply.

A = Hard news photograph. 4.4%

B = Feature photograph. 16.5%

C = Photographic illustration. 46.8%

Overall acceptance rate 50.6%

Alteration-acceptability index 0.68

The respondents were very critical of multiple alterations involving human beings. The comparison between the alteration-acceptability index in Content Example (0=1.32) in which multiple alterations were done to a flag and that in this example (0=0.68) further supports the hypothesis that altering a photograph involving a human being is less acceptable to the respondents than altering objects.

The alteration-acceptability indices varied greatly among content-alteration examples. Most of the time respondents made their decision on whether to accept alterations by considering whether an alteration had changed the original meaning or if the alteration involved a human being. In both cases, they would oppose the alternation.

One respondent automatically made a comparison between technical alterations and content alterations by writing: " [P]hotos should be used as recorded by the photographer. Changes in visual content or meaning should not be acceptable.

Minor changes to contrast + cropping could be accepted for printing purposes with no change to content." A second respondent said: "Digital imaging should be used primarily to enhance the quality of a photograph without altering its content". Another respondent said that digital-imaging technology should only be used "to make the whole picture easier to view".

COMPOSITE IMAGES

A composite image is something like a painting. It usually starts with one photograph, or sometimes with a blank painting board. Different elements are then added to the photograph from different sources to compose a brand new image. The elements added are normally not trivial.

For instance, two persons from two different photographs are combined to become the subjects of the new photograph; or a head of a person is added onto another person's body. Composite images could look unrealistic because of incommensurate scale or impossible combinations of elements such as a pig with airplane wings, but sometimes they can look very real as the four examples shown below will demonstrate.

A lot of criticism from the respondents has focused on the practice of forging realistic-looking composite images without letting readers know what has happened. The respondents reported feeling deceived. The overall acceptance rates for this category of alterations in hard news photographs were extremely low (3.2%-7%). The highest alteration— acceptability index value (1.12) was simply the mean (1.1) and the lowest was close to 0. This category contains four real-life examples all taken from the media. The names of the publications and all other linguistic information shown over these images were digitally eliminated.

Composite Example described its alteration by stating:

In this image, three separate images were combined: skywriting planes, the Chrysler Building, and the words "New York." In which of the following photograph types would you accept this computer editing change? Circle all that apply.

A = Hard news photograph. 7.0%

B = Feature photograph. 25.3%

C = Photographic illustration. 79.7%

Overall acceptance rate 85.4%

Alteration-acceptability index 1.12

Because of the ease and the undetectability of digital-imaging alterations, media professionals may find it difficult to resist the temptation of combining images. The above example, taken from the cover of the October 1988 issue of Conde Nast Traveller magazine, depicted airplanes flying over the Chrysler Building together with the words "New York" that was supposedly written by the airplanes. The fact is that these were two separate photographs shot by the same photographer and later combined by an editor.

This example received a very low acceptance rate for hard news photographs and a fairly low acceptance rate for feature photographs, too. However, the overall acceptance rate and alteration-acceptability index were both high. Reaves's 1993 study used exactly the same example and she found that 19.5% of the editors would accept the use of this composite image.

Composite Example described its alteration by stating:

In this image, separate photos of two celebrities were combined because they were not at the same place when a photograph of them together was needed. In which of the following photograph types would you accept this computer editing change? Circle all that apply.

A = Hard news photograph. 3.2%
B = Feature photograph. 24.1%
C = Photographic illustration. 46.2%
Overall acceptance rate 55.7%
Alteration-acceptability index 0.73

The alteration in this famous example of composite image got highly negative feedback from the respondents.

In order to get further support for the finding that altering human being tends to get lower alteration-acceptability index than altering objects, a comparison was made between the object alteration in Composite Example (0=1.12) and the alteration involving human being in Composite Example, (0=0.73) which got the highest alteration-acceptability index of all the composite images containing human beings. As a result, this two-relatedsamples t-test showed a significant difference.

Again, Reaves's 1993 study used exactly the same example and she found that 12% of the editors tolerated the use of this composite image.

Composite Example described its alteration by stating:

In this image, separate photos of two notable athletes were combined because it was impossible to photograph the two skaters together. In which of the following photograph types would you accept this computer editing change? Circle all that apply.

A = Hard news photograph. 4.4%
B = Feature photograph. 14.6%

C = Photographic illustration. 38.6%

Overall acceptance rate 45.6%

Alteration-acceptability index 0.58

Composite Example described its alteration by stating:

In this image, a photograph of a celebrity's face was combined with a photograph of a model's body because the celebrity would not pose for a portrait. In which of the following photograph types would you accept this computer editing change? Circle all that apply.

A = Hard news photograph. 3.8%

B = Feature photograph. 3.2%

C = Photographic illustration. 11.4%

Overall acceptance rate 15.2%

Alteration-acceptability index 0.18

Both to the readers in this study and the editors in Reaves's 1993 study, the procedure of combining one person's head with another person's body was the least acceptable digital-imaging alteration.

The respondents were very offended by this kind of practice. One of them wrote: "(Media) should respect the wishes of the people whose pictures are being printed - for example pasting a celebrity's face over model's body without the celebrity's consent is totally unacceptable. Digital altering should not misrepresent the facts". Another female respondent wrote that she would be very upset if she knew that her head had been added onto another person's body without her permission.

She wrote that "the Oprah Winfrey picture is absolutely unacceptable. She should sue!" "Keep the fine line of freedom of speech in perspective," warned Respondent. Again, many respondents adopted an empathetic approach to such an alteration: "Would they care if they were in the picture"? "Would the editor feel comfortable if the alteration published in the paper was about himself"?

For all three categories of alterations, composite images obviously were least acceptable. Much of the concern the respondents had was targeted at this category of alterations because readers are unaware of the alterations. The respondents obviously expected a realistic-looking picture to both iconically and indexically refer to the objects or persons depicted.

By running a general linear model ANOVA for repeated measure (since respondents were allowed to circle more than one choice in each question) on the means of alteration-acceptability indices for technical alterations chi=11.3038, content alterations (chi=1.1297) and composite images, significant difference was found to exist among them. The confidence interval for each population (mu) was

Technical alterations: 1.239 <=(mu) 1.3038 <=1.369

Content alterations: 1.065 <=(mu)= 297 <=1.195

Composite images: 0.589 <=(mu)= .6535 = <0.718

The confidence interval for each population (mu) showed no overlapping; each mean was significantly different from each other. Readers would be most likely to accept technical alterations in general, less so for content alterations and the least for composite images.

Associating respondent acceptance indices with their demographic data produced interesting results. It was found that respondents who were aware of the fact that most photographs published in newspapers and news magazines are digitally processed tended to be more accepting of digitalimaging alterations.

It was also found that the more pairs of types of photographs (hard-news photograph - feature photograph; feature photograph - photographic illustration; hard-news photograph — photographic illustration) the respondents could distinguish when reading newspapers or news magazines, the more they would accept digital-imaging alterations.

Those who could detect no difference or detect difference in only one pair of types of photographs tended to be critical of alterations, while those who could distinguish two to three pairs of types of photographs tended to be more accepting of alterations. This finding tells us that the respondents had different expectations for different types of photographs in terms of alterations. The respondents' sensitivity to the context in which an alteration was used determined, to some extent, their attitude toward that alteration.

Respondents' photographic education played a big part in their attitudes toward digital-imaging alterations. The more photographic education a respondent had received, the more she or he could accept alterations. However, a respondent's frequent exposure to digital-imaging technology did not necessarily mean that she or he would be more likely to accept alterations.

No significant associations were found between the respondent acceptance indices and other demographic data including media-reading breadth (number of types of print media read), newspaper-reading frequency, magazine reading frequency, computer-use frequency, computer literacy, educational level, and age. However, it was found that the more frequently the respondents read newspapers, the more frequently they used a computer, the more knowledge they had about computer uses, and the more digital imaging experience they had, the more they were aware of digital imaging in media.

Cross-tabulating respondent acceptance indices with awareness by controlling demographic variables such as newspaper-reading frequency, computer-use frequency, computer literacy, and digital imaging experience revealed a different perspective of associations.

First, respondents' awareness was significantly associated with acceptance indices, but only on the level of high newspaper-reading frequency (every day or almost every day). Fifty-five out of 127 respondents (43%) were not aware of the uses of digital images in print news media in spite of the fact that they read newspapers every day or almost every day. These respondents tended not to see digitalimaging alterations in a favorable way.

However, more respondents (57%) were aware of such uses and most tended to approve of alterations. The Pearson X value shows that those differences are significant. For those who read newspapers less than once a week (low frequency), however, no such association was found. This finding suggests that readers who read newspapers frequently tended to be aware of the uses of digital images at least in newspapers and they might know something about digital-imaging alterations. Such knowledge gained from daily newspaper reading enabled most respondents to make informed decisions about the alterations and made them more tolerant toward the practice of altering photographs.

This explanation found support in the findings about magazine reading frequency and breadth regarding the association between respondent acceptance indices and awareness. For those who read magazines less than once every two weeks (low frequency), no such association was found.

However, those who read news magazines at least once a week (high frequency), they tended to be more accepting in their attitudes toward alterations. For those who read more than three types of print news media, if they tended to be aware of digital image use and were also more accepting of digitally altered photographs.

Computer literacy, computer-use frequency, and digital imaging experience were three more variables that support the findings discussed above. The study demonstrates no associations between respondent acceptance indices and awareness in the levels of "no computer literacy" and "low computer literacy."

This makes sense since typing or word processing does not help make a computer user sensitive to the uses of digital images. On the other end, those who often surfed the web, used graphics software, or had more knowledge about digital-imaging technology tended to favour digitalimaging alterations.

The more respondents used a computer and the more they were aware of digital image uses in media, the more tolerant they were of alterations. However, such an association existed only on the level of "high computeruse frequency" and not on the level of "low use frequency."

Finally, in terms of digital imaging experience, the results showed that when respondents knew very little about digital images, chances were they were aware that digital images were being used in media and they tended to accept potential alterations. This was even true with those who had more digital imaging experience. However, for those who claimed to have no experience with digital imaging, no such association existed.

In conclusion, the reader's knowledge about digital images acquired from frequent computer use, prior exposure to computer science, and frequent and extensive print news media readings has a direct bearing on the extent to which they could accept digital-imaging alterations.

Despite the fact that no significant correlation between respondent acceptance indices and age and education was found, the younger the respondents were, the more types of print news media they were exposed to, the more often they read newspapers, the more often they used a computer, the higher their computer literacy was, and the more digital imaging experience they had.

It was also found that the higher the respondents' educational levels were, the more types of print news media they were exposed to, the more often they read magazines, the more often they used a computer, the higher their computer literacy was, and the more digital imaging experience they had.

These findings tell us that the respondents' age and education were directly related to the extent of exposure to digital images in certain pattern, although not directly related to the extent to which they could accept digital imaging alterations.

RESPONDENTS' CONCERNS OVER DIGITAL IMAGING ALTERATIONS

The respondents' biggest concerns about digital-imaging alterations were that media would enhance or distort an image without informing readers that an image had been altered. As a result, media could intentionally or unintentionally - change the meaning of a picture. This, in turn could affect the media's impartiality, create bias, project a viewpoint, sway opinions, and mislead readers.

The respondents were concerned and frustrated by the potential of not knowing whether an image had been altered. Respondent 33 said: "We are getting someone else's clouded view of what's actually happening, and that's my biggest concern, I think. We won't be allowed to make up our own minds about what's going on." Respondent 46 asked: "Do I have to hunt for the truth? Do I have to sort things out?" They were afraid that they could not believe what they saw. If digital image alteration becomes commonplace, they said, it would leave little to believe in.

Some alterations were perceived as unfair to the people whose pictures were altered. One respondent worried that her perceptions of people or stories could be manipulated anyway the editor chooses: "Since not many people are looking over their shoulder to make sure they do not overstep their boundaries, alterations could get way out of hand".

Voicing the sentiment of many readers, a respondent said: "As they say, a picture is worth a thousand words; words elicit ideas, perceptions and emotions. Photojournalists who alter images which alter the commonly understood meaning of a picture, do so at their own peril".

GUIDELINES AND PRINCINLES PROPOSED BY RESOONDENTS

Sixty-five per cent of the respondents suggested guidelines and principles for using altered images in documentary contexts. Summarizing what they wrote, the following guidelines and principles were identified.

First, digitally altered images should generally not be used. This finding suggested that even if the overall acceptance rate was high for a specific alteration, the high rate should not be interpreted to mean that editors can alter images with impunity. The respondents could tolerate specific alterations to a certain extent, but they did not want to encourage alterations.

Respondent said: "The software looks pretty easy to use and the results are spectacular. However, I am far more impressed with a fabulous un-altered photo anyway." Respondent agreed by saying: "I would like to be able to pick up a newspaper or a magazine or whatever, and know what I am looking at really is what took place at that point.

Second, if the media have to use an altered image, they should let readers know. When asked the question: "After an editor has decided to use a digitally altered image, he or she should let readers know that the image was altered. Do you agree?" Almost 100% of the respondents said yes in one way or another.

Fifty-nine per cent of them unconditionally agreed that they had the right to know of alteration and 24-30% said it depends on how much alterations were involved or what motivation was involved. Respondent 30 wrote: "Biggest concern is misleading viewers by not stating an image has been altered. Documentation suggests truth. Documentation is equated with truth. When reporting news it is important to inform viewer that a level of veracity was compromised."

Third, the respondents demanded that the media need to consider context when using an altered image, using alteration only to clarify characteristic in hard-news photographs, make alterations judiciously in feature photographs and photographic illustrations. They demanded that the media apply the highest and strictest standards to hard-news photographs because In]ews is no art" (Respondent).

The respondents did not agree on whether stricter standards should be applied to feature photographs than to photographic illustrations. They found real-life-like photographic illustrations in the form of composite images problematic. If the alterations are not obvious but are significant, the respondents suggested that they should be noted.

Fourth, many respondents suggested that the media should try to reduce alterations to the technical minimum. Some respondents warned that digital imaging should not become the easy way to correct photographic incompetence or laziness. As one respondent wrote: "If they want better photos (without objects that are distracting), they should get better photographers that know how to take good photos and know how to click their cameras more than once". On the other hand, the respondents believed that content and meaning of a photograph should not be changed to misrepresent a subject or to mislead readers. Rather, the media should present facts and truth accurately and honestly in images

Fifth, respondents believe that media professionals should put themselves in the subject's shoes to see how they would feel about an altered picture of themselves. They should consider the subject's wishes when altering an image. Some of the respondents singled out the cases of the darkened O.J. Simpson police mug shot and the Oprah Winfrey composite image as examples to illustrate the inappropriateness of altering an image without consulting the person.

Finally, many respondents mentioned morality as a guideline. They believed that media should consider moral-ethical guidelines and not be guided by what is strictly legal. As one respondent wrote:

I do not think you can restrict editors from doing this kind of journalism without crossing the line of the freedom of press. If we have the technology to alter photos, then it is up to the editors' conscience to guide them. I think it is a moral issue more than a legal issue.

These guidelines and principles proposed by the respondents indicate that respondents had different expectations for using digitally altered images in different contexts.

The results of this study failed to support the five hypotheses that were generated from Reaves's 1993 editors study. However, the findings of this study about the relationship between readers' backgrounds and their acceptance of digital-imaging alterations are significant. Editors are exposed to digital images every day and they know very well what digital alterations are about. Therefore, they were able to give informed answers to Reaves's questions. When the readers are asked similar questions, their answers, to a large degree, depend on their knowledge of digital imaging and their awareness of the uses of digital images in media.

The respondents are made aware of digital-imaging alterations mainly through their photographic education, digital imaging experience, computer literacy, computer-use frequency, and print news media-reading breadth and frequency. There was a marked tendency among these respondents to accept digital alterations.

Almost all of the respondents expect the media to let them know if a digitally altered image is used. So far, few magazines or newspapers have used a sign or symbol to indicate that an altered image was used in a documentary context. The media probably should reconsider their current policy of using digitally altered images without making it known to readers. The quantitative analyses in this study demonstrate that such awareness plays a big part in readers' acceptance of digital-imaging alterations.

The respondents' acceptance of alterations is limited. They tend to give more freedom to editors to do alterations in photographic illustrations and feature photographs but are much less accepting of alterations of hard news photographs.

They regard photographic illustrations appearing in places like news magazine covers as art, feature photographs as semi-art and hard news photographs as factual. The respondents generally welcome the new technology because of its efficiency in processing photographic images, but they do not expect it to be used to misrepresent a subject or to mislead readers.

One of the respondents' primary concerns is that once editors start making alterations, it is hard for anyone to know where they will draw the line. It is interesting to note the tension between the respondents' concerns and their high acceptance rates for many types of alterations..

This study suggests that a clash exists between the respondents' wish to hold on to the traditional values and their perhaps grudging acceptance of some negative results introduced by new technology. The respondents care greatly about potential alterations of reality. Therefore, the guidelines and principles for using digitally altered images they propose are:

- Whenever possible, do no alterations.
- Raise the ethical standards.
- If using any altered images, identify the alterations.
- Try not to alter hard news photographs; try not to alter human beings; and try not to alter the meaning of a photograph.
- Do unto others as you would have them do to you.

The respondent-proposed guidelines and principles indicate that they expect self-discipline, factuality, honesty, fairness, and as few alterations as possible from the media.

Chapter 3

Unwriteable Discourse and Interpretive Practice

In most of this literature journalists serve either as channels through which interested institutions speak or as agents whose actions are overdetermined by institutional constraints. Whether one regards them as vehicles which provide "officials a place to elaborate interpretive webs as part of a negotiating and signaling process" or as relatively unconscious agents of the "everyday practices of domination", analysts taking such views effectively erase the agency of journalists as social actors and interpreters.

Journalistic accounts of journalism, on the other hand, portray journalists as almost entirely free agents. In its most extreme articulations this journalistic self-representation takes the form of reports of often epic proportions, in which journalists draw from an American cultural metanarrative of "the fiercely independent, intelligent, and brave male, who by virtue of those qualities is able to overcome insurmountable obstacles" to construct themselves as flawed but persistent heroes (or, alternatively, as trickster figures) on a quest for truth in a landscape of obstructions, illusions and dangers?

A phenomenological account of journalists, describing the world from "the native's point of view" would describe journalists are relatively free agents who struggle against institutional authority, sometimes reluctantly compromising with but never giving in to, hegemony.

One of the ways to deal with this structure/ agency

problem is to see journalism as a form of language-in-use. To the understanding of journalism as a socially structured practice and a view of journalism as a struggle to represent social dynamics existing "out there," a structure-in-use approach adds a further insight: journalism embodies social creativity. It is an interpretive practice.

Journalists interpret the social world in the act of representing it and they do this by interpreting the social contexts through which they apprehend the world they are representing. Furthermore, this interpretive creativity is not random but both constituted by and constitutive of social epistemologies. Finally, it is out of these interpretive practices that the regularities perceived by media sociology as structures, emerge.

Journalism as interpretive practice can be viewed as supplementing or, perhaps, even bridging, other perspectives on the press as a social institution. Certainly there are social dynamics that structure the ways in which the work of journalism is done and which thus contribute to the reproduction of social formations.

At the same time, journalism makes truth claims that are read as such and evaluated as such according to widely-accepted cultural epistemologies which belong not only to a journalistic subculture but reflect widely shared American cultural knowledge about the referential nature of true statements.

In this chapter I offer a view of journalism as interpretive practice by focusing on the series of speech acts by which news stories are constructed. In particular, I examine off-the-record discourse, as a particular site where accounts of social dynamics are contested and negotiated between journalists and their sources and institutional agents (such as editors) before written representations are generated.

OFF-THE-RECORD

"Off-the-record" is a domain of discourse between newsmakers and their sources in which public disclosure of what is said is ethically forbidden. The overt purpose of off-the-record communication is to enable journalists to learn information which will help the journalists to contextualize a story. It is also used as a means of supplying journalists with information that, if sourced, might cause problems for the source.

The ethical taboo on mimetic reproduction of off-the-record discourse allows responsibility for the content of what is said to be deferred. It therefore serves not only as a safe site for the disclosure of "sensitive" information, as journalists themselves tend to see it but is even more important as a discursive space in which sources can try-out different explanatory scenarios as part of the rhetorical process of "getting to the story."

Off-the-record messages are frequently clearly delineated by a marker: "this is off the record," "this is just for background," or "this isn't for publication." Either the source or the journalist may initiate such discourse (as when a journalist asks, "look, off the record, what's really going on here?")

In interaction, off-the-record discourse is frequently coded by intimacy markers. These include the use of first names by both parties, a softer more intimate (or perhaps conspiratorial) tone of voice and mutual courtesies: "I've been very impressed with your work, you've written a couple of good stories, I wouldn't want you to get this wrong . . . " and "Look, you've always been straight with me . . . .

The utility of off-the-record discourse is linked to the complex construction of authority, responsibility and voice in American newspaper writing. American journalism is mimetic; it seeks to represent the world by iconically reproducing it, using propositional descriptions and quotations.

These constitute "facts" about the event-object being represented. Journalistic authority is established through sourcing, the verbal representation of indexical relations between facts and the people and events from which these facts are drawn. The byline serves as a master trope that names the journalist who uncovered and arranged these facts for us. Journalists thus do not take responsibility for the truth of the facts they represent; they take responsibility for the accuracy of the mimetic reproduction: getting the names right, having the events accurately described and so forth. The responsibility for truth about the world lies in the object world itself, including the social actors in that world (like Congressional staffers) who serve as sources.

Because these actors have interests which lead them to privilege certain facts and interpretations, truth is never completed in journalism but must ever be (re)represented. Off-the-record discourse allows the sources an opportunity to enter the privileged world of the reporter and editors, that is, to speak outside of representation. To speak off the-record is to have the opportunity to speak without being discursively responsible for the truthfulness of one's words.

Professional sources like those hired by congressmen to represent them to the press are quick to make use of off-the-record discourse as a strategic resource. Going off the record encourages breaches in the normal processes of turn-taking and narration. Since responsibility for the truth of the content is deferred, off-the-record discourse offers a means to transform normal journalistic interview procedures and shift them to processes of co-narration.

Ochs and others have argued that co-narration of events leads to significant cognitive reframings in adultchild relationships. My sense is that among professional sources it is employed toward a similar effect, but often as a specific rhetorical strategy, one in which journalists, because of their need to "get to the story" are complicit. At the very least, going off the record undermines the journalist's ability to use the power of the question-andanswer format to structure the interactions.

Journalists commonly speak of two levels of off-the-record discourse: "off the record" and "deep background." The distinction involves issues of sourcing. Normal off-the-record discourse allows attribution but at a remove from the individual making the statements. This is textually marked by phrases like, "sources close to the President said . .

...Background means the journalist may use the material to understand what's going on but cannot attribute it, even generally. In my experience these distinctions are negotiated rather than constituting clearly marked frames.

The general rules for off-the-record discourse are well understood by newsmakers, both journalists and their professional sources. Messages disclosed may not be broadcast, published or otherwise recorded. They may, however, be gossiped about. A good deal of the conversation of reporters meeting at the press club over drinks is a sharing of off-the record information.

This exchange is understood to be part of how reporters stay current on what .is going on "behind the scenes." Thus I refer to off-therecord discourse as unwriteable rather than unspeakable; it can be gossiped, shared and debated but never mimetically recorded and attributed. Indeed, when off-the-record discourse is mimetically reproduced orally as gossip, it retains this essential feature. Going off-the-record thus protects sources from the consequences of mimetic reproduction of their words as they seek to define and interpret facts and events in order to produce coherent representations for public consumption.

NEGOTIATING THE NEWS: A CASE STUDY

He handed me a packet of materials including copies of two bills introduced by Republican Congressman Alpha, two press releases from Democratic Congressman Beta (of the same state) criticizing one of the bills (HROO01) and endorsing the other (HR002), and a press release from Alpha's office listing supporters and cosponsors for the first bill. My editor said he'd intended to write the story himself but to his unspecialized eye, both bills looked exactly the same. He'd called Alpha's office but no one there had been able to explain the difference between the two bills. Since I had previously covered stories on the political issue concerned, and knew both Congressmen, he asked me to "see what the story is."

After reviewing the materials, I went back to my editor and told him that on the surface it appeared that

Congressman Alpha had introduced a bill, Congressman Beta had attacked it in the home state papers and the next day Congressman Alpha had introduced a revised version of the bill. We agreed that such a story would make good copy and since the attack was detailed in the press releases, I estimated I could complete the story by the 3-hour deadline if I could get Congressman Alpha's "side of the story"-that is, his response to Beta's attacks. The editor-in-chief called me into his office to provide "some additional background: Alpha was running for governor of an East Coast state and Beta considering running against him. He urged me to keep this in mind as a possible angle. I called Alpha's office but his press secretary was not in.

The chief legislative aide was also out and no one else in the office could explain the differences between the two bills. More importantly, no one in the office was authorized to speak for the congressman. I warned the secretary again that I was under deadline and that the office needed to call me back as I had strong statements from Congressman Beta and I wanted to give Alpha the opportunity to respond. I spoke with my editors, telling them it looked to me as if Beta's criticisms might be justified.

After all, how could a Congressman create a bill and almost no one in his staff know what it is about? How could a congressman introduce two different bills on the same issue? I began sketching out the body of the story, using Beta's press release and incorporating background on Alpha from the morgue (the newspaper's archive of previous stories, clippings, and press releases).

Bert said he was glad he'd reached me because my angle was "all wrong." He explained that Alpha had written and introduced the first bill and that he was actively seeking cosponsorship and support for it. He introduced the second bill to get the chief lobbying organization's position into Congress, not as a result of the criticisms by Beta, which he claimed not to have heard. I read him the strongest language by Beta (accusations of political one-upmanship) and got back even stronger language (Congressman Alpha has forgotten more about this issue than Beta ever knew). I led my story with the "fact" of Congressman Alpha having introduced two bills with different legislative intents, described the bills and their current status in the calendar, then introduced Beta's criticisms and Alpha's office's rebuttal.

The story was read and passed without further changes by my editor and the editor-in-chief and ran on the front page the next day. Brinkmanship, after all, can go on indefinitely. Ernie insisted that I needed more "background," and that Alpha's office was not telling the truth. I suggested that if he would give me details we might consider a follow up story.

Ernie went off the record and made a number of accusations, specifically that: 1) Alpha had introduced two contrary bills so he could claim support from both sides of the issue; and 2) Alpha lied about his second bill (HROO02) being supported by the chief lobbying group for this issue. He suggested I call the lobbying group for "verification," that is, for on-the-record support of his off-the-record allegations.

The spokesperson for the lobbying group provided a different story. She said that her group did support HROO02, but that they had they had not written the bill and that it did not contain their preferred language. They had, however, provided input to Congressman Gamma, who, she said, had actually written the bill, even though Alpha had introduced it. She added that they had not been asked to support the bill until after it had been introduced. Dropping off the record, the spokeswoman told me that in fact Alpha had stolen the bill from Gamma and that Gamma's office would confirm this. She said that this "theft" had prevented the lobbying group from building broad support for the bill before it was introduced.

Gamma's office did not confirm this. The spokesperson said that while Congressman Gamma did write HROO02, he had cosponsored it with Alpha "in a move of bipartisan support" on this issue. Asked to comment specifically on why Alpha had introduced a bill Gamma had written, the spokesperson merely said that "everything moved very quickly." Off the record, he said that Gamma had been working with the lobbying group to create a bill acceptable both to the Congressional leadership and to the lobbyists. Gamma's office appraised Alpha because he was the minority leader of the committee that the bill would be reported to. After Alpha read the bill, it was introduced a day later. This had taken Gamma's office by surprise as they had planned to slowly build support before introducing it.

On the face of it, this story seemed to support Beta's allegations of political brinkmanship by Alpha, but since no one in Gamma's office would say so on the record, it was not a writeable story.

I called the lobbying group again, and this time spoke "on background" to an official with whom I had a long-term relationship. She repeated what her colleague had said and told me I could quote her as a source within the lobbying group but could not print her name or title. I called back Ernie and told him that the story he'd fed me didn't pan out. He asked me if I would talk to Congressman Beta when he returned to Washington that evening. I asked what more the congressman could add, but Ernie was evasive. We scheduled a time for the congressman to call me at my home that evening.

My editor was out, so I spoke to the editor-in chief and told him what was going on. He reminded me about the state political angle and suggested I see if I could get Beta to admit on the record that he was going to run for governor.

Beta called me at home that evening and I brought up the political angle suggested by my editor. Beta told me for the record that he would run for governor and called this introduction of two opposing bills "a symbolic move" by Alpha that showed "lack of real concern" for the issue.

The next morning I called Alpha's office and offered Bert Beta's charges that Alpha was playing politics. From Bert I again obtained dramatic quotes for the record, and allegations of political chicanery off the record.

The story generated from these interactions was passed

by the editor without further changes and appeared on page three as a "news analysis."

JOURNALISM IN THE SUBJUNCTIVE MODE

To analyse this series of interactions I want to treat each interaction between a set of participants as a separate speech act with its own set of messages, goals and outcomes and media of transmission. Cumulatively, these acts form a speech event that culminates in the production of a written text, a news story. In this case, reactions to the first news story generated a second speech event culminating in the production of a second news story. Space precludes a detailed analysis of each of the twenty acts that comprise these two speech events.

What I will focus on here are the epistemologies and heuristics that give order to the process. In the first speech event, I was, as the journalist, charged with the project of "seeing what the story is." This project emphasizes several of the points of the underlying epistemology of journalism: that there is an object world that can be represented verbally, that the object world is constituted by social events and that previously-inscribed discourses (press releases, bills introduced) constitute events in this object world. Most importantly, the use of the definite article points up a central assumption of journalistic practice: that there is a best possible account and that the production of this best account is the project of journalism.

"Getting the story" thus involves recovering, or uncovering, referential meaning. This search for truths, however, is only the first step; truthful reports must be further organized around the truth, a main point that can serve as an "angle," or master frame, for construction of a story.

This distinction between reports and story draws on the insights of Livya Polanyi, who defines a story as a narrative in which a teller describes events which took place in one specific past time world in order to make some sort of point about the world which teller and recipients share.

Reports on the other hand, are not supposed to be trying to make a point but rather to recount past, present or future events in a more-or-less non-evaluative way. Reports are usually elicited by the recipients or in response to circumstances that require an accounting of what went on. It is the context of reporting that supplies the framework in which the relevance of the states and events being reported can be ascertained.

In fact, the recipients may even apply relevance to very specific pieces of information whose importance escapes the narrator. The burden of assigning differential weighting to the various narrated propositions thus falls on the receiver of the report. The reporter himself may implicitly tell the elicitor, "O.K., you wanted to know. You figure out what it means".

News stories clearly lie in between these two genres, as is suggested by the terminology used by journalists: reporting is what journalists do, but stories are what they write. A news story is like a report in that it is not written—or, at least, it is not supposed to be written-specifically to make a point. Instead, it is supposed to be a non-evaluative recapitulation of events whose meaning is inherent in the events themselves.

The choice of what is reported is not supposed to be actively chosen by the reporter; rather it is dictated by circumstances. Some things are news, and some are not. But a news story is a story in that these events must be organized and arranged according to their relevance, that is, their point. For example, although bounded by specific time lines, news stories are rarely told in chronological order. News stories seek to open (or lead) with the most "relevant" information, which may or may not coincide with the most recent information.

In reporting, the facts are seen as lying within the sources and the goal of the reporter is to extract these from him or her as directly as possible.

The truth value of the source's statement is measured according to its correspondence to the real object out there in the real world of objects. However, the interaction is complicated by two problems.

First, the journalist usually does not have direct access to the event-as-object being represented but can only get to it through the discourse of his or her sources. He or she cannot check what a source has said directly against the phenomenological world but only against other sources. Second, all these sources are known to have "interests" which will bias their subjective (that is, emotional and mental) attitude toward the objects and so shape the representations the source offers the reporter. This problem, that the truth is out there and is writeable but the people who know the truth have reasons for not telling it to you accurately, is the paradox that drives the journalistic enterprise.

A central problem of interpretive practice for journalists, then, is handling the polyvocality of multiple reports to produce a coherent story. To handle this, journalists treat the event-object of their representation as something to be uncovered so that it can be represented. Sources are treated as people who know about the event-object but for various reasons of their own (including simple misunderstanding) seek to obscure or mask that knowledge. "Getting to the story" is largely a process of sifting through reports to see what's "really going on" so that it can be represented.

My own efforts to get to the story involved both interpreting the written documents according to my own competence and in seeking sources who could explain them. This is typical of political journalism in Washington where it concerns actions of the legislature. As one colleague told me, "the bill isn't the story.

The story is what I find out about the bill on the phone after I get back [from the press conference where the bill was introduced]." Beginning with a set of faxed press releases and copies of the actual bills (brought in by newspaper staff from the Government Printing Office downtown) I began not by simply reporting the two newly introduced bills but by looking for the story behind the bills.

This story came to me couched by my editor as a puzzle. Normally, we would expect to see two conflicting bills on the same subject by two rival Congressmen, a situation for which there are standard story frames. Here we had two different bills on the same subject written by the same Congressman. The press release criticizing the first bill from the rival Congressman offered a clue for interpreting these bills: Perhaps Alpha introduced the second bill in response to the criticisms made by Beta as described in Beta's press release.

This interpretation is a transformation of the existing interpretive frame and "makes sense" given the assumptions of that frame. It was endorsed tentatively by my editors but we agreed that in order to present it as a story, that is, as a statement of referential truth, it needed to be confirmed by Alpha's office. At least, Alpha's "side of the story" would need to be included in our representation.

Bert was able to use my effort to "balance" the news to go off the record and offer me an entirely different frame, one that would entirely exclude Beta and his allegations. My final story positions these two frames in tension, describing Alpha's actions, offering Ernie's/Beta's interpretation of them and concluding with Bert's/Alpha's rejoinder.

Had I not been working under such a tight deadline, a call to a political scientist as to how common the strategy of introducing two bills on the same topic is, a call to some other lobbyists and perhaps an academic expert on the topic of the bills might have fleshed out the story. As it was, the lead was rather prosaic-it was the dramatic exchange of insults in the fifth and sixth paragraphs on a slow news day that made the editors consider the story for the front page.

There are several anomalous elements to the first speech event, not the least of which is the fact that the story was given to me by my editor as a story. In the normal course of events a reporter is expected to handle his own beat, uncover and recognize stories as they arise, and keep the editor informed of what he is working on. The abnormal number of editorial conferences in the first speech event reflects the odd genesis of the bill, although it seemed natural at the time. The second story is a more reflective of routine processes of newsmaking. In the initial telephone call, Ernie attempts to hook me by suggesting my published story is wrong or incomplete.

Such conversation is de facto off the record since he can be certain a reporter will not make use of such casual criticisms. He goes formally off the record in order to offer a new interpretation of what is going on and offers me a suggestion as to where I can get this confirmed.

This leads to a sequence of interactions in which I seek to discover the "true" state of affairs. Each source has an official statement to offer me "for the record" and an interpretation of or claim about the events to offer off the record. The official statements are insufficiently newsworthy to justify a new story but any of the off-the-record allegations would, if true, make a good story. In the end, I called Bert to tell him there's no story not simply as a courtesy but in an attempt to coerce him into saying something interesting for the record.

This led to my conversation with Congressman Beta and his allegations that Alpha's actions were simply political machinations. Yet Beta's allegations were not sufficient to justify running the story as "hard news." In the end, the story that ran as a "news analysis" mimetically reproduced this bickering to highlight the theme (denied by both Congressmen as applying to themselves) that political rivalries over gubernatorial and other stakes can impact federal legislation on issues largely unrelated to those stakes.

One of the most interesting aspects of both series of speech acts is that each act is contingent. Each speech act has a dynamic of its own driven by the need of the participants to negotiate a frame, the relations between speech acts, and the dynamic of their constitution as a speech event which produces a written text.

The journalist seeks continually to discover a story that

can be the story, that is, which can be understood as true by reference to the objective world. The journalist abrogates to himself the right to determine which story, or synthesis of stories is the story, but only through reference to prior representations offered by sources, whether documentary or oral. As a result, each speech act produces an interpretation of events whose validity as the story is held in check while the reporter pursues additional sources, which lead to additional interpretations.

These interactions also expose the degree to which the interpretive practices of journalists are social and how much of what they write as having been uncovered is in fact negotiated. These negotiations are excluded from the written news story" yet they are an essential part of interpretive practice. In order to arrange for such negotiations, journalists and their sources, particularly professional sources, recognize off-the-record discourse as a special register of talk specifically used for such negotiation.

Off-the-record discourse offers a site within which journalists and sources can handle polyvocality by trying out different explanatory scenarios.

In setting out to get to the story, the journalist is engaging in a series of encounters that take place within a structured "field" of journalism, "a microcosm which has its own rules, which is constituted autonomously and which cannot be understood from external factors".

To understand what a journalist writes, it is necessary to understand his or her place in the journalistic fieldthe status of the newspaper for which the journalist writes (and hence the authority with which he or she speaks and asks questions), the journalist's specific competence in the writing technologies privileged within the field, the position of the journalist within the sets of roles within the newspaper, and the history of the journalist's prior relations with the social actors he or she is constituting as sources.

The journalistic field is in turn bordered by other fields; the problematic overlap between these fields is also a necessary context for understanding interpretive practice.

Each of the twenty interaction/ negotiations described above, then, can be more thickly described in terms of situated interests within overlapping social fields.10 From the journalist's perspective, much of the story lies in interaclions taking place in these fields-in this case, particularly, the political.

Perhaps more importantly, the engine that powers these interactions derives from the fact that the representations ultimately fixed in textual form constitute a form of capital in these overlapping fields. For the journalist, the story becomes part of a portfolio that may be used in seeking promotions or new jobs or simply increased status within the field. For professional sources like Ernie and Bert, these texts, if they can be framed as supportive of the politicians and their agendas, are likewise sources of economic and social advancement.

In talking about the negotiations of the story in off-the-record discourse it seems to me that neither structural/ institutional nor free-agent theories are useful, as both obscure elements of this process. Negotiations take place as a result of interests on the part of various social actors within structurally constrained fields.

The interpretive practice of journalists is further affected by the fact that they are not seeking to write against normative frames of understanding. They instead offer accounts of the world that can be read by their audiences as natural, that is, according to the "common sense" frames of interpretation in circulation in the society for which the accounts are intended." These practices are largely unreflexive.

One way to articulate this is with Bourdieu's term habitus, which he has defined in one place as an "art of inventing." Life is a series of confrontations between the social actor and situations; habitus makes it possible to produce an infinite number of practices, each situational and thus "relatively unpredictable" but also "limited in their diversity".

Habitus is the product of our prior encounters with the world, our successes (positively sanctioned behaviors) and our failures (negatively sanctioned behaviors) and hence it "tends to generate all the `reasonable,' `common-sense,' behaviors (and only these) Which are possible within the limits" of the regularities of our life experiences.

Practices-like the practice of journalism-are the outcome of an encounter between one's professional habitus and a particular social field:

The Kabyle woman setting up her loom is not performing an act of cosmogony; she is simply setting up her loom to weave cloth intended to serve a technical function. It so happens that, given the symbolic equipment available to her for practically thinking her own practice-in particular her language which constantly refers her back to the logic of plowing-she can only think what she is doing in the enchanted, that is to say, mystified, form . . ..

Similarly, the journalist, sitting down with her computer and telephone, is not engaging in a process of cultural reproduction or of resistance; she is trying to write a story about people and events that her readers, as she imagines them, will read and understand.

The symbolic equipment available to the journalist for making sense of the world in order to define and get at the story is much the same as other members of her cultural background, including her sources, and in the U.S. constantly refers her back to the logic of the market, of free choices and rational calculation. The professional habitus that informs her writing practices, the language in which she commits her story to words, is further organized by a particular cultural logic: a logic of objectivity.

To understand what a journalist writes, it is necessary to understand his or her place in the journalistic fieldthe status of the newspaper for which the journalist writes (and hence the authority with which he or she speaks and asks questions), the journalist's specific competence in the writing technologies privileged within the field, the position of the journalist within the sets of roles within the newspaper, and the history of the journalist's prior relations with the social actors he or she is constituting as sources.

The journalistic field is in turn bordered by other fields; the problematic overlap between these fields is also a necessary context for understanding interpretive practice. Each of the twenty interaction/ negotiations described above, then, can be more thickly described in terms of situated interests within overlapping social fields.10 From the journalist's perspective, much of the story lies in interaclions taking place in these fields-in this case, particularly, the political.

Perhaps more importantly, the engine that powers these interactions derives from the fact that the representations ultimately fixed in textual form constitute a form of capital in these overlapping fields. For the journalist, the story becomes part of a portfolio that may be used in seeking promotions or new jobs or simply increased status within the field. For professional sources like Ernie and Bert, these texts, if they can be framed as supportive of the politicians and their agendas, are likewise sources of economic and social advancement.

In talking about the negotiations of the story in off-the-record discourse it seems to me that neither structural/ institutional nor free-agent theories are useful, as both obscure elements of this process. Negotiations take place as a result of interests on the part of various social actors within structurally constrained fields.

The interpretive practice of journalists is further affected by the fact that they are not seeking to write against normative frames of understanding. They instead offer accounts of the world that can be read by their audiences as natural, that is, according to the "common sense" frames of interpretation in circulation in the society for which the accounts are intended." These practices are largely unreflexive.

One way to articulate this is with Bourdieu's term habitus, which he has defined in one place as an "art of inventing." Life is a series of confrontations between the social actor and situations; habitus makes it possible to produce an infinite number of practices, each situational and thus "relatively unpredictable" but also "limited in their diversity". Habitus is the product of our prior encounters with the world, our successes (positively sanctioned behaviors) and our failures (negatively sanctioned behaviors) and hence it "tends to generate all the `reasonable,' `common-sense,' behaviors (and only these) Which are possible within the limits" of the regularities of our life experiences.

Practices-like the practice of journalism-are the outcome of an encounter between one's professional habitus and a particular social field:

The Kabyle woman setting up her loom is not performing an act of cosmogony; she is simply setting up her loom to weave cloth intended to serve a technical function. It so happens that, given the symbolic equipment available to her for practically thinking her own practice-in particular her language which constantly refers her back to the logic of plowing-she can only think what she is doing in the enchanted, that is to say, mystified, form . . ..

Similarly, the journalist, sitting down with her computer and telephone, is not engaging in a process of cultural reproduction or of resistance; she is trying to write a story about people and events that her readers, as she imagines them, will read and understand.

The symbolic equipment available to the journalist for making sense of the world in order to define and get at the story is much the same as other members of her cultural background, including her sources, and in the U.S. constantly refers her back to the logic of the market, of free choices and rational calculation. The professional habitus that informs her writing practices, the language in which she commits her story to words, is further organized by a particular cultural logic: a logic of objectivity.

My final story positions these two frames in tension, describing Alpha's actions, offering Ernie's/Beta's interpretation of them and concluding with Bert's/Alpha's rejoinder. Had I not been working under such a tight deadline, a call to a political scientist as to how common the strategy of introducing two bills on the same topic is, a call to some other lobbyists and perhaps an academic expert on the topic of the bills might have fleshed out the story. As it was, the lead was rather prosaic-it was the dramatic exchange of insults in the fiJournalists are not entirely unaware of their epistemological dilemmas. Commentary on these issues constitutes a heterodox zone within journalism, sometimes characterized as "the new journalism." Most journalists run up against situations that expose these dilemmas at some time in their careers. In stories they tell, reporters attempt to speak as direct observers about matters of empirical fact and are squelched by editors, who as gatekeepers of journalistic objectivity, are quick to suppress such behaviour.

Unexamined by journalism is the possibility that the object world perhaps cannot be neutrally represented or that journalism is a particular form of knowledge whose truthfulness lies not so much in its reference to the object-world as in the mode of production which engenders it.

The importance of objectivity as a conceptual framework is marked by every ethnographer who examines the American press. The problem is the relationship of objectivity to journalistic practice. Tuchman has looked at objectivity as a "ritual practice," a repetitive series of actions through which journalism is produced. Iyengar has presented objectivity as a system of frames.

Both these concepts largely ignore the creative, performative and negotiated aspects of journalism, particularly since Iyengar's notion of frames is a cognitive one quite different from the attention given to the ongoing negotiation of framing activity proposed by the originators of the term. More recently, Pedelty has offered the notion of objectivity as a "disciplinary apparatus," one of several which organize the social fields in which journalism takes place.

This is a useful notion, particularly since it draws attention not only to constraints but to the pleasures-"pay, promotion, notoriety, identity, fantasy"-that draw journalists toward the reproduction of cultural forms favored by institutions.

However, it tends to draw attention to the structure of the field in which practices take place rather than the unfolding of the action. My own effort here is to draw attention to the links between epistemologies and the heuristics that social actors use it interpreting situations so that they can act in them. For this reason, I am here considering objectivity as a practical logic.

A "practical logic," Bourdieu says, "understands only in order to act". Faced with the subjunctive, contingent nature of reporting, a reporter finds that objectivity provides a generative logic that can produce a universe of action without reporters being under the burden of carrying about an imaginary "file of prefabricated representations". Off-the-record discourse offers a privileged and perhaps necessary site for much of this action to take place. Faced with the unsubstantiated but attractive claims offered by sources (and editors) off the record, the logic of objectivity allows the reporter to act creatively in order to bring negotiations around to a writeable story.

Chapter 4

The Origins of the Right to Privacy

From the seventeenth-century Puritans to the current culture warriors, many Americans have heen determined to set standards of moral conduct for others. Much of the country's first two centuries of printing was concerned with monitoring prohibited actions and making religious and ethical pronouncements. Colonists and then citizens of the new nation were anxious not only about political maneuverings, but also about the vices associated with profit making and popular culture and the prospects of more autonomy for women and the working class.

Not knowing how their experiments in government would turn out, many worried about liberty and opportunity generating dissolution and disorder. The founding principles of the United States included the assumption that the survival of republics depended on public virtue that in turn required private morality.

Proper public and private behaviour frequently was seen as relying on parental guidance, religious beliefs, enlightened education, or beneficial economic arrangements. Public activity could be subjected to press criticism when not in accord with the common good and thwarted by the mechanisms of government when necessary. Societal decisions were supposed to be shaped by a reasoning process that could be understood as relying on the chilly calculations of the Madisonian head and the innate moral sense of the Jeffersonian heart.

Private judgment, which was usually not subject to public surveillance, was supposed to be shaped to a large extent by moral suasion within the home. Domestic hierarchy and the influence of women were regarded as sacrosanct, stabilizing influences.

The ideal of republican self-discipline and the belief in moral nurture did not disappear in antebellum America, but the nation's politics and culture became more romantic and individualistic. The personal became more prevalent in mass communication.

Publications paid more attention to human desires and frequently dwelled on struggles between conventional morality and powerful impulses. Inexpensive newspapers, pamphlets, and books gave lurid accounts of lust, intoxication, and laws breaking that were often ostensibly for edifying purposes, but that, in any case, offered opportunities for voyeuristic contemplation of the conduct being examined. The popular fare inspired Edgar Allan Poe, Herman Melville, Nathaniel Hawthorne, and other literary figures to portray dark and irrational reaches of the human mind.

Schooled in the era's competitive print culture, they managed to turn stories of subversion and suggestiveness into memorable texts of moral turbulence and ambiguity. Poe went as far as making saleable writings out of the morbid and mentally deranged. Answering objections to the publication of his "Berenice," a tale of an obsessed lover who digs up a woman's coffin and extracts her teeth, Poe told the proprietor of the Southern Literary Messenger that he should want more pieces of the same kind in order to be successful.

"But whether the articles of which I speak are, or are not in bad taste is little to the purpose," Poe wrote. "To be appreciated you must be read, and these things are invariably sought after with avidity." Fiction and poetry were found in antebellum newspapers, but were being displaced by fact by mid-century. News stories offered constant novelty and a sense of experiencing real characters and plots.

Newspaper narratives about people's conduct increased during the nineteenth century without general agreement that the revelations served as cautionary tales or spurred needed change. As immigration, industrialization, urbanization, partisan strife, and other stresses shook the society, fears of losing class privilege, gender roles, common propriety, and personal security made life seem more precarious and less predictable. Religious revivals, reform movements, social experiments, and moral regulations were ways of coping with conditions that could seem too free and frightening.

Victorian moral discourses promoted an ethos of respectability in which men of character maintained control of themselves and others while women took special responsibilities for piety, etiquette, and integrity in the domestic sphere. Public pressures and prescriptive literature, however, could have only limited effects on what people did. Even as the nineteenth-century home became a more sentimentalized, privatized place in idealized conceptions, illicit behaviour by all categories of citizens made images of decency and decorum difficult to preserve.

Prostitution, pornography, drinking, gambling, and other vices thrived in an underworld that was an inversion of bourgeois values. Market-driven newspapers moved beyond the traditional political topics to delve into the details of private lives being touched by scandal, crime, or other events. Stories about sin and self-indulgence named names in high society. Social deviance became harder to hide or ignore.

The transatlantic culture of Victorianism valued order, progress, and self-control in a competitive world without many safeguards other than resolute personal rectitude. Victorian ideals were espoused as well as assaulted in print media that were themselves going through tremendous changes. Attention-grabbing material and low costs made the number and circulations of publications soar.

Metropolitan dailies began using high-speed presses, telegraphy, photography, new designs, and expanded features. Human-interest stories and society news revealed aspects of people's lives that usually had been thought inappropriate for journalism. As the press became more commercial and more interested in exposing the personal, journalistic competition intensified and reporters could be regarded as too intrusive.

Admitting that an '"interviewer"' occasionally could be a nuisance in the pursuit of a story, an admiring appraisal of urban journalism in Harper's in 1877 said that "the characteristic attaché of the city staff is a polite, shrewd, and intelligent gentleman" who was mortified at having to bother people in order to satisfy readers' appetites. Such complimentary assessments of reporters, however, were not as common as condemnation.

While some observers defended or excused the coverage, others identified invasion of privacy as a problem to be solved by self-regulation or by carving out a new exception to constitutional protections for publications.

Two hallowed principles, a right to know and a right to be left alone, were being contested between 1833 when Benjamin Day began publishing the nation's first successful penny daily, the New York Sun, and 1890 when a much-acclaimed Harvard Law Review article by Samuel D. Warren and Louis D. Brandeis formalized arguments for an invasion of privacy tort that courts and legislatures would gradually develop in the following decades.

"The press is overstepping in every direction the obvious bounds of propriety and of decency," Warren and Brandeis wrote. "Gossip is no longer the resource of the idle and of the vicious, but has become a trade, which is pursued with industry as well as effrontery." The two authors wanted a freedom from the communication of degrading facts in order to preserve "incorporeal rights" and "intangible property" in pleasant and profitable mental processes.

They portrayed revelatory journalism as a loathsome business that should be held responsible for violating "man's spiritual nature" and "the sacred precincts of private and domestic life." Trivializing personal gossip had a "blighting influence" on better thoughts and feelings, Warren and Brandeis maintained, and were procured with a "modern enterprise and invention" that violated the home's necessary retreat from an increasingly intense, complex world.

Historians have noted the existence of complaints about the press before 1890 and have begun to consider and connect the multiple intellectual and cultural dimensions of the disputes over control of personal information and space. Particularly in need of closer examination are the professional and legal questions that were at stake at a time when both Victorian manners and moneymaking ventures were valued in American society. Religious and moral frameworks of meaning were being pitted against an emerging gospel of consumer gratification.

As the more commercial approach to journalism became more common, many commentaries asserted that the market-driven stories could be detrimental to morals30 and that the reporters themselves could have unsavory characters. A number of the era's leading journalists and public intellectuals dramatized a need for protecting people from the prying practices and debasing influences of journalism. Like the eighteenth-century newspaper contributors who pondered the meaning of press freedom before the First Amendment was ratified, they reflected on rights and responsibilities.

Their public discourse often applied Victorian rules of decorum and typically assigned blame to economic pressures on journalists to satisfy vulgar appetites. Some of the writers endorsed more self-regulation while others sought a legal remedy in the years before Warren and Brandeis published their version of the idea.

The contours of the contention over privacy rights can be traced in the thought-leader periodicals of the late nineteenth century. Prestigious magazines dedicated to elitist or reformist values presented essays on the issue as they sought to set a high standard for expression in print. Publishers vied with each other to reach new levels of excellence and had notable success.

Paul Blouët, a French visitor to the United States, wrote in 1889 that some American magazines had "attained a perfection which is the highest utterance of journalism, as understood by the educated world." His main examples were North American Review, Forum, Atlantic Monthly, Century, Harper's, Scribner's, and Lippincott's. Essays from these and other magazines with intellectual commentary were located for this study with the help of volume indexes, Poole's Index to Periodical Literature, databases, and the Making of America digital library. The purpose of the research is to delineate the pre-history of one of the most vexing issues in democratic theory.

What did press proponents and critics before Warren and Brandeis conclude about a right of privacy, what rationales did they develop, and what resistance did they meet? The differences of opinion on journalistic disclosure illustrate the difficulty of developing any consensus on constraints for commercial mass communication. Assertions about social morality and individual well-being can be at odds with a market economy and freedom of expression.

SENSATIONAL NEWS, SOCIAL RESPONSIBILITY, AND PERSONAL RESPECTABILITY

Before the rise of sensational journalism in the 1830s, newspapers were often celebrated as informative and socially beneficial vehicles of enlightenment. Later assessments of the press frequently found some kinds of subject matter distinctly improper. One constant for the nation, however, was that political conflict could be a motive for newspapers to cross the boundary between the public and the private.

"Party spirit has entered the recesses of domestic retirement, violated the sanctity of female character, invaded the tranquility of private life, and visited, with severe inflictions, the peace of families," Governor De Witt Clinton complained in his annual address to the New York legislature in 1828.

Throughout the nineteenth century, publications sought partisan gains with stories about the sexual behaviour of opponents such as Thomas Jefferson, William Henry Harrison, and Grover Cleveland. One of the journalists who had more general purposes in mind while exposing private wrongdoing was Anne Royall, who worked within the moralistic and rationalistic framework of the Enlightenment.

She regarded herself a prophetic voice against the vices that would doom democracy and the bigotry and priestcraft that kept women from exercising their civilizing influences. She made little money and at one point was convicted of breaking a colonial-era law against being a common scold. Her Paul Pry, a Washington weekly founded in 1831, muck-raked and revealed personal failings. Royall said that the aim of her successor publication, The Huntress, was to "expose corruption, hypocrisy, and usurpation."

When Alexis de Tocqueville, the French social theorist, was sent to the United States in 1831, he found Americans uninterested in press restrictions even though party newspapers were routinely ready "to assail the characters of individuals, to track them into private life, and disclose all their weaknesses and errors." He thought that any wrongs of journalism were too difficult for courts to handle and were outweighed by the role of free expression in preserving liberty and civilization.

Censorship was absurd, Tocqueville said, where popular sovereignty presumed people could make their own judgments about facts and opinions. Women, he observed, were "confined within the narrow circle of domestic life," but were regarded as having understandings as sound and intellects as clear as men's.

In the following decades, however, anxieties about personal belief and behaviour deepened as expanding cities made temptations more available and wrongdoing less detectable. Publishers responded by selling materials about the misdeeds, mysteries, and moral geographies of urban life. Confidence in democratic communication, meanwhile, appeared to wane as such content was regarded as harmful to vulnerable minds or as the result of questionable motives or methods.

The commercial press phenomenon emerged in the

Jacksonian era with penny dailies that appealed largely to urban artisans with egalitarian sentiments. Increasingly inexpensive publication costs and mushrooming metropolitan markets allowed print culture to become more diverse and, some feared, more degraded.

The public sphere was splitting into separate, antagonistic public sphericules. Penny papers and religious publications did detective work on the furtive immoralities of the elite in the 183Os. New York's "sporting press," publications with names such as Flash, Whip, and Rake, gleefully covered individuals in the world of commercialized sex in the early 1840s.

Journalists who wanted reform, who articulated defenses of prostitution, or who simply treated illicit intercourse as news were reviled as lewd intruders on privacy and were subjected to a variety of sanctions ranging from withdrawal of financial support to criminal or obscene libel prosecutions.48 They and other writers on "racy" or "society" topics were accused of blackmailing people who did not want indiscretions disclosed or invented.

A New Hampshire newspaper contributor stated that if journalists wanted to publish such "sacrilegious" and "unholy" violations of family feelings, "then the liberty of the Press needs very much some kind of restriction."

Reporters could observe urban social codes and provide inside information to parvenus, poseurs, and the public at large. James Gordon Bennett's innovative New York Herald achieved its popularity in the 183Os and 184Os partly through sustained attention to the upper crust.

Sources were inclined to cooperate because the paper, which was too republican not to notice the flaws and follies of American aristocrats, could damage or foster reputations. The advantaged perceived a greater access to facts about themselves as a danger to their status and power and scorned the purveyors even if the public well-being was involved.

Philip Hone, a wealthy, courtly New Yorker who objected to reporting on social activities, made diary entries that recorded his consternation at how Bennett and his reporters covered balls and dinners with a sense of entitlement and how politicians sought their company. Hone deplored newspaper disclosures about stock swindling as disgraceful to the city and insulting to "the moral sense of the community." Yet, he observed, even those who denounced such publications bought copies.

"Licentiousness, no matter how disgusting, lies, however glaring, personal abuse without a shadow of foundation, must be served up to gratify the taste of the people," he wrote, "or the papers will not sell." He saw that libel cases had little or no deterrent effect on Bennett's determination to report on the lives of others and that street beatings and social ostracism only encouraged public sympathy for the editor. Hone thought that a reform society should be established to eradicate the evils of the penny press.

The Herald and other papers justified shocking reporting on the vices and corruption of the poor and the privileged as a guide to social conditions in need of reform. When a prostitute named Helen Jewett was brutally murdered in an elegant New York brothel in 1836, Bennett visited her room, interviewed the madam, and described the beauty of the corpse.

Class friction was evident in the courtroom and in the press as one of Jewett's customers, Richard Robinson, was tried and acquitted. Journalists pointed to a conspiracy of the prosperous and powerful. Philip Hone, who was active at the highest levels of Whig politics, attended part of the trial and had no doubt that Robinson was guilty, but noted that the defendant had influential friends as well as skilled attorneys who could raise doubts in the minds of the jurors.

Circulations shot up as even the most sobre sheets covered the crime and news accounts of Jewett's life and death presented conflicting details. Bennett's moral thunderings and his unreliable, inconsistent, and strangely incomplete reporting raised suspicions that he was taking protection money from citizens who could have been embarrassed by their connections to the case.

Bennett's wit, enterprise, disdain of prudery, and self-promoting championing of truth and justice made him popular enough to prosper in spite of detractors who portrayed him as a vulgar wretch. A boycott of Bennett by clergy, journalists, and business leaders in 1840, which was dubbed the "Moral War," met with little success.

A letter to the Macon Daily Telegraph in 1860 said that the Herald's kind of gossip about the leisure activities at Newport or Saratoga was a "growing evil" that Northerners might accept, but not the ladies and gentlemen of Georgia who had the "same right to privacy" at a resort as at home. When Bennett died in 1872, Appleton's Journal reprinted a sarcastic London Saturday Review obituary congratulating New Yorkers and lamenting that the Herald survived him. He was described as an unprincipled peddler who served the "prurient appetites and mean jealousies" of "the worst side of a democratic society."

An 1873 essay in Overland depicted Bennett as desiring wealth while New York Tribune editor Horace Greeley had sought influence. The coarse, cynical, and mercurial Bennett "did not hesitate to exhibit his own private and domestic life" for his paper's benefit, the writer observed, while the reformminded Greeley "aimed at something higher than mere money-grubbing."

Invasive journalism upset notable writers who said they wanted print culture to be more high-minded. "To a philosopher all news as it is called, is gossip, and they who edit and read it are old women over their tea," Henry David Thoreau grumbled at Walden Pond.

"Yet not a few are greedy after this gossip." In his novel Martin Chuzzlewit (1843), Charles Dickens, who had toured the United States in 1842, depicted New York City newsboys shouting the names of the fictional publications: the Sewer, Stabber, Family Spy, Private Listener, Peeper, Plunderer, Keyhole Reporter, and Rowdy Journal.

Walt Whitman, who had edited or contributed to more than 30 New York area newspapers by 1855 when his Leaves of Grass appeared, singled out Bennett's newspaper for aspersions. Writing as the editor of the New York Aurora in 1842, Whitman decried the Herald as "a scandal to the republic." He said that its editor was worse than any Dickens villain "inasmuch that the poison he diffuses is gilded, and allowed to pass by common suffrance." He described Bennett as a "reptile marking his path with slime wherever he goes, and breathing mildew at every thing fresh and fragrant; a midnight ghoul, preying on rottenness and repulsive filth."

When Whitman left the .Aurora and briefly edited the New York Evening Tattler, he wrote a paragraph calling his former paper "trashy, scurrilous, and obscene" and its two owners ignorant, coarse, selfish, and illmannered vagabonds and blackmailers.

A nationalistic and radically democratic American, Whitman could be as indignant about disreputable commercial journalism as any privileged moralist. His journalism promulgated Jeffersonian principles and regarded freedom of expression as sacred even if subject to some restrictions based on necessity or outrage. He contended that inexpensive reading material could be a means of common education, but was anxious about public morality being affected by "the general character for scurrility that marks the American newspapers."

In 1842 he and other editors reprinted a bogus letter supposedly written by Dickens to a London paper to criticize Americans as greedy, uncouth, and foolishly devoted to "the very silliest kind of mock exclusiveness" rather than to a simplicity of manners.

The letter expressed disgust at the overwhelming attention Dickens had received as he traveled in the United States and complained, "I never thought that I was petted, merely for myself, but as a kind of monster, to look at, and be gazed about, and imbue my keepers with somewhat of the notoriety that enveloped myself." Whitman praised the letter for attacking public curiosity and "the flimsiness of our American aristocracy."

Hone, one of the dignitaries who had welcomed the famous novelist with elitist flourishes and social exclusions that dismayed the more democratically minded in the press, wrote to Dickens and received a reply saying that the letter was a wicked, infuriating forgery. A year later, however, Hone was perturbed by the disparaging way the luminary he had defended described the United States in Martin Chuzzlewit, a book the New York gentleman denounced as "an exceedingly foolish libel upon us, from which he will not obtain credit as an author, nor as a man of wit, any more than as a man of good taste, good nature, or good manners."

As the editor of the Democratic Brooklyn Daily Eagle from 1846 to 1848, Whitman concluded that the benefits of the press were being sacrificed to profit and partisanship. "We have little fine, hearty, truthful writing in our papers," he wrote. "We have, (it must be from want of public encouragement,) little high-toned gentlemanliness or elegance-little politeness even." He editorialized against publishing private letters in the press and said those who did should be socially ostracized.

Such betrayals of confidence by "sneaking stabbers, who violate every dictate of honour and gentlemanly feeling," he said, were worse than highway robbery. Not seeing an entirely bleak picture, Whitman commented in an 1848 editorial that American newspapers were generally better behaved than those in England and that he hoped they would improve.

Yet, he said that publishers were too concerned with immediate financial rewards and too willing to serve up the superficial. Whitman again disdained the Herald's "flippant, sneering, exclusively selfish and sordid method," but did appreciate its "example of newspaper enterprise." Less than two weeks later, despite helping the Eagle prosper and gain the respect of other newspapers, Whitman was dismissed for taking anti-slavery positions at odds with his publisher's opinions.

Despite his protests about the press, Whitman himself produced sensational journalism and fiction early in his career and, as the attempts to censor Leaves of Grass indicated, his later work tested the boundaries of propriety.

The heterogeneity of the nation was reflected in a large array of newspapers representing diverse economic, social, political, and cultural interests, but some of the metropolitan dailies revolutionized journalism and gained large audiences by devoting unprecedented amounts of coverage to crime and personalities. Anyone with a societal, professional, or personal reputation to uphold could fear coverage or complain of being victimized by crass journalistic conduct.

Privacy proponents attributed intrusive newspaper reporting to moral failures associated with uncivilized character and unconstrained commerce. In an 1886 issue of North American Review, attorney Augustus A. Levey said that too much newspaper reading "is a mild form of mania which needs regulation and control as much as other petty vices of human nature."

He insisted that the "highly cultivated and educated few" scorned the scandal, sensationalism, and superficial thinking of newspapers. Low standards were the result of private enterprise, said another contributor to the magazine, because "if readers did not enjoy and demand these things they would not be printed." The Nation commented in 1889 that "the doctrine is being more and more accepted that the sole function of the newspaper is to make money" and that enterprising publishers were indifferent to the growing tendency to discuss "personal and domestic life."

Reporters had a legendary drive to gather personal information about the lives of the prominent and the distresses of the poor. "Happily for them, no false and mechanistic objectivity interfered with their belief in the sharp eye, the immediate impression, and the insolent question," historian M.H. Dunlop has remarked.

"The dailies snapped and popped, they offered up a confusing and uproarious world unfiltered by rumination, and they thereby saved the world from the deadening middle-class gentility of the periodicals." Jaded amusement could be one reaction to their exploits. "For the interviewer, nothing is sacred," Paul Blouët wrote in a jocular 1889 book. "Audacity is his stock-in-trade; the most private details of your daily life are at his mercy, and unless you blow his brains out-which is not lawful in New York State-you have no means of getting rid of him." In a more serious vein, Blouët admitted that he had admiration for the newsgatherers' persistence, personalities, and reporting skills. He did treat a female interviewer with some condescension, however.

Women were, nevertheless, widely accepted in the field of society reporting, a task that was seen as suitable for their gender and within what one writer called the "natural limits" of those who took jobs outside the home.

The elite and their lifestyles could be commodified for the masses in ways that catered to curiosity and sparked envy or resentment. Emotionally charged fiction sought to portray the secrets of the rich and poor. Journalism similarly intruded on the physical and psychological isolation of comfortable and well-ordered lives with stories that had the potential to raise issues of race, gender, and class domination.

Press exposure of private activities could make consumption too conspicuous. In 1886 author William H. Bushnell lectured the readers of Inland Printer on "the sacredness of social and, particularly, home life." His essay, "Journalistic Barbarism," accused "gossipmongers" of pandering to "base appetites" with "morbid curiosity" and "appalling" newsgathering techniques that included bribing servants and placing an "ear at the keyhole."

Wedding coverage, he said, included facts on bridal trousseaux "to a fraction the size of her corset" and "can scarcely be shut out from the bedchamber." Bushnell wrote that houses might as well have "speaking tubes leading from every room into the street" and was indignant about how a reporter's "fertile imagination magnifies the most minute and innocent mole-hills."

Journalists live by the "self-made law" of profit rather than "common decency," Bushnell said. The legal principle that "the house of a man was his castle, has become a mockery." Thinking the press should be subject to some penalty for violating privacy, Bushnell only asked that reputable journalists condemn the "cancerous ulcer" eating away at their profession and that good citizens wage "unceasing warfare" against the "hideous monstrosity."

The prying and prevarications of reporters had apparent economic incentives. Newspaper workers often were depicted as drunken, skeptical Bohemians who would work long hours for low pay. They were suspected of taking bribes or conducting blackmail operations to supplement their incomes. Reporters received bonuses for writing especially exciting stories.

The extra payments were, in effect, an inducement to fabricate facts and quotations. James Parton, a journalist and biographer, published a lengthy history and analysis of press falsehoods in Harper's in 1874. He blamed proprietors who prostituted themselves to political and business interests and who failed to pay wages that would attract a staff of character and intelligence.

In a North American Review essay on "The Decline and Fall of the Press" in 1887, the dramatist Dion Boucicault complained that newspapers made money by pandering to degraded tastes and by taking "the craft of misrepresentation to the level of a high art." Reporters, he wrote, are "sent into the houses of private citizens to obtain the offal of society-the filthier the better."

An "Editor's Easy Chair" column in Harper's a year later remarked that reader demand had made journalism largely gossip about the private lives of the rich. Recognizing "the natural interest of man in man," the column said, interviewers with "impertinence" and "impudence" were willing to "seize any person whose name for any reason is known to the public, and to turn his life inside out to the public gaze." Any coverage of personal peccadilloes could threaten the social standing and moral authority of eminent individuals whose lives were arranged by a complex assortment of rituals, courtesies, and recognitions. Minot Judson Savage, an author and Unitarian minister, questioned editors who thought they were taking over the instructional roles of churches and schools.

Writing in the North American Review in 1885, Savage said newspaper journalists were not distinguished for their morality or educations and yet seemed to speak "out of the clouds" once they entered a newspaper sanctum. Large-circulation dailies, he maintained, actually do a kind of catering that "does not imply a very delicate sense of either smell or taste on the part of those it is supposed to feed."

Savage cited the example of recent deathbed coverage of Ulysses S. Grant that described his personal habits including "the state of his teeth, the accumulations of tartar upon them, and his neglect of the tooth-brush." Reporters could be praised for their fact-gathering abilities, Savage said, but they made their sources envy "Daniel in the lions' den, because the mouths of the lions were 'stopped.'"

Press speculation about his wedding plans made President Grover Cleveland ask why he should be treated any differently than others and why pure, unprotected womanhood should be subjected to cruel publicity. "The President should have some right of privacy you might respect," he told a reporter. "Your class give me none." After Cleveland married twenty-one year-old Frances Folsom, reporters posted themselves outside the honeymoon cottage at a resort in Deer Park, Maryland.

The surveillance of the newlyweds and the reporters' detailed stories sparked controversy. Some press opinions on the coverage regarded the president's life as, in effect, public property, but others described the stories as a violation of sanctified private rights and touched on the hazy legal issues.

Joseph B. Bishop of the New York Evening Post gave an account of the press siege in a commentary on "Newspaper Espionage" for The Forum. Such ungentlemanly actions, he wrote, had made the press "a positive terror to respectable citizens" who were a majority and could assert their rights. Bishop described invasions of privacy as a public nuisance and compared scandal-mongering to selling obscene books and pictures.

"The profession becomes the lowest of human callings-

lower than brothel-keeping or liquor-selling," he said, "for these make no pretense to respectability, while the journalist pretends to be a public guide and teacher."

Similar statements were made three months later in a Lippincott's piece, "Newspaperism" by Condé Benoist Fallen. A writer who had a doctorate in philosophy, Fallen portrayed the press as arrogant, shallow, and morally degrading. Sensational news for the masses, he said, is "the common sewer for public and private immorality." Violations of sacred privacy rights could hardly be redressed with libel suits, Fallen wrote, because they brought "a detestable notoriety and the expense of a wearisome litigation with a soulless, conscienceless corporation."

His solution was better moral principles in journalism and in society generally. Junius Henri Browne, an author and newspaper correspondent, wrote in the next issue of the magazine that Fallen exaggerated privacy problems and that journalists often censored themselves. Browne said that the press was becoming more professional and was, in fact, constrained by concerns about profits and public popularity. Admitting that abuses occurred, he contended that having the press "shackled in the least," even in extreme cases, would be a "greater evil" than surrendering some individual rights.

A popular romance novelist, an English woman known by the singlename pseudonym Ouida, reached a contrary conclusion in an 1887 North American Review essay. A main difference between "ill-bred and high-bred persons," she stated, is the vulgar curiosity of the crowd and the detached dignity of the more cultured.

A newspaper's intrusiveness on private matters may be profitable, Ouida said, but "it is alike a curse to those whose privacy it poisons and a curse to those whose debased appetites it feeds." Readers had to take ultimate responsibility for supporting the "carrion flies" of reporting, she warned, and had to understand that stories about personal lives were as addictive and dangerous as absinthe.

"The best characteristic of the best society would be that they should be absolutely forbidden in it," she advised. Later in 1887 The Journalist urged the use of obscenity law against "unnecessary dirt" in newspapers and demanded the dismissal of a "leperous outlaw" editorial writer at the Minneapolis Tribune who said Mrs. Cleveland was apparently older than reported and described her as "a woman who would sell herself to so gross and repulsive a man as Grover Cleveland, and one with a private record so malodorous, for the bauble of a brief social ascendancy."

Popular journalism brought the ills and inquisitiveness of the world into the romanticized and privatized Victorian home that was often described as hallowed space for the family. "The right of privacy is sacred, and should always be respected," a manners manual stated in 1863. Reporting on personal lives could be a jarring note at a time when house design itself could be dedicated to refuge, ritual, and religious nurture.

Magazines referred to "sacred" privacy being violated by impudent reporters and uncultivated nouveau riche sources. "Our 'dailies' at present are rarely fit for home-reading without thorough expurgation," said an 1882 North American Review essay. The writer, George T.

Rider, depicted the fourth estate as superficial, intrusive, insincere, duplicitous, partisan, dogmatic, imperious, slangy, corrupting, prurient, and gossipy. He expressed disgust at how crime stories removed the "wholesome secrecy" of life in the lower depths of society and how "profane" and "hungry eyes peer into private houses" to report on banquets, balls, and teas.

One well-known etiquette and home culture book of the time discussed a duty to object to "pandering to plebian tastes" in news stories about respectable people, but was generally fatalistic about such journalism.

Being good was not always expected in Victorian America, but appearing well-mannered and irreproachable could be de rigueur for those who wanted to maintain respectability.

Even if their hiding of disconcerting matters from public view could be considered hypocritical, their pronouncements on the thwarting of human curiosity and impulses acquired shibboleth status. Such scruples preserved social capital linked to commerce and acceptance in a community.

Many patrician writers deeply resented news stories that looked behind the theatrical facades of propriety or that exposed the miseries of the lower classes. The coverage may have been a kind of resistance to a hegemonic culture, but also presumably catered to an enduring fascination with how others live in a society that did not value familiarity.

People were not supposed to get too close to each other in public. Women often were expected to create, willingly or not, a domestic sanctuary of purity, piety, and tranquility and did not have the same rights as men in the external world.

Houses were divided into public, private, and service zones, and women were to avoid attention outside the home. Class privilege was to be upheld against the assaults of a populace seen as too democratic and as too likely to produce swindlers, blackmailers, and unsuitable suitors. Etiquette experts explained how privacy and social exclusion were to be retained.

An essay in Appleton's Journal, for example, described the woman as the "gatekeeper of society" who makes rules for her own protection and convenience. The writer said that when seeing a man, a woman "must speak first, or not at all, if she wishes to guard herself against intrusion, unconventionality, and social irregularity of every order." Even women's clothing went to extremes in restricting movements and displaying status.

The rigid restraints, the fears of faux pas, the demands of domesticity, and the resentment of men's double standards for behaviour inside and outside family life created severe strains in the supposed refuge of the home. Henry Ward Beecher, the country's best-known clergyman, declared that a family had "a sacred right of privacy" and that talebearers should be treated as "moral outlaws" who did more harm than thieves who stole the silver.

Sex radicals, meanwhile, wrote articles documenting

conflicts within marriages and extolling the benefits of being together without commitments.

In 1872, Victoria Woodhull's free-love newspaper exposed an adulterous affair that Beecher had with Lib Tilton, the wife of a close associate. The same November 2 issue of Woodhull & Claflin's Weekly gave an explicit account of orgiastic behaviour at New York's French Ball and, in an apparent attempt to conduct blackmail, referred to embarrassing information the newspaper had about men of all kinds named in the records of a high-class house of prostitution.

Woodhull explained that privacy could be invaded to reveal the hypocrisy of marriage customs equivalent to monarchy and slavery. When the anti-vice crusader Anthony Comstock had the editors arrested on an obscenity charge, a court ruled that the federal statute did not apply to newspapers.

He was successful, however, in lobbying Congress to pass a more comprehensive statute. The Comstock Act of 1873 barred from the mails anything that could be deemed obscene, lewd, lascivious, or indecent. Comstock was immediately appointed a special postal agent to enforce the statute, and the New York legislature chartered his New York Society for the Suppression of Vice to help authorities obtain vice law convictions.

He and others prosecuted not only pornographers and their distributors, but also birth control activists, medical writers, free-lovers, and freethinkers. Judges rejected defendants' arguments about persecution and violations of liberties by applying precedents allowing the suppression of almost anything considered a bad influence on morals.

Opinion leaders and officials were alarmed by the profusion of pornography, uninhibited literature, and sensational journalism in print culture. Some thought that women and the lower classes in particular were being influenced by solitary reading that undermined the standard expectations learned and enforced within society. Dime novels, story newspapers, and similar fare appealed to the powerless with tales of criminal notoriety, improbable wealth, and elite corruption.

Such narratives could be inspired by news accounts and could display the differences between street standards and the genteel culture. Comstock and similar censors largely relied on middle- and upper-class fears that the availability of information about sex and crime would produce the moral corruption and eventual social downfall of the young. They sought extensive powers over private reading and had broad notions of what should be illegal.

Newspapers feared that Congress would pass legislation outlawing depictions of lawbreaking. Writing in the North American Review in 1882, Comstock said that the press advertised illegal activities and published "sickening details of hideous crimes" that corrupted the young as did popular entertainment, half-dime novels, and "the blasphemies of infidel publications."

The ultraliberal clergyman O. B. Frothingham wrote a response saying that Comstock should rely on education and moral power rather than belligerence and asking whether his organization should be inspecting newspapers or imposing its moral sentiments on others. Others went as far as questioning Comstock's respectability as they objected to his devious methods of entrapment and overzealous use of vague legal standards.

Anti-vice societies, religious organizations, and women's groups campaigned against various forms of high and low culture that they condemned as dangerous to morality. Believing that impressionable minds would be influenced by depictions of wrongdoing, they were instrumental in the passage of federal laws to control obscenity and state statutes to restrict the sale of sex and crime newspapers such as the National Police Gazette.

The purity movement, which spanned genders, races, classes, parties, places, and times, placed propriety over profit and pleasure.

Adherents advocated public manners and respect for the sanctity of the private sphere. Saying that social interchange should be kept on a high level and that domestic life should be undefiled, they condemned explicit material in newspapers, novels, and sex education as tawdry, indiscreet, and even dangerous. Journalists, authors, and free-lovers who discounted such scruples defended exposure as informative or liberating.

They had a common cause in portraying their moralistic opponents as repressive, ignorant, and dirty minded. In 1883 Joseph Pulitzer's New York World, the nation's foremost sensational newspaper, described Comstock as unfit for his legal authority and as man "whose zeal to reform the world is largely in excess of his intelligence."

A similar profile in the Atlanta Constitution complained that Comstock "hates sinners for the love of virtue" and that he suppressed art photographs while allowing "the worst of cheap papers to flourish their bawdy pictures on the public news-stands." The Constitution later published an editorial that said "everything in his eyes is corrupt."

Moralists were particularly offended by the frothy brew of gossip, crime, fashion, high society, sports, human interest, and political chicanery in Pulitzer's paper in the 1880s and 1890s.

A Sunday World front page in 1883, for instance, featured detailed stories on William K. Vanderbilt suffering social embarrassments from financial losses, on a fifteen-year-old African-American girl drowning herself rather than be disgraced by an incident at school involving a vulgar song, and on gamblers being swindled by phony telegraphic accounts of horse races.

New York's state school superintendent declared that such reading weakened and blackened young minds. The state's press association endorsed purity resolutions adopted by the National Editorial Association that said depictions of misconduct lowered moral standards and incited others to reenact the wrongdoing.

Reacting to assertions that news of lawbreaking and immorality fostered imitation, The Journalist, a trade paper founded in 1884, contended that crime stories informed the public about dangers and punished the perpetrators with publicity and that readers regarded revelations about the escapades of well-known people as merely common incidents involving human nature. The Journalist, nevertheless, cited potential injuries to morally degraded classes in campaigning for decency laws to use against the tawdry Police Gazette and the thinly veiled prostitution advertisements in the World.

Papers like the World took professional pride in publishing circulation building stories that shamed people and put problematic practices under surveillance. In the late 1880s female journalists launched a fad of undercover reporting on the hardships of working women and the vices, failures, and corruption of unsuspecting men. Nellie Bly, a World reporter, posed as a fallen woman, chorus girl, and asylum inmate.

Pretending to be the wife of a patent medicine manufacturer who wanted a proposed law blocked, she exposed a powerful lobbyist who asked her for $1,000 to pay off New York legislators. Addressing the Wisconsin Editorial Association in 1888, Charles A. Dana, editor and owner of the New York Sun, placed journalistic success above any scruples about privacy.

Dana defined news as "everything that occurs, everything which is of human interest, and which is of sufficient importance to arrest and absorb the attention of the public or of any considerable part of it." Rejecting the notion that "certain kinds of news ought not to be published," he said that he had "always felt that whatever the Divine Providence permitted to occur I was not too proud to report."

A Scribner's essay later asserted that the "socially and intellectually half-cultivated" masses were acquiring detailed knowledge they needed to survive and thrive in a fluid democratic society. The loss of privacy and intellectual delicacy, the writer said, was only a "temporary eclipse during transitional conditions."

Victorian legal and reform reasoning, however, was

often premised on perceptions of melodramatic Jekyll-and-Hyde moral struggles within human nature. Personal vices and pernicious publications rather than social and economic structures were blamed for the shortcomings of the "vicious" classes.

Scholars were among those who articulated anxieties about the intentions and influences of the commercial press as it evolved from the 1830s to 1920s. A college textbook that had extraordinary success in the nineteenth century, Francis Wayland's The Elements of Moral Science, said that journalists had no greater privileges than others and took the position that press freedom meant only the right to publish truth with good motives and justifiable ends, a test proposed by Alexander Hamilton in 1804 and adopted by many states in the following decades. Wayland declared that journalists did not have "a right to publish cases of individual vice, unless the providence of God has made them public before."

A sociology textbook published in 1894 observed that a "newspaper may lead its public positively, but it must adapt itself, in a measure, to that public's opinions, tastes, and prejudices." The authors, Albion W. Small, the chairman of the sociology department at the University of Chicago, and his doctoral student George E. Vincent, warned that sensational stories stimulated pathological thoughts and feelings. They wrote that coverage of topics such as vice, divorce trials, and brutal crimes sullied the minds of the nation and that the typical newspaper is simply "the old-time gossip in print."

LEGAL PRINCIPLES, PROPOSALS, AND PITFALLS

When journalists took a flippant, libertarian, or utilitarian stance, they were not addressing issues of professional responsibility and natural rights that conceivably could be brought to the legal system even if a public official was involved. When interviewers asked New York's Boss Tweed about his nerves when he was charged with government corruption in 1871, one essayist stated that the right of privacy was a self-evident, inalienable right not enumerated in the Declaration of Independence and that invasive interviews were a nuisance that ought to be abated.

Privacy can be connected to the human dignity of maintaining one's self in solitude, the personal autonomy of controlling knowledge about intimate matters, and the property right to a life that includes close relationships.

The defenders of privacy could assert, in essence, what Warren and Brandeis eventually did in 1890, that "the right to life has come to mean the right to enjoy life,-the right to be let alone," that "the right to liberty secures the exercise of extensive civil privileges," and that "the term 'property' has grown to comprise every form of possession-intangible, as well as tangible."

Nineteenthcentury Americans had relied on relatively intangible perceptions and responsibilities to restrict various kinds of expression. They used libel suits to defend reputation, wartime repression to preserve morale, and obscenity laws to restrict tastes. Yet, such concerns, as well as the especially "ethereal" harm of invasion of privacy in news reporting, contended with an ideology of the press as a potent and constitutionally protected instrument of democracy and progress.

The First Amendment's prohibition of laws abridging freedom of the press and corresponding provisions in early state constitutions were based on an Enlightenment endorsement of reason, popular sovereignty, and distrust of government power, but conceptions of journalistic liberty often made distinctions between a broad freedom of opinion on public issues and a narrower right to deal with private matters and character. Reasons for restrictions on communication content also included general social control.

Americans could cite Sir William Blackstone, the reactionary eighteenth century compiler of English common law, who denied that press freedom protected words that could be considered dangerous or offensive.

Blackstone, a defender of British oligarchy, declared that liberty of the press meant only freedom from censorship prior to publication, not freedom for bad sentiments with bad tendencies.

British and American law valued the ability of free, white males to maintain honour in public life and autonomy in private affairs. Reverence for a right to be left alone was often summarized by the maxim that "a man's house is his castle." By the end of the nineteenth century, privacy protections had been recognized in the United States in areas such as trespass, eavesdropping, "peeping Toms," mail, wiretapping, telegraphy, self-incrimination, spousal testimony, attorney-client communication, and the census.

Libel suits could be brought against journalists who disseminated false and defamatory statements of fact that damaged reputation, but plaintiffs lacked a precise legal weapon to use when accurate, intrusive stories about their private lives were published. Some who complained about journalists invading privacy hinted at a new branch of law by referring to the pithy Blackstonian observation that the liberty of the press did not protect the licentiousness of the press. A private sphere largely shielded from individual and government action, they seemed to suggest, might also be secured from intrusion by the news industry.

Nineteenth-century legal scholars often used Blackstone's formulations when they supported suppression. In his constitutional commentaries published in 1833, Supreme Court Justice Joseph Story cited Blackstone and the conservative New York jurist James Kent as saying that press freedom could be used but not abused. Story insisted that journalists could not be allowed to violate a citizen's rights or to disturb public or domestic peace. "Civil society could not go on under such circumstances," he said. The Michigan justice and law professor Thomas M. Cooley reached similar conclusions in an 1871 treatise.

"The constitutional liberty of speech and of the press, as we understand it, implies a right to freely utter and publish whatever the citizen may please, and to be protected against any responsibility for so doing," he wrote, "except so far as such publications, from their blasphemy, obscenity, or scandalous character, may be a public offence, or as by their falsehood and malice they may injuriously affect the standing, reputation, or pecuniary interests of individuals." Cooley showed that the language on press freedom in most state constitutions made an exception for the "abuse" of the right.

Journalists, however, had popular newspapers, political power, and constitutional and prudential rationales for their actions. They could present themselves as properly protected custodians of social conscience. "No censorship nor restraint, save those of public opinion, have tended to impede the full and free development of the energies of Journalism," observed a magazine essay in 1842.

The writer said that a newspaper should be a "guardian and guide of public morals," but was concerned about the press being too busy pandering to public tastes to be a lofty profession. Critics argued that the decency of journalism itself needed guarding.

One of their options was to urge, as a Southern Literary Messenger essay did in 1848, that the press devote itself to moral uplift and be "its own guide, monitor and censor." Another was to say, as the Southern Quarterly Review did in 1851, that liberty of the press did not protect press licentiousness and was never meant to include abuses such as to "invade the sanctuary of the domestic fireside."

The critics of the news industry pondered causalities and countermeasures. An essay in the American Whig Review in 1848 said that journalistic violations of privacy created opportunities for extortion and occasionally provoked acts of revenge.

The writer, who used the penname Athenion, said that the press was in the predicament of having a primary duty to the public and a lesser obligation to consider the feelings of individuals.

Noting that the vaunted press freedom envisioned by the founders was checked only by libel suits and violence, the essay called on journalists to exercise their rights with discretion and prudence or risk rendering themselves "much more of a nuisance and pest, than a benefit to the community."

A disgruntled former editor, Lambert A. Wilmer, published a book in 1859 that catalogued the failings of the press and compared the profession to the vice of prostitution and nuisance of public filth. Depraved newsmongers who defy the social compact, he said, should not think that the liberty of the press provided them with constitutional "rights, prerogatives, immunities or exemptions, which do not belong equally to every other class of citizens."

Beating editors might be effective and might even be acceptable in the absence of adequate punishment for calumny, Lambert wrote, but stronger laws were needed to deal with what he described as "invading the sanctuary of private life, disturbing the peace of families, giving extensive circulation to groundless and malicious slanders, calumniating the worthiest and most honorable men and the purest and most innocent women, driving many objects of its detraction to phrenzy and desperation."

Conclusions about journalistic invasions of privacy involved not only general understandings of press rights and effects, but also statements about specific legal problems and public predilections. Going to court for relief from reporters could make the situation worse.

In addition to the usual disincentives for litigation, potential plaintiffs risked a further exposure of private information. When an Albany newspaper advised presidential candidate Grover Cleveland to sue for stories about his sexual indiscretions, The Journalist noted that he would be "compelled to go on the stand and answer to a searching and impertinent scrutiny into matters the privacy of which ought to be inviolable."

Achieving a moral victory in court might prove incomplete because a story could be considered reprehensible by some and gratifying by many. Publications in England charged that the indecent prying of cheap, popular newspapers in the United States was attributable to the unwholesome vices of a reckless young republic. An 1867 essay in Galaxy, a New York magazine that was absorbed by Atlantic Monthly in 1878, regretted the intrusive aspects of modern democracy and recommended seeking solitude from newspapers, telegraphs, and other inventions that fostered a "vulgar spirit of fusion, of familiarity, of ignoble curiosity, of prurient gossip."

Advancing techniques of illustration allowed the public to gaze at personal images with a heightened sense of intimacy.168 Engravings and eventually photographs placed individual likenesses in an unrestricted, commercial context. In 1874 the New York Times questioned the use of pictures without the subject's consent and said the issue would make "a most interesting" issue for a court.

"In cases like these it is difficult to draw the precise line where liberty ends and license begins," the paper said. "Men of right feeling and true delicacy know by instinct what is correct and what a violation of personal rights and domestic privacy is." Caricatures ridiculed personal appearance and idiosyncrasies.

In 1873 a Ladies' Repository piece by William Winters expressed amazement at the enterprise of the press and its technological developments, but objected to invasions of domestic solitude and to the effects of sensational writing and illustrations on children and the lower classes.

He blamed Thomas Nast's humiliating cartoons and other journalistic abuse for the death of the unconventional editor Horace Greeley a month after he lost the mudslinging presidential election of 1872. Yet, Winters explicitly ruled out legal restrictions on journalists. "Until the press voluntarily and from principle desists from such unwise and ungenerous criticism," he wrote, "it is best to allow it to continue."

Some periodical essayists prescribed peace of mind or better manners. In 1870 the poet H.T. Tuckerman said in Atlantic Monthly that personal revelations were the staple of daily newspapers and that "for this infringement of what was once understood to be a social law there is no legal remedy." Tuckerman advised his readers to seek sacred inspirations in silence rather than pay attention to "the perpetual proclamation of news from everywhere and about everything."

A similar commentary in Century in 1888 said that newspaper standards had been sinking since the founders' era and that editors published "cruel and impertinent gossip." Yet, the writer thought that the press ought to be able to reform itself while championing other reforms. An Overland piece a year later stated that invasions of privacy were condoned because of a fear of impairing the legacy of the First Amendment, but that the spirit of Constitution was violated by a press that "invades the sanctity of private life" and searches for sensation in "social waste heaps and cesspools."

A number of press critics were too exasperated with some kinds of reporting to settle for self-regulation. In a plea for legal restraints he published in Scribner's in 1872, Whitelaw Reid disdained "that reckless trifling with character and that invasion of personal concerns which make so marked a feature of many of our most successful newspapers."

Reid, an editor at Greeley's New York Tribune, asked the "respectable press" to welcome every justifiable libel suit as a gain for decent journalism and advocated making the trials easy and inexpensive. Libel defendants, however, might be able to use truth as a defence when reporting on public or personal topics.

During the nineteenth century most states adopted constitutional provisions recognizing a truth defence in defamation cases. One type of language required good motives and justifiable ends, and another stipulated that the information be proper for public information. Libel law thus had vague standards for journalists to follow and could allow privacy invading stories that met the qualifications applied to truthful statements. In an 1876 issue of International Review, the law reformer David Dudley Field observed that the "secrets of families," even if true, "should not be published." He criticized personal journalism, called for more stringent laws, and advised patience until the press improved.

As efforts were made to delegitimize prying stories, some of the more morally outraged and law-minded periodical writers developed general lines of reasoning for a legally enforceable right of privacy to restrict journalists. One was Richard Grant White, a noted Shakespeare scholar who had studied law and who had been troubled by stories he had read and perhaps by his own experiences with interviewers. In a two-part article, "The Morals and Manners of Journalism," that appeared in the December 1869 and January 1870 issues of Galaxy, White argued that impolite journalists should be taken to court for the psychic and social harm they caused.

The first part said the press had the public at its mercy and should be "held responsible under heavy penalties for any injury which may be inflicted, even through carelessness." The responsibility of publications is "voluntarily assumed," White wrote, and the harm of falsehoods could "in some cases bring ruin not only upon individuals, but upon whole classes."

In addition to being limited by libel law, he thought, the press should be held responsible for candor, good faith, and decency. White contended that journalists should be judicious enough to be above commercial considerations and to reject gossip and attacks on the personal reputation or private life of an opponent.

White's second installment focused on invasions of privacy by the "personal journalist" whose "breathings taint the social atmosphere, and develop in us all a moral disease, the seeds of which are in every heart." Such a pest, he said, "passes the bounds set up by personal reserve with the daring and the dash of a swine running at a swill-trough."

White was especially contemptuous of wedding engagement announcements that reached strangers and that sometimes proved wrong and therefore "shocking to a woman of any delicacy."

He also denounced mentions of women's ages and descriptions of their physical attributes. White admitted that some vain people supplied trivial information about themselves in order to appear socially prominent and fashionable.

He believed that an unwanted "breach of good taste," however, should not be permitted. White concluded by proposing a privacy tort under defamation law: "For the journalist to pass the barrier of private life, whether to praise or to blame, should be by law, in itself, a libel; to bring suit for which would be, of course, at the discretion of the person whose privacy was invaded."

The idea of invasion of privacy legislation was presented in a North American Review article in 1880 by John Proffatt, an author of legal treatises. The article reasoned that a person could prevent trespassing and warrantless searches at a home and therefore should be able to stop a reporter who would "drag to public view its intimacies, its privacy, and its confidences." Proffatt said Americans should be protected by a law similar to a French one that allowed journalists to discuss public character, but not domestic matters.

"We could hardly expect outside of Anglo-American communities such a high regard for the inviolability and the sanctity of the family," he wrote. "Yet to-day in France, under the law of the 11th of May, 1868, any publication in a periodical relating to facts of private life is prohibited under a fine of five hundred francs."

A court decision, he said, had interpreted the law to apply even in public places. Proffatt, who also thought civil or criminal libel cases could be brought for privacy invasions, believed that liberty of the press simply did not protect licentious violations of private life and character. A year later France's comprehensive Press Law of 1881 abrogated the 1868 privacy provision, a fact that apparently escaped Warren and Brandeis in 1890 when they referred to the 1868 statute.

Americans, however, often resisted attempts to legislate public or private morality. Some magazine writers were content to propose good educations for journalists, subscription cancellations, or a lenient attitude about the press. Others described interviewers as aggressive, but considerate enough to get cooperation from sources. In an

1881 essay in the North American Review, a young lawyer said that laws had to be adjusted to the times and that invitations to morality were more attractive than commandments on matters such as equivocation, defamation, and pure living.

"All mankind-even the best-do in fact transgress; and it is surely wiser to permit them to do what we cannot prevent," he argued. The lawyer, who wrote under the protection of a pseudonym, said he had only a hedonistic outlook left after having "given up the theological, the intuitive, and utilitarian ethics."

Having enforceable press restrictions made sense to others, particularly John Bascom, a professor and philosopher who had some legal training. A pioneer of progressive thought who was an ardent prohibitionist, labor advocate, and backer of women's rights, he believed that laws should evolve to give greater support to moral causes. Bascom complained in an 1887 sociology book that civil law generally failed to protect injuries to feelings and that benevolent change could be difficult to achieve.

"The undue hold of professional sentiment, the force of legal custom, eager interest in an intellectual tournament, and pride in the symmetry of a system," he wrote, "should all be softened by virtue, a heedful response to human happiness." In a Bibliotheca Sacra article published in 1872, Bascom described popular newspapers as overwhelming distractions that replace serious analysis with the trivial and transient.

The evils of the press, he said, are "a perpetual trespass on the privacy of individuals, a useless consumption of leisure, a fretting tyranny of public sentiment, a reduction of individuality, a loss of political influence, a fresh trial of moral integrity, and the vanity of apparent power springing from the mere fact of publicity."

Bascom, whose personal characteristics were sometimes disparaged in the press while he served as president of the University of Wisconsin from 1874 to 1887, made a fervent argument for a right of privacy in the July 1884 issue of

Education. He said that the community should use civil law to control a lawless press not being reined in by public opinion.

"Privacy is among the most primitive of rights," Bascom stated. "We will not allow a street-tough to fling open our own front door; but we take it very resignedly if the press throws open all the doors of our neighbor's house and invites a curious public to enter and to criticize, to gossip and to sneer, within its desecrated rooms." Saying that every person is entitled to personal faults that do not affect the public, Bascom maintained that the press should not be able to use its increasing powers in order to proclaim "private facts which are injurious to character" from the housetops, that new conditions required new laws.

Some writers regarded the possibilities for privacy law as resting on fundamental freedoms that were disregarded and difficult to assert. "In all the rights and equities of the natural man, the privacy of his personal and family life stands foremost," North American Review contributor John Dudley said in 1888. "Yet there is no right more continually and recklessly violated, more deliberately assailed, and less adequately protected."

Dudley declared that the whole "system" of profiting from "the pungent, personal, racy paragraph" was to blame. "The nominal responsibility under the law of libel an unscrupulous newspaper chief laughs at," he wrote. "The average futility of a suit against a powerful journal makes it a safe hazard, not to be weighed against value as a popular advertisement." Dudley was also apparently skeptical about the prospects for privacy law because he advised waiting for less callous and cynical times in journalism.

Edward J. Phelps, a law professor at Yale University, made comparable, but even more disdainful claims in Scribner's in 1889. He said that newspapers had "put an end to all human privacy" with the remorseless reporter who believed that "every circumstance and incident in every man's and woman's life is the property of the public" and that people have "no rights that he is bound to respect." Phelps, who had recently been the United States minister to Great Britain, said that America tolerated journalistic invasions of privacy as no other country would and that defamation of personal character was too common to attract much attention. He wrote that libel law existed in theory but had no force because defence attorneys were "quite able to make the remedy of the plaintiff much worse than the injury complained of."

Phelps declared that the unchecked "purveyor of garbage" in the press contributed to crime, suicide, and social decay by influencing susceptible minds.

Journalists who sided with the forces of respectability denounced their down-market competitors and declared that the gentlemen of the press had a moral responsibility to maintain the proper social atmosphere. The dignified New York Times summarized its position in an 1889 editorial, "The Right to Privacy," that expounded on the concept as a "real right" to keep "properly private affairs" from disclosure and that described curiosity about the lives of others without their consent as "an emotion of which well-bred people are rather ashamed, and which they try to suppress."

Noting that under libel law "it is not lawful to print lies about your neighbour, or even to print truths maliciously," the paper said, "there is no doubt that an effective prohibition against the publication of unauthorized gossip about the private life, even of public characters, would be an excellent thing if such a prohibition could be devised." The Times had been arguing for decades that private matters should remain private and that people should not enjoy or assist intrusive reporting.

"If the barriers that have been gradually built about the affairs of the family and of individuals are to be tumbled over whenever an 'interviewer' presents himself," the paper said in 1874, "one of the strongest incentives to honorable respect for each other and for ourselves will be weakened."

Distinctions between the private and public, usually with particular implications for women and children, arose with families and societies recognizing they could have differing values and competing purposes. Liberal democracy in the United States was founded with the recognition that moral principles would be in conflict and provided for negotiation processes that ideally would involve moderation, mutual respect, and reasonableness.

Principled accommodation rather than consensus was expected. Comity, however, was challenged by the growth of commercial enterprises dedicated to objectives other than being comme il faut. A century after their Constitution and Bill of Rights had listed and limited federal government powers over the lives of citizens, Americans were trying to tame freewheeling corporations that were producing both enormous profits and public outrage.

In 1890 Congress passed the vaguely worded Sherman Antitrust Act in an attempt to control predatory monopolies and Warren and Brandeis wrote their impassioned and influential Harvard Law Review article, "The Right to Privacy," to advocate tort liability for invasions of privacy in the information industry.

The article by the two Boston lawyers appeared in December after a year of particularly pointed national debate on intrusions by reporters. The freedom of the press was being weighed against freedom from unwanted curiosity and exposure. Journalists had to admit that ethical infractions infected their profession, but they could have mixed feelings about accepting legal restrictions and difficulties reaching common ground.

The January 23, 1890, issue of The Open Court, for instance, presented a pair of essays that accepted the Hamiltonian test of restricting journalistic freedom with the qualifications of truth, good motives, and justifiable ends. However, the two writers, both of whom had legal training, had differing perspectives on veracity, intentions, and purposes.

Slason Thompson, an experienced metropolitan editor, objected to the characterization of the press as "the heartless inquisitor into the sacred privacy" of people's lives and emphasized the socially beneficial role of the press in exposing wrongdoing. He argued that the usual attention to the dark side of life was comparable to Christ's parable about a shepherd leaving the herd to find one lost sheep.

Saying that newspapers knew where to draw the line between individual privacy and the society's right to information, he contended that "the rights of the public have to be governed by the broad principles of universal good and not by the hardships, or even the heart-breaks of particular cases." Thompson acknowledged that a newspaper with filthy news and corrupt opinions was a "public enemy" and that its patrons were "particeps criminis," but remarked that such publications could use the excuse that a market existed for their tainted goods.

He said that by far the most common complaints about journalism involved conflicting versions of the truth that were difficult for anyone to resolve. A reply by Matthew Mark Trumbull, a humanitarian activist and assistant editor of the magazine, said that Thompson had an idealistic notion of the press as a "moral guide" and should have practical and gentlemanly concerns about editorial cruelty and greed as well as blackmail and quack advertisements. "The rights of a newspaper are limited by the moral code and the usages of enlightened society," Trumbull insisted.

Social value judgments can produce laws restricting power inside and outside of government. Tests of utility and moral legitimacy can be applied. In April 1890, Charles Dudley Warner, an urbane literary figure who had practiced both law and journalism, published an essay in The Forum that decried defamations and invasions of privacy by the press. "We are paying the penalty of cultivating the ability to read in advance of the taste to discriminate," he said, adding that even the more reputable people found sensational reporting difficult to resist.

Some of the publicity might seem harmless, Warner wrote, but was, in fact, "injurious, wanton, painful, indescribably brutal, sowing suspicion as to character and motive that can never be overcome, sometimes driving the aggrieved to suicide." Newspapers do both services in informing public opinion and harms in damaging reputation and privacy, he said. "But the public has its legal remedy for the injury, or can have it, and it need not read that which is vulgar and indecent."

An anonymous essayist in the June 1890 issue of Century offered similar arguments, including the charge that the press incites suicide, and made an appeal for action. Contending that invasive journalists lacked conscience and that legislators were afraid of them, the writer described newspapers as "the dumping-ground of the moral filth of a whole continent" and as the source of information on illegal prizefights and gambling.

The essay said the public could demand that publishers care not only about making profits and playing the role of public protector, but also about publishing "newspapers which they, as private individuals, would be willing to indorse, in every part, as men of character, refinement, and self-respect." Saying that new restraints were needed for the new conditions in the press, the writer predicted that "the present tendency towards trivialities and personalities will continue until private rights and public morals are better protected by the laws."

At the same time H. Elton Smith wrote in Overland that vulgar tastes should not be indulged like a spoiled child's. Referring to stories about marital problems and deathbed scenes, he asserted that many lives were "ruined by the publication of facts with which the public had no concern." Smith asked, "What higher right has the newspaper to cater to the brutish side of humanity than the vendor of prurient literature?"

Some periodical essays in 1890 tried to deflect the attacks on invasive journalism. In the July issue of The Forum, the famed Civil War newspaper correspondent and Lincoln hagiographer Noah Brooks noted the criticism that had been appearing in magazines and suggested that the monthly periodicals were becoming so competitive among themselves and with the dailies that they too were developing a tendency toward trivialities. He attributed shortcomings of the press to deadlines, partisanship, and public demand. "Invasion of the privacy of the individual is frequently held up to scorn as one of the grossest abuses of the press," Brooks said. "But that is nothing when compared with the habitual, persistent, and malevolent misrepresentation of public men who happen to be political leaders."

He urged his readers to be patient with the journalistic experiments of the time and to hope that the bottom had been reached. Brooks looked forward to future newspapers that would be "clean, bright, honest, impartial, accurate, painstaking, and absolutely just (allowing for the frailties of poor human nature)."

Other journalists pointed out that legal actions against the press were hazardous and evaluated the possibilities for reform. A.E. Watrous, a Philadelphia city editor writing in Lippincott's in February 1890, was so disgusted by the unsatisfactory outcomes for both parties in libel cases that he suggested everyone "frankly acknowledge that the law of the land is incompetent to deal with the relations of the individual to the newspaper."

Watrous proposed setting up an extra-judicial body with a journalist, a lawyer, and a leading citizen to determine the proper functions of the press and to punish its abuses. Another journalist, Franc B. Wilkie, replied that finding censors with the necessary wisdom would be difficult, that any defects in libel law could be cured by legislation, and that "the reform of bad newspapers must be applied to the root of the evil, that is, to public sentiment." Wilkie had been employed for many years by Wilbur F.

Storey's sensational and lucrative Chicago Times. "Scandals in private life, revolting details from the evidence taken in police-court trials, imaginary liaisons of a filthy character, reeked, seethed like a hell's broth in the Times' cauldrons, and made a stench in the nostrils of decent people," Wilkie wrote in his 1891 memoirs. "All this was done with a purpose: it was to attract attention to the paper, to secure notoriety, advertising and circulation."

He recalled that the Times was not deterred by having

to pay the small damages awarded at its frequent libel trials and responded with retaliatory coverage, continual delaying tactics, and threats to expose the personal misbehavior of its antagonists. When the paper was indicted on an obscenity charge for a story about a nude dance at a brothel, for instance, the Times published embarrassing information about the private lives of two young men on the grand jury and berated the rest.

Wilkie told one of the spectators at the brothel, a city editor at another paper, that he would be called as a witness if he did not use his influence to have the case dropped. Wilkie did not know what he did, but no trial was held.

E.L. Godkin, the lawyer and newspaper correspondent who founded the Nation in 1865, showed little enthusiasm for invasion of privacy law in two articles published in 1880 and 1890. The first one, which appeared in the Journal of Social Science, attributed the French prohibition of reporting on private life to an attitude that the press is a nuisance. Americans, Godkin said, respected the role of journalism and indulged its mistakes, but should pay attention to intangible sensitivities and do "something" to protect the right of privacy.

Lacking a specific, satisfactory solution, he observed that editors often managed to resist public tastes and that courts could create more problems. The second article, published in the July 1890 issue of Scribner's, noted that libel cases brought against the press were confusing, slow, and sometimes frivolous. Godkin said that invasions of privacy bothered some more than others, that social curiosity was a common trait, and that publishers gained prestige with the money they acquired from their journalistic excesses.

French law had responded to public concerns about insult and privacy, he said, but in the United States any such sensitivity "has been destroyed by the number and enterprise of the newspapers and the extremely democratic condition of American society." People in a country without recognized social classes often enjoyed being known for something, he remarked, and those who "love the shade of private life" seemed somewhat incomprehensible. Juries could punish damage to a person's reputation, Godkin thought, but were "not disposed to make much account of mere wounds to his feelings or his taste."

The Warren and Brandeis article that appeared in December 1890 said that for years "there has been a feeling that the law must afford some remedy for the unauthorized circulation of portraits of private persons; and the evil of the invasion of privacy by the newspapers, long keenly felt, has been but recently discussed by an able writer."

The writer was identified as Godkin in a footnote that cited his Scribner's article. Warren and Brandeis otherwise did not directly acknowledge periodical essays while giving serious attention to the defunct French privacy law and weaving together Anglo-American cases and commentaries in an effort to show a solid foundation already existed for recognizing the "intangible" spiritual interests involved in "the right to be let alone."

The authors tried to distinguish between libel as a matter of harm done to external relations with others and invasions of privacy that caused internal mental pain "far greater than could be inflicted by mere bodily injury." Warren and Brandeis, like a number of earlier writers, were alarmed about "a lowering of social standards and of morality" and joined those who reasoned that new mass communication practices required a corresponding development in the law. As some courts and periodicals already had done, their article paid particular attention to the implications of new camera capabilities. Taking a picture, the authors pointed out, no longer required a person to pose. Photographs taken "surreptitiously," they insisted, should not be reproduced without consent.

The authors of the Harvard Law Review article were close friends, former law partners, and members of the same polo club. Warren and Brandeis had been among the independent Republicans who rejected the party's 1884 presidential nominee, the ethically tainted James G. Blaine. Like other Mugwumps, they believed the nation needed men of education and rectitude to guide moral and political reform. Looking back in 1905, they agreed that the idea for their 1890 article had been Warren's and was prompted by his "deepseated abhorrence of the invasions of social privacy." According to an early Brandeis biographer who did extensive interviews, Warren was outraged when photographers snapped baby carriage pictures of his children.

Another well-informed biographer attributed his resentment to society coverage of relatives. In any event, Samuel Warren, a stiff, sensitive, proper Bostonian, valued the privacy of his unconventional, feuding family of great wealth.

His brother Fiske was a nudist who lived in a commune, and his brother Ned was an uninhibited homosexual who quarreled with Samuel over policies at the Boston Museum of Fine Arts. Samuel shot himself in 1910 after Ned hired an attorney and began to expose Samuel's questionable handling of the family trust. Brandeis helped the family handle the press inquiries and cover up the cause of death. Criticism of his role in setting up the Warren trust was a factor in the fourmonth confirmation ordeal Brandeis endured in 1916 when he was nominated to the Supreme Court of the United States.

Cultural expectations about privacy can be translated into law, but creating exact boundaries of toleration can be challenging because of clashing values. Brandeis himself was disappointed as he read the Harvard Law Review proofs and felt the article was not "as good as I had thought it was." When his second cousin and future wife Alice Goldmark read the article, she and Brandeis discussed the possible lack of support in public opinion.

"Most of the world is in more or less a hypnotic state-and it is comparatively easy to make people believe anything, particularly the right," he wrote to her. "Our hope is to make people see that invasions of privacy are not necessarily borne-and then make them ashamed of the pleasure they take in subjecting themselves to such invasions." Two months later Brandeis told her he would have been more interested in writing an article on the duty of publicity than the one he wrote with Warren. "If the broad light of day could be let in upon men's actions," Brandeis said, "it would purify them as the sun disinfects."

Progressive Era Americans sought to improve professions such as journalism with more self-regulation and, when necessary, more laws. The right that Warren and Brandeis were influential in launching was later criticized as vague, exception-riddled, frustrating for plaintiffs, and detrimental to freedom of the press.

Early indications of the trouble ahead were not only the mixed feelings of Brandeis himself, but also the polarized views published before the Harvard Law Review article finally attempted an in-depth legal analysis. Previous defenders of privacy rights had made little effort to devise specific legal formulations while proponents of self-regulation could not promise rapid, reliable, or comprehensive results.

The conflict between freedom of the press and the right to be let alone apparently had seemed too convoluted for any simple, fully satisfactory solutions. Periodical essays reacted to the Warren and Brandeis proposal with the same lack of agreement that was apparent earlier. Some supported more protection for feelings. Others suggested that particular people were being too sensitive. Godkin's Nation said that plaintiffs would get more unwanted publicity, that juries would not respect privacy rights, and that public demand for personal tales would remain high.

Nevertheless, the Warren and Brandeis article was regularly referred to in decisions about privacy issues and became one of the articles cited most often in law journals. After initial setbacks, support for the tort grew in the following decades as courts and legislatures established four types of invasion of privacy: intrusion on a plaintiff's seclusion or solitude, disclosure of embarrassing private facts about the plaintiff, publicity placing the plaintiff in a false light, and appropriation of the plaintiff's name or likeness for the defendant's advantage. A writer in a 1905 issue of the American Law Review praised the authors not only for their reasoning and results, but also for their "originality of conception."

Legal scholarship ever since has habitually credited Warren and Brandeis with originating the idea of a right of privacy. A communication law book said in 1933 that "prior to 1890 the possibility that such a right existed was scarcely contemplated." Twenty-first-century media law textbooks have not only regarded the two authors the "foundation" or "fountain" of thought on the subject, but also described their joint effort as "often considered the most influential law review article ever published."

Their article may have been a prominent piece of legal reasoning, but was not path breaking in its basic contentions. Warren and Brandeis did not so much create the idea of legal protection from invasion of privacy by the press as synthesize existing thoughts, extend the logic, and supply citations. The renowned Warren and Brandeis article thus can be seen as a milestone in the development of a tort rather than as the starting point.

Legal historians have made the authors the patriarchs of privacy law, but restraints on press freedom are more likely to materialize from the sensitivities of a compelling social order than to spring suddenly from a single act of stirring scholarship.

Earlier rhetorical battles over press exposures exhibited a variety of fissures over liberty, taste, manners, and values in Victorian America. Nineteenth-century periodical essayists had promoted moral panic by cataloging the ethical shortcomings of journalism, reworking the narrative of the newspaper as public servant, and arguing that press freedom was less valuable than virtue.

How much Warren and Brandeis knew about the continuing controversy is a subject for conjecture, but their article, like earlier ones, moralized at length about journalistic impropriety and its injurious effects on a person's valued feelings and sense of sacred space. They described a commercial, pandering press that dwelled on the sexual, the domestic, and the trivial in ways that appealed to the weak-minded and crowded out the important and uplifting. Placing the public debate in a much more detailed legal framework than others had, they portrayed a potential plaintiff as having anguish akin to that produced by an unlawful threat, public nuisance, or disruption of family relations.

Warren and Brandeis did not accept truth as a defence, but gave some leeway to journalism by outlining defenses such as consent, privileged communication, and legitimate public concern. The authors admitted that drawing "the exact line at which the dignity and convenience of the individual must yield" would be difficult, but asked why the courts should recognize "a man's house as his castle" at the front entrance and "open wide the back door to idle or prurient curiosity."

Although the social construction of the privacy right was incomplete and would change over time, law did emerge from the prudish and progressive impulses of Americans who saw themselves as moral guardians of the nation's ideals. "The makers of our Constitution undertook to secure conditions favorable to the pursuit of happiness," Justice Brandeis wrote in dissent in a government wiretapping case. "They recognized the significance of man's spiritual nature, of his feelings and his intellect."

He called the right to be let alone "the most comprehensive of rights and the right most valued by civilized men." Brandeis and like-minded contemporaries distinguished between the sacred and the profane and thought that laws could improve the performance of the press. Their polemics placed invasions of privacy on the level of public nuisances, obscenity, or trespassing and therefore could treat them as beneath legal protection.

They maintained that popular newspapers undermined necessary virtues and those social interests could be served by restrictions on press rights. Facing the pressure, journalists reflected on their practices and sometimes adopted ethical principles to preserve their professional status.

In order to make a distinction between itself and its less reputable local rivals in the 1890s, The New York Times adopted its slogan "All the News That's Fit to Print." The Journalist said that journalism schools could "teach the difference between genuine enterprise and keyhole journalism."

In challenging public tastes and journalistic decisions with some success, nineteenth-century privacy advocates showed how standards of civility can be used to limit civil liberties. Constitutional protections for expression can be overshadowed by community norms and demands for personal dignity.

The firm "no law" language of the First Amendment sometimes has been overcome when journalism is classified as threatening to society and broadcast content is considered a violation of the public interest. Some types of expression have been restricted because of the experiences and expectations of the private sphere. In 1978, for instance, the Supreme Court of the United States upheld broadcast indecency rules by comparing the intrusiveness of "filthy words" on daytime radio heard by children to the nuisance of a pig in a parlor.

Supporters of the privacy tort did not have major legal obstacles to surmount. They could establish a new area of law but not ensure that the application of such a conflicted idea would be easy or effective. Later uses of the privacy concept in areas from procreation to electronic commerce have produced perplexing and sometimes paradoxical outcomes Controversial issues of informational and decisional privacy have permeated the legal system, but the roots of the right remain in rather nebulous standards of social politeness and personal spirituality.

Chapter 5

Hiring and Training of Photojournalists

The technology of newspaper photography has changed dramatically in the last decade from predominantly chemical to predominantly digital processes. The technology used in educating prospective newspaper photographers has changed somewhat less dramatically. Many journalism programs continue to focus on chemical rather than digital processing. Is this discrepancy a cause for concern?

Are there implications for traditional as well as new media jobs in an age of digital journalism and increasing media convergence? This chapter, which is based on a national survey of daily newspaper photo editors, details the degree of technological change in newspaper photography. It looks at the importance placed on digital imaging and photography competencies, and it examines the implications for the training and hiring of journalists.

Digital imaging burst on the newsroom scene in the early 1990s, but its roots in the news production process are deeper. In the early 1980s, about the time National Geographic was electronically realigning the pyramids for a cover, newspaper pagination pioneers were starting to digitize photos for full-page assembly and output.

Electronic picture desks were used throughout the 1980s by the wire services, but they did not become common in daily newspapers until 1990. Early that year, the Associated Press (AP) announced that it would make a digital darkroom system the standard receiver for Photostream, its new high-speed digital photo transmission system. By early 1992, AP Leaf Picture Desks had been installed at nearly all of the 1,000 AP photo clients.

In a parallel development, many papers began using relatively inexpensive off-the-shelf hardware and software, such as Macintosh computers and Photoshop, for processing staff photos as well as the image files received on Leaf desks. Many of those images were passed to pagination systems or to desktop computers loaded with page-design software such as Quark Xpress.

The shift to all-digital handling of photos at many papers raised questions about storage and indexing of image files, and by 1994, a growing list of vendors offered digital archiving hardware and software. "The world and, more importantly, the industry are changing rapidly," he said. "The academy must introduce and teach new learning, or to paraphrase Eric Hoffer, our students will find themselves beautifully equipped to deal with a world that no longer exists."

An innovation such as the digital camera might necessitate some changes in emphasis in photo training. Irby pointed out that shooting with a digital camera is more akin to shooting colour transparencies than it is to shooting with the much-more-common, and more forgiving, colour negatives. Consequently, photographers who use digital cameras must learn to pay greater attention to correct exposure and lighting.

Whether an emphasis on technology training is good or bad as far as journalism education is concerned is a fair question. It is difficult to ask the question intelligently, though, without having first answered several others:

How widespread is the use of the technology in the industry that most of these students plan to enter?

How important is it for photojournalists to be conversant with digital technologies? Another way of asking the question is: How vital do the people who hire photojournalists think the new technical skills are?

Hiring Standards and Convergence. There are

indications that technological know-how is becoming a de facto hiring criterion for many newsroom positions. A 1996 Dow Jones Newspaper Fund survey of 489 newspapers found that more than 85 per cent said computer skills were either very or somewhat important in assessment of job applicants for reporting, editing, and design positions.

The study found that internships, work for a campus publication, a degree in journalism or mass communications, and, to a lesser degree, good grades also were important. Another recent study reported that although managing editors rated pagination experience relatively unimportant when asked what skills future journalists need, job advertisements provided a different picture - they placed considerable emphasis on pagination know-how.

The head of a newsroom training firm has said that writing, editing, and design skills should be taught first but that computer page design technology "has become a tool of the trade and should be better taught by our colleges and universities."

Since the advent of newsroom computerization, it has become increasingly difficult to disentangle the tools used by members of the journalism profession from the nature of the work that they do. A copyeditor, for example, is defined by a traditional set of competencies, such as word editing, headline-writing, and page-layout skills, and, increasingly, by whether he or she knows how to use Quark Xpress. As trade journal ads clearly indicate, graphics professionals are closely associated with the software and systems that make newspaper graphics practical in a digital age.

The kinship between photography and technology has long been the closest among newsroom specialties. Indeed, as far back as the 1930s, newspaper photographers struggled to convince their newsroom colleagues that they were professionals rather than mere technicians; some suggest that the struggle to convince reporters and editors that "picture people" are journalists too is not over yet.

Digital technology may be forcing the issue. Some photographers and photojournalism teachers say that because digital imaging enables photographers to get out of the darkroom and into the newsroom, it will create opportunities for photo staff members to take their rightful place alongside reporters and editors. The flip side of that argument is that the new technical demands of computer-based image-processing may make photographers appear to be even more specialized and even more out of touch. Another issue on the horizon is one of control.

Because digital imaging can be done in the newsroom, some photographers and photo editors have expressed concerns that photojournalism may be increasingly shaped by people who have little photo training. This question has been raised in the context of online journalism as well. Beckman commented in 1995 that "the very technology that brought us digital darkrooms, high-speed access to photo databases and desktop computer graphics and pagination has now led us into a reality of poorly designed electronic newspapers sparsely illustrated with low-resolution photographs."

In the intervening two years, hundreds of papers have developed online sites, many of them offering staff photography. Are photojournalists typically involved in preparing photography for the web, or has photography become part of the job of separate online staffs?

It also is becoming more difficult to distinguish roles within news operations. Digital imaging technology makes it possible, though perhaps not practical, to promote a convergence of jobs within the newsroom. Computer picture processing has largely eliminated the need to have a separate physical location where photo handling is performed.

Many papers continue to shoot and develop film, but every point in the process beyond developing can be done outside the physical environs of the darkroom. Another step, the digital camera, eliminates the need for any darkroom. In effect, digitization of text and photos has made it possible for photographers to take on reporting and visual-presentation tasks typically done by reporters, editors, and designers and, at the same time, for editors to take on roles traditionally held by photographers and even production camera operators.

Some newspapers have institutionalized cross-training for staff members, including photographers, who may do a stint as reporters, copyeditors, or designers, learning new tasks and new technologies. Moss argues that such training will become increasingly important. At smaller papers, staff members have always worn many hats; is digital imaging helping make that approach more important at mid-size and large papers?

If digital imaging has led to intraorganizational convergence, one indication is whether photo editors consider nonphoto skills of growing importance in the hiring of photographers. A parallel issue is raised in various forums about the extent and rapidity of cross-media convergence and whether journalism schools are prepared to train students for careers that may require skills that cut across traditional media industries. Video skills are the best example.

Some programs have shifted to a model in which students learn both print and visual reporting in expectation that media convergence will continue to dissolve the distinction between print and electronic reporting as it has in some online or multimedia news operations. More and more journalism programs are creating electronic publishing courses that deliberately blur the distinction between traditional industry practices.

Friedland and Webb, for example, talk about a course at the University of Wisconsin that requires students to learn a variety of online skills, including how to take digital pictures and process them for web use. Paul Lester of the University of California, Fullerton, sees technological change and convergence as a challenge to be met as well as an opportunity in journalism education:

"It will be standing room only in photojournalism classes when we teach our students the fundamentals of visual communication- how to sense, select and perceive a visual message - and how to work a camera, a computer and the software, how to use database research methods, how to create informational graphics, how to combine words with your stories, and how to make layouts and designs for print and interactive media."

Few newspaper web sites now contain video clips, but many observers expect the use of video to grow in the near future, as bandwidth improvements enable faster transmission times. Several questions emerge: To what degree are newspaper photojournalists involved in online still photography at their papers, and to what degree do photo editors, many of whom work at papers with web sites, see the need for photographers to be skilled in video?

Whatever form new media take, images will almost certainly play a major role. The crystal ball used by photo editors in not necessarily clearer than others'; photo editors do, however, have the clearest image of newspapers' imaging needs for the present and, because they deal with ongoing technological change (and hiring), they have a valuable perspective on the near future.

This study examines the attitudes and issues photo editors face when dealing with new technologies. It deals with five general areas:

- What is the extent of digital imaging use at U.S. dailies? Included in this section were questions dealing with the preferred platform and software, the extent of digital camera use, the percentage of papers that have web sites and use local photos on those sites, and the role photo staff members play in web photo work.
- What skills are most important for photographers today? Included in this section were questions asking editors to rate the importance of traditional photo skills, processing skills, digital imaging and digital camera skills. Photo editors also were asked about the importance of skills that reflect convergence of jobs within the organization, such as design and graphics skills and skills that reflect convergence with other media forms, such as web skills and video camera skills.

- What skills are likely to be important in five years? Here, editors were asked to predict future skill needs. This section made it possible to compare current skills with predicted future needs to examine whether chemical darkroom skills will be less important and whether digital skills would remain the same or increase in importance.
- Are there shifts in skills toward convergence? We assume that skills dealing with the world wide web will increase in importance. Articles in the trade press as well as in academic journals have noted the blurring of lines between media and the blurring of lines within the academy and the newsroom. Do photo editors see a similar shift? Will video skills, for example, be more important in the future?
- Finally, to what degree do photo editors consider digital imaging skills as hiring criteria? How do those skills rank in perceived importance among other job criteria? Is there a difference based on newspaper size? It is possible, for example, that digital imaging skills may be of greater importance at entry-level papers than at larger papers. Smaller papers do not have the resources to train extensively and thus may want new employees to begin work with experience in the technology. If so, this information would be of particular importance to journalism educators.

Data come from a mail survey of photo editors at daily newspapers in the United States. Newspapers and addresses were selected from the 1996 Editor and Publisher International Yearbook through a systematic random sample.

Only newspapers with circulation of more than 7,500 were surveyed. Newspapers below 7,500 circulation use digital image processing, but they are less likely to have a photo department as such and less likely to use certain digital technologies, such as Leaf Desks.

Because we wanted to examine attitudes and issues photo editors faced because of new technologies and in the hiring of photographers, we felt eliminating smaller papers was justified. The initial mailing took place on 28 February 1997. A second mailing, with a follow-up letter and another copy of the questionnaire, was sent two weeks later. Both mailings were addressed to each newspaper's photo editor, chief photographer, or photo department director as listed in Editor and Publisher International Yearbook.

If a newspaper's listing in the ESP Yearbook did not list a supervisory position for photo, the mailing was addressed to "Photo editor."

A total of 225 newspapers out of 362 responded, for a 62.2% response rate, which is acceptable, according to Babbie. The survey instrument asked a variety of questions dealing with the importance of chemical and digital photographic skills, other newsroom skills such as graphics and page design, and new web-based and video skills.

Photo editors were asked to indicate whether they thought each of 17 skill areas was important on a scale ranging from "not at all important" to "extremely important". They also were asked to indicate the importance of 9 possible criteria for entry-level hiring on a similar scale.

1. Digital imaging use. Digital imaging is almost ubiquitous at U.S. dailies whose circulation is more than 7,500. Only 5 papers out of 225 indicated no digital imaging use, 78.7% were 100% digital, and 94.7% used digital imaging for at least 90% of their images. For most of the papers that still print negatives in a darkroom, prints represent a small fraction of their output. Most papers that use digital image processing scan negatives rather than transparencies, because negatives, particularly colour negatives, are more forgiving in exposure than transparency film. Ninety-five per cent said they primarily scanned negatives; 2% said they primarily scanned transparencies.

A great majority of papers use Photoshop software on a Macintosh platform for digital imaging, as industry observers have been reporting anecdotally for several years. Nearly 95% said they used Photoshop, and 87% said they used a Macintosh platform. Only 10% of photo editors said their imaging was done on a Windows platform. About 6% of photo editors said they used other systems, such as Scitex, for image-processing.

Digital camera use is surprisingly high - at 28.9% of papers - though the percentage of photos shot with those cameras remains relatively low. Among papers that use digital cameras, the mean was 23% of staff photos shot with digital cameras.

Most shoot only a small fraction of their photos electronically (60% of the 65 papers that reported digital camera use said they shot 10% or fewer photos electronically). Eight photo editors said their papers took 80% or more photos digitally.

One-hundred twenty-seven photo editors, or 56.4%, said their papers had online editions. Of papers with online editions, 83.5% indicated that they use staff photos. Of those, 62% said online photos were prepared by a separate online staff, 27% by the photo department, and 8% by the news department. These findings suggest that observers who have expressed concerns about photographers' control of their images online may have a point.

2. What skills are important today? Photo editors ranked traditional photography skills such as shooting and providing accurate caption information highest among the 17 skills listed, and another traditional skill, picture editing, is also high. Two digital processing skills (scanning and using Photoshop) are next in importance. The picture is somewhat mixed on traditional chemical darkroom skills, with developing film ranked very high and printing considerably lower. These rankings reflect the reality of photo processing in dailies today, where negatives are still used for the majority of pictures but prints are almost nonexistent. Several other digital skills - using the Leaf Desk, using an electronic photo archive and using a digital camera - are considered somewhat important today.

3. What skills are likely to be important in five years? The picture changes somewhat for the near future. Photo editors again ranked traditional skills of shooting and providing caption information highest and picture editing quite high. But they indicate that a wider constellation of digital imaging skills will be very important. Those are Photoshop use, scanning, using digital cameras, and using digital archives. Traditional processing skills drop far down in ranks, with film developing only "somewhat important" in five years and printing very unimportant.
4. Do shifts, if any, reflect convergence within the organization and between media forms? Photo editors consider skills such as page design and graphics, which would reflect convergence of photo jobs and other newsroom jobs, of little importance in photo hiring today.

In five years, photo editors indicate, those skills will increase somewhat in importance. Photo editors at entry-level papers place slightly more emphasis on those skills than their counterparts on larger papers do, which may be a reflection of the importance traditionally placed on versatility at small papers.

Web skills, which include using the web and preparing photos for the web, move up from "slightly" to "somewhat" important in five years. There was no difference between entry-level and larger papers on the importance placed on these web skills.

There was little difference between papers that had web sites and those that didn't on the importance photo editors placed on web skills both now and in five years. The results suggest that photo editors attach greater importance (though still not much) to a convergence of skills within their organizations than between media.

The increasing importance placed on web skills may be more a reflection of photo editors' desire to gain more control over how images are used in online editions than it is an indication of cross-media convergence.

Video skills were ranked lowest of the 17 listed skills both for the present and in five years. The difference in means on this item is statistically significant, but even at five years, the mean score fails to rise to the level of "slightly important." Moreover, there is no significant difference between entry-level and larger papers on this question for either the present or five years from now.

And there is no difference between papers that had web sites and those that did not. It may be that photo editors as a group are dubious about the likelihood of a near-term solution to the bandwidth problems that inhibit the delivery of video on the web. It also may be the case that photo editors at U.S.

dailies do not believe that media convergence is occurring as quickly as some observers within both the industry and academia suggest. For journalism educators, a prudent course might be to keep one eye on the light at the end of the tunnel and the other on the track immediately ahead.

5. Hiring criteria. The results indicate that digital-image-processing skills currently are an important criterion for hiring at the entry level. Digital darkroom skills ranked second only to having a good portfolio, which photo editors consider of great importance. The mean for a good portfolio was 4.55 - midway between "very" and "extremely" important and the mean of 4.01 for digital darkroom skills was "very" important. The ranking of criteria is generally consistent with the findings of the 1996 Dow Jones Newspaper Fund survey of hiring criteria for reporters, editors, and designers.

Breaking the sample into three circulation groups (less than 25,000, 25,000-75,000, and greater than 75,000) shows a high level of consistency in assessment of the importance of entry-level criteria.

Only three significant differences emerged: Larger papers were more likely to rate a photo internship very important, and smaller papers were more likely to rate chemical darkroom skills important. Large papers also ranked good grades slightly more important.

Another question offers additional evidence of the importance of digital imaging skills. About 2 out of 5 photo editors say they are either somewhat or very unlikely to hire a photographer with no digital imaging experience. Here, too, no significant difference emerged between photo editors at the entry level and those at mid-size papers (25,000-75,000) and large papers.

There are no industry-standard definitions of "entry-level paper," but the lack of relationship holds when papers are grouped in other ways, such as two groups (less than 25,000 and greater than 25,000) and two somewhat different groups (less than 50,000 and more than 50,000.

The shift from chemical to digital processing has led to a relative lack of concern among photo editors about the need for chemical skills, in particular, printing. Very few of the photos used in newspapers today are printed in a darkroom. Many journalism programs, however, continue to focus on those skills, for reasons of cost and, perhaps, as LeFleur and Davenport found with database reporting, inertia.

Certain new skills are growing in importance, such as the use of digital cameras, use of the web, and preparation of photos for the web. Skills that reflect convergence between photo jobs and other newsroom jobs, such as design and graphics arts, appear to be growing in importance. The key skill that reflects cross-media convergence - video - increases in importance, but not to the level of the others.

For the most part, photo editors at large and small papers agree on both the criteria for entry-level hires and on the importance of specific skills. One might expect greater variation between circulation groups because of the greater resources and higher degree of specialization found at larger papers. The similarity suggests that a technology such as digital imaging affects papers and photographers in largely the same ways.

An analysis of skills photo editors consider important

now is vital in curricular planning. A glimpse at what skills might be important in five years also will be useful to journalism educators, who need to prepare students for the near future as well as the present.

How soon do journalism programs need to think about moving from chemical to digital training? Based on this survey, the message from photo editors is that the digital revolution has already occurred, particularly in image processing, and that it is well under way in image capture. By implication, their message to journalism educators seems clear as well: It's time to join the revolution.

Chapter 6

Next Generation of Journalists for Converged Media

The news industry has been undergoing a fundamental paradigm shift since the end of last century. An increasing number of media companies around the United States, such as the Washington Post in Washington, DC, Media General in Virginia, the Tribune Company in Chicago, and New England Cable News, have taken solid steps to merge different media such as newspapers, television stations, radio stations, and online journalism companies to disseminate news content on multiple media platforms.

As a result, in a metropolitan area, one company would own print, TV, and online venues. Media call this industrial trend "media convergence," though the concept means much more than media mergers. Media convergence muddies the lines among broadcast journalism, print journalism, and online journalism, leaving college journalism educators to wonder whether traditional journalism programs have become dinosaurs.

After surveying 200 newspaper publishers worldwide, the World Association of Newspapers (WAN) found, "Despite a somewhat gloomy outlook for wholesale convergence in media companies worldwide in the near term, convergence is already being implemented with varying degrees of enthusiasm and speed among the world's media companies". The Innovation International Media Consulting Group estimates that at least 100 of the world's multiple media companies are planning and implementing integration strategies. South and Nicholson (2002) drew a sketch of a converged media company:

Daily journalists need to embrace the 24-hour news cycle, with continuous deadlines. And the story needs to be reported and produced for a multi-platform audience. That may mean delivering content first to the Web and cell phones, a streaming video broadcast later in the day, a TV talk-back interview still later, and a "second day" interpretive story for the next morning's newspaper.

Dominic Gates (2002) pointed out, "Convergence with broadcast and online media is the shape of things to come for newspapers." The trend remains controversial. Critics complain that such cross-ownership of both a television station and a newspaper in the same market is a threat to democracy because it limits the number of voices.

Delegates of the Communication Workers of America, a 60,000-member guild, passed a resolution in June of 2002 at the group's annual convention in Las Vegas, pledging to increase public awareness about the risks of ongoing media convergence. The delegates complained that shrinking media markets are a threat to editorial diversity and job security.

In 1975, the Federal Communications Commission (FCC) ruled that no new broadcast licenses would be granted to companies that own a major daily newspaper and a local television station in the same city. Fairness & Accuracy In Reporting (FAIR) calls on the FCC to roll back limits on media consolidation.

The Newspaper Association of America (NAA), on the other hand, has asked the FCC to appeal the rule. On June 2, 2003, the FCC voted 3 to 2 to relax or eliminate some ownership restrictions, such as a rule barring media companies from owning television stations in markets where they publish daily newspapers. Although some lawmakers and advocacy groups are still fighting in the courts and on Capitol Hill to overturn the FCC's new media ownership rules, these rules will be likely to encourage cross-media ownership in the years to come.

The mergers have raised questions about whether they

are good for the craft of journalism itself. Critics complain that by requiring journalists to be jacks of both trades, print and broadcast, the journalists will be masters of none. Robert J. Haiman, president emeritus of The Poynter Institute, compared the media convergence trend to an Amphicar, a cross between a boat and a car. The Amphicar, hawked in Florida during the 1950s, flopped. "It flopped because people quickly discovered that while it really was an ingenious combination of a car and a boat, it was a lousy car (because it also had to be a boat), and it was a lousy boat (because it also had to be a car)".

Willingly or unwillingly, many news practitioners' functions are gradually changing or are expected to change as media convergence rolls on. For a reporter in a converged media environment, knowing how to write is probably no longer enough. S/he could be expected to write the same story for different media in a timely manner.

Ideally, s/he can readily talk in front of a video camera. As a photographer, knowing how to tell a story both in video and in still images is more and more in demand. A designer should know how to prepare still graphics for print, moving graphics for television and dynamic graphics for the Web.

At the online version of the Chicago Tribune, for instance, staffers are supposed to cover stories, take pictures, operate video cameras, and create digital pages. The editors, too, need a wider variety of skills than the traditional paper editors. Along with infrastructure changes and the attempt to create synergy among the various media outlets, a new breed of journalists-digital or multimedia journalists-is expected.

As media jobs become more demanding, some news practitioners are beginning to team up to complete projects. At the same time, fear, confusion, and frustration from news practitioners are creeping into newsrooms. Carr (2002c) wrote: "Convergence frightens many people who wonder whether their current skill sets have prepared them for-or will even be needed in-that great undiscovered country, the future. This is probably the primary reason why I still find such great hostility to convergence among certain journalists." Killebrew, a mass communications professor from the University of South Florida, suggested that "journalists must be prepared to either crosstrain themselves or seek training from other sources while management must be prepared to give them the opportunities and time to do so."

The 1999-2000 president of the Association for Schools of Journalism and Mass Communication (ASJMC), Shirley Staples Carter, questioned whether, in the midst of the "Internet revolution," programs are prepared to educate journalists of the future.

When specifically talking about writing, Keith Hartenberger, manager of news and programming for Tribune Regional Programming, said that journalism schools should make their students aware of the many ways to present the news. "It's a multimedia world out there," he said. "If you're just being prepared to write newspaper stories, you won't be prepared". "At some point, this [cross-media training] is something we're going to expect from everyone".

Media convergence, as a trend that is gradually shaping the landscape of the media industry in the new century, has called into question the conventional journalism school practice of having separate tracks-print, broadcast, etc. Journalism educators around the country also are trying to figure out what they should do, if anything, to better prepare students for the converged media.

For instance, should journalism educators consider merging different sequences such as magazine, newspaper, broadcast, and photojournalism, or still teach all such courses as if they were unrelated media? "Traditionally defined segments of the communications industry are less and less distinguishable for technological and market convergence," observed Moon (2001).

Are college journalism educators themselves both theoretically equipped and technologically prepared to teach their students for converged media? What do media companies expect from future news practitioners? What do current news practitioners in converged media feel is lacking? For both news practitioners and professors, the two most urgent questions cry for answers: Should journalism schools train specialists or fit for-all generalists? And how should college journalism education balance the teaching of critical thinking and technical skills?

Apart from all these education-related questions, we are also interested in finding out what are the driving forces behind the media mergers, who are regarded as the beneficiaries of this trend, and how people's political beliefs are related to their attitude toward teaching media convergence in colleges? These questions pertain closely to college journalism education, which has been the subject of debate and criticism for two decades.

A national survey was conducted among colleges, daily newspapers, and commercial television stations to explore the issue of how journalism schools should prepare students for the trend of media convergence from the perspectives of news editors, news professionals, and journalism professors. The study measured the level of general support for convergence education and determined if a new model of journalism education was called for.

If so, it examined whether consensus existed among the three groups on the direction educators should take when revisiting programme designs. Where consensus was not apparent, divisions among the sample of educators, editors, and reporters were defined. The goal of the study is to provide evidence that will help journalism educators make informed decisions about how to respond to media convergence in their curricula and courses and lay an empirical foundation for further discussions and conversations about media convergence.

The search results show that media convergence is a comparatively new topic in media research, though articles about it have inundated the Internet, magazines, and newspapers. Most research writings appeared no earlier than

1998. Articles about the relationship between media convergence and higher education are rare and have shown up more recently in trade magazines. A few research writings were found in academic conference (i.e., AEJMC) proceedings.

Many writings have addressed one of the toughest questions: What is media convergence? How to define "media convergence" had a direct bearing on how we conducted this study. Out of these writings, we identified four categories of media convergence that directly affect how journalism will be taught in colleges.

CONTENT CONVERGENCE

As Tremayne noted, decades ago, the term media convergence referred to the content convergence between competing newspapers and even among newspapers, magazines, and television. Today, pure content convergence continues on the Internet. For instance, the St. Petersburg Times has incorporated local Channel 10's TV news into its online newspaper though they are independent business entities. In other words, media convergence may not necessarily be tied to media merger.

Form convergence (or technological convergence). Around the mid-1990s, as Tremayne and Wurtz (2000) noted, computer technology and Internet technology made possible the convergence of all forms of mediated communications including video, audio, data, text, still photo, and graphic art for "on-demand" audiences.

Using these different forms to tell news stories on the World Wide Web has been widely regarded as the future of mass communication regardless of the fact that most online news sites have had a hard time making ends meet, let alone making a profit. Form convergence, often called technological convergence, has been a fundamental force to guide and lead convergence in the market, industry, and regulation.

CORPORATE CONVERGENCE

Since the late 1990s, media convergence has been escalated to the level of media mergers. The News Centre located in Tampa, Florida, owned by Media General, and the Tribune Interactive, owned by the Tribune Company, for instance, are the products of media mergers. In The News Centre, WFLA-TV, The Tampa Tribune, and Tampa Bay Online operate out of the same building.

They share daily tips and information, spot news, photography, enterprise reporting, franchises, events, and public service. Each of the three entities in The News Centre has its own independent newsroom, but they issued a joint statement of coverage principles, titled "News Centre Pledge".

The Tribune Interactive has brought together the interactive functions of the company's four newspapers and more than a score of television stations including WGN-TV and CLTV. The individual media outlets have their own newsgathering staff, but their coverage is enhanced by their multimedia desks in the Chicago Tribune newsroom and the Tribune Media Centre in Washington.

"A synergy-team of print editors and TV news veterans at the Chicago Tribune work together to manage resource sharing and the relationship". Media merger has made both content convergence and form convergence handy. Corporate convergence via vertical and horizontal integration, mergers, alliances, and acquisitions will make traditionally defined segments of the communications industry less and less distinguishable.

ROLE CONVERGENCE

Russial identified several examples of role convergence in newsrooms. For instance, the roles of reporter and librarian, the roles of copyeditor and compositor, the roles of graphic artist and Web designer, and the roles of photo editor, darkroom technician, and photographer are all converging in different media.

In more recent years, content convergence, form convergence, and especially corporate convergence have sparked more in-depth role convergence among news practitioners. For instance, Victoria Lim from The News Centre in Tampa revealed at a February 2002 conference on media convergence at the University of Florida that she primarily works as a television reporter for WFLA-TV, but she also has to write for the company's newspaper, The Tampa Tribune, as a senior consumer investigative reporter and for the Web company TBO.com on a daily basis; at the time of the conference, she was working on 31 stories.

A newspaper reporter may also produce a newspaper in QuarkXPress or serve as a TV news anchor, while a newspaper photographer may shoot video stories or produce interactive online stories in Flash. Role convergence requires that both reporters and editors re-equip themselves both journalistically and technologically.

Of the four types of convergence, role convergence has the most direct effect on future journalism education. Within the media industry, there are serious doubts about whether training cross-media journalists are possible or desirable. When asked whether reporters of the future must be equally skilled in print, TV, and online, Forrest Carr, news director of WFLA-TV at The News Centre in Tampa, said no. He said he believed that there would always be areas of specialization and students may still choose specialties, but said that it no longer makes any sense to pretend print journalists and electronic journalists are in different professions.

On the other hand, he said that journalists who have skills in TV, print, and online media certainly will be more valuable to their employers; and he emphasized that prospective employees must be willing to work in an environment where reporters cooperate across platforms. In most cases currently, he said, cooperating across platforms simply comes down to the sharing of tips and information.

Charles Kravetz, the vice president for news and station manager of New England Cable News (NECN), the largest regional news network in America, concurs with Forrest Carr. When asked "Do you see a time when all journalists will have to be able to file stories on all platforms (print, TV, radio, online)?" Kravetz said: "I am not sure that is the way it is going to work out.

This notion we had that one-journalist-fits-all-media is perhaps not that realistic. ... There are very few people we will talk about in the future that are TV/newspaper/internet reporters". Gates agreed, "The 'backpack journalist'-a superhack master of multimedia who can do it all and who routinely packs a laptop and a video camera along with the tape recorder and steno notebook-may be the subject of avant-garde j-school courses, but it's not likely to become the norm."

Some other media executives have tried to define the extent to which role convergence is expected. Gil Thelen, executive editor and senior vice president of The Tampa Tribune, for instance, gave suggestions to journalism educators based on his two years of experience in The News Centre.

"The fully formed, all-purpose, multiplatform, gadget-laden journalism grad is NOT what we're looking to hire. ... Journalism schools must continue to produce graduates who are competent in one craft area: reporting, design, producing, directing, editing." However, Thelen encouraged journalism schools to train writers to write for print, online, and broadcast and train print photographers to learn how to shoot and produce TV packages. Thelen said that cultural resistance is the biggest hurdle for converging newsrooms, and that employees or current journalism students need to learn to cooperate and collaborate across newsrooms.

What is unclear is whether these media administrators' predictions are limited by the status quo of the current generation of news practitioners who might not be very well prepared for convergence or who might even resist the notion of media convergence.

At Brigham Young University, students with multiple skills are more valued and feel more comfortable in the converged media environment. In addition, sharing tips and information does not entail convergence. Reporters have been doing this for decades. It seems that keeping convergence only on the level of sharing tips and information can hardly justify the high cost of rebuilding infrastructures like The News Centre. We are interested in finding out what expectations media companies have for future journalists. From news professionals' self-evaluations of their preparedness for media convergence, we should also be able to infer what is most desirable in the media industry nowadays.

In the face of increasing demand for technically skilled journalists-conversant with QuarkXPress, Photoshop, Avid, and Dreamweaver and able to crunch statistics using spreadsheets and other statistical methods in order to uncover the hidden story-should longstanding staples such as ethics, law, and theory remain at the heart of journalism curricula? Or should such materials, commonly grouped together as "critical thinking", share equal hilling with technology or "skills" training?

In other words, how should journalism schools balance the teaching of professional skills and that of critical thinking in an era when technology penetrates every facet of news gathering, preparation, editing, production, and delivery.

Convergence further complicates this age-old battle in journalism education.9 Abraham noticed that the goal of most restructuring in journalism institutions is to provide an integrated skills environment where students would get the chance to practice the skills of multimedia production. Abraham argued: "The role of journalism academy should be very different from that of the industry. Its role should not simply be to inculcate skills that will help students to flag down jobs.

They should aim to provide a scholarly background for a deeper intellectual understanding of our lives, media forms and of communication in general". The dean of the University of Nevada at Reno thinks the ability to use multiple media skills is essential. Brigham Young University, which has built a working converged newsroom into its curriculum, expects students to graduate with multiple skills.

University News Director, Dean Paynter, said, "We expect our students to more than anchor, more than report, and more than produce. The best ones can do it all, including write for the newspaper". Mitchell Stephens, professor of journalism and mass communications at New York University, holds up the other end.

"In a world where corporate pressures on 'content providers' seem to be increasing and civic affairs decreasing, the argument for emphasizing the basics does have much to recommend it." Thomas Kunkel (2002), dean of the Philip Merrill College of Journalism at the University of Maryland, sums it up: "Today's journalists, first and foremost, must be strong critical thinkers who know enough about geography, history and the human condition to understand why events play out as they do. They must be intellectually curious. They should speak a second language. They should read something other than Jim Romenesko's MediaNews site. They ought to have a world view."

A controversy in late 2002 at Columbia University demonstrates how volatile the argument is currently. The debate arose when the graduate school of journalism at Columbia University halted its search for a dean. The new university president, Lee Bollinger, wanted to re-evaluate the school's mix of craft versus theory, and the move created a flurry of opinion about the journalism school's existing curriculum.

This critical curriculum question is often reflected in the questions of whether and how new technology classes should be included in the existing curriculum and how they should be taught. Some journalism schools are preparing to embrace the wave of media convergence in their new curricula by converging print and electronic media sequences to adapt to the industrial trends and the new technological environment.

Blanchard and Christ warn that universities with limited resources will no longer tolerate duplicating specializations with separate courses such as writing for television, writing for newspapers, writing for public relations, and writing for advertising. Blanchard and Christ add that the communications revolution (the media's convergence and related trends) is making journalism and mass communication's traditional sequences obsolete. Actually, Blanchard and Christ's opinion is not something new. Early in 1972, the University of Iowa School of Journalism already eliminated its sequences but at the expense of being denied reaccreditation by ACEJMC. About thirty years later, their decision seemed to be finding more sympathy.

Many schools are still exploring where to go. In October 2001, seventeen professors and leaders of new media from thirteen journalism programs across the country gathered in Berkeley, California, and had a discussion about new media in journalism education. The University of Nevada, Reno, offered several different elective courses in new media, but it did not have a special sequence.

It was struggling with how to incorporate them in other classes. The University of Florida had a concentration in online media, which was equivalent to other concentrations such as reporting and editing and photojournalism. Students who were not in that concentration couldn't always squeeze in the online media courses because they did not have any leftover électives they could take in the school.

American University had three divisions, journalism, public communication, and visual media, but they did not work together very well most of the time. The University of South Carolina was restructuring its graduate masters programme in newspaper leadership and was focusing it on convergence.

The University of Maryland had an online curriculum, but it was not formally structured as such. Northwestern University had an introductory New Media course at the undergraduate and graduate level, which was offered as an elective. It was packed with everything from new skills training to wrestling with the business issues of new media to actual production. After three admission cycles, enrollment declined.

The University of Minnesota established the Institute for New Media Studies, which merged broadcast journalism and print journalism programs to make them a concentration with the idea that future journalists would work in a multi-channel environment and should know how to operate within all those channels.

Although editors and academics sometimes agree on the qualifications a journalism student needs, an ideal curriculum doesn't always include convergence preparedness courses. In a 2000 poll, editors and educators agreed "on the same five of 14 types of knowledge considered most necessary for journalism graduates and listed them in the same order of importance".

Technical skills were not mentioned in the top five, surpassed instead by "understanding of a journalist's responsibility to the public, understanding of the ethics of journalism, knowledge of current events, broad general knowledge, and knowledge of government".

With so much variance across universities, we are interested in finding out how many journalism schools have revamped their curricula to prepare students for the trend of media convergence, what professors' attitudes are toward teaching critical thinking vs. teaching technical skills and training generalists vs. training specialists, and what editors' and news professionals' attitudes are toward the same issues. In this regard, several scholars and news practitioners have tried to give advice to journalism professors and students in the context of media convergence.

In 2002, David Bulla from the University of Florida presented his "Media convergence: Industry practices and implications for education" to the AEJMC annual conference in Miami. This is the first research writing of its kind. The theme of the paper is the closest to that of this study. Bulla's study looked at the changing nature of contemporary mass communications practices, focusing on multimedia or converged journalism.

It described what scholastic journalism scholars are doing to prepare their students for these changes and provided recommendations to educators about how to update curricula to account for convergence. The research questions for that study were: (1) what are journalism educators currently doing to incorporate convergence into their curricula; and (2) what abilities, skills, and attitudes do professional journalists expect from their newest employees? Media convergence in Bulla's study was defined as multimedia journalism, which means reporting, writing, and disseminating content in two or more media platforms.

Because of the controversy about media mergers, Bulla tried to find answers to some hot issues concerning democracy including: Does corporate media merging reduce public discourse and hinder democracy? Will it ultimately mean the need for fewer and fewer reporters, as the development of other technology has meant a decline in the number of employees in other areas of the production process? All these questions pertain to our study.

Bulla obtained a sample of 114 news practitioners working at newspapers, television stations, wire services, magazines, radio stations, and online publications in the United States. The sample was randomly selected from Editor & Publisher and Yahoo lists of media companies in the U.S. Media Web sites. With a response rate of 36 per cent, Bulla interviewed 41 news practitioners. Bulla also interviewed college educators, but he did not state how he sampled them.

What is unclear is the extent to which the Yahoo list and Editor & Publisher list overlap each other and if a sample from two potentially overlapping lists is any longer a random sample. In addition, since Bulla's questions were almost all unstructured, that is, he conducted interviews, he did not really need a random sample.

Researchers strive for depth rather than breadth and don't mean to claim external validity in the statistical sense by conducting interviews. Finally, if he did need a random sample, a sample of 114 people with a 36 per cent response rate could be statistically defective because of big statistical errors. Bulla needed a better research design to make his study valid and reliable.

Some scholars doubt whether journalism school professors are theoretically and especially technologically prepared to teach media convergence. In an article written for Journalism Education magazine, John Irby, a professor from Washington State University and a veteran newspaper editor and publisher, for instance, was concerned about the disconnection between the newsroom and the classroom. Irby (2000) asked:

Are universities and educators effectively preparing students for the work force? Do educators understand what newspapers are looking for in future reporters and editors? Does the newspaper industry have a responsibility in the division between educators and professionals? Are journalism educators "discounted" by professionals who believe those who teach couldn't succeed in newspapers?

Irby said older generations of newspaper reporters also appeared on radio and television periodically though they had no training; they never even felt like it was part of their job and thus did not take it very seriously. But now, he continued, print journalists do need to take it seriously; journalism educators need to re-evaluate, and probably modify, the separatetrack approach in training print and broadcast journalists. Irby believed that there is still a need for specialization, but he told students to take both broadcast and print courses and told them that computer literacy is as crucial as the old-fashioned kind.

In October 2001, seventeen professors and leaders of new media from thirteen journalism programs across the country gathered in Berkeley, California, and had a discussion about new media in journalism education. The University of Nevada, Reno, offered several different elective courses in new media, but it did not have a special sequence. It was struggling with how to incorporate them in other classes.

The University of Florida had a concentration in online media, which was equivalent to other concentrations such as reporting and editing and photojournalism. Students who were not in that concentration couldn't always squeeze in the online media courses because they did not have any leftover électives they could take in the school. American University had three divisions, journalism, public communication, and visual media, but they did not work together very well most of the time. The University of South Carolina was restructuring its graduate masters programme in newspaper leadership and was focusing it on convergence. The University of Maryland had an online curriculum, but it was not formally structured as such. Northwestern University had an introductory New Media course at the undergraduate and graduate level, which was offered as an elective.

It was packed with everything from new skills training to wrestling with the business issues of new media to actual production. After three admission cycles, enrollment declined. The University of Minnesota established the Institute for New Media Studies, which merged broadcast journalism and print journalism programs to make them a concentration with the idea that future journalists would work in a multi-channel environment and should know how to operate within all those channels.

Although editors and academics sometimes agree on the qualifications a journalism student needs, an ideal curriculum doesn't always include convergence preparedness courses. In a 2000 poll, editors and educators agreed "on the same five of 14 types of knowledge considered most necessary for journalism graduates and listed them in the same order of importance". Technical skills were not mentioned in the top five, surpassed instead by "understanding of a journalist's responsibility to the public, understanding of the ethics of journalism, knowledge of current events, broad general knowledge, and knowledge of government".

With so much variance across universities, we are interested in finding out how many journalism schools have revamped their curricula to prepare students for the trend of media convergence, what professors' attitudes are toward teaching critical thinking vs. teaching technical skills and training generalists vs. training specialists, and what editors' and news professionals' attitudes are toward the same issues. In this regard, several scholars and news practitioners have tried to give advice to journalism professors and students in the context of media convergence.

By implication, their message to journalism educators seems clear as well: It's time to join the revolution. -Ì¨a¢ayne noted, decades ago, the term media convergence referred to the content convergence between competing newspapers and even among newspapers, magazines, and television.

Today, pure content convergence continues on the Internet. For instance, the St. Petersburg Times has incorporated local Channel 10's TV news into its online newspaper though they are independent business entities. In other words, media convergence may not necessarily be tied to media merger.

Form convergence (or technological convergence). Around the mid-1990s, as Tremayne and Wurtz (2000) noted, computer technology and Internet technology made possible the convergence of all forms of mediated communications including video, audio, data, text, still photo, and graphic art for "on-demand" audiences.

Using these different forms to tell news stories on the World Wide Web has been widely regarded as the future of mass communication regardless of the fact that most online news sites have had a hard time making ends meet, let alone making a profit. Form convergence, often called technological convergence, has been a fundamental force to guide and lead convThe questions concerning teaching skills vs. critical thinking and training specialists vs. generalists are not new.

They have been contextualized in ongoing conversations across disciplines over decades on many campuses in the United States. But such conversations take on new meanings in journalism schools when many reporting jobs today are becoming high-tech-oriented and many news companies are demanding high-tech skills from new hires upon their graduation.

The impact of such industrial demands on universities brings us back to the core issue-the role of the university in the shaping of the young souls in its charge. In other words, how should a university achieve the desired product-a truly educated human being for newsrooms.

The question of teaching skills vs. critical thinking winds

down to a perennial competition between acquiescing pervasive vocationalism with its emphasis on skills training in an attempt to enable college students to survive outside academic institutions and establishing the relevance of the broad spectrum of knowledge to the career goals and lives of individuals. E. D. Hirsch argues: "Narrow vocational education, adjusted to the needs of the moment, is made ever more obsolete by changing technology... What is required is education for change, not for static job competencies". Probably no one has better expressed than Joanne G. Kurfiss the importance of imparting critical thinking as skills of analyzing and constructing arguments, as construction of meaning, and as the manifestation of a contextual theory of knowledge.

"Critical thinking can result in a new way of approaching significant issues in one's life or a deeper understanding of the basis for one's actions. Or it might result in political activity".

Along the similar line as Kurfiss's critical thinking theory and unlike Allan Bloom, who condemns the introduction of non-Western materials into the university curricula so as to protect the curriculum from the contamination of ideological conflict, Jerry Herron also highly promotes the teaching of critical thinking by calling on faculty to bring their conflicting ideologies into open engagement so that students can discover what is at stake in different ideas and can see their representational meaning.

The questions are whether universities should totally give up the teaching of skills today and how the needs of the job market and the goal of college education can be in harmony. In other words, can the teaching of common traditional content and the teaching of higher order skills join forces? Patracia Graham, ex-dean of the Harvard Graduate School of Education, argues that we need both commonality and flexibility in American education and there is no reason we cannot have both at once.

The question of training specialists vs. generalists is an extension of a larger conversation about reforming the fragmented curricula in higher education. Often classified as "cultural right," Ernest Boyer, Allan Bloom, and E. D. Hirsch share similar views about the problems in higher education. They point out that the university now is anarchistic. There is no vision of what an educated human being is. The curriculum is disjointed and disciplines are fragmented into smaller pieces.

Undergraduates find it hard to see patterns in their courses and relate what they learn to life. Careerism conflicts with the liberal arts. And finally, schools have failed to thoroughly carry out the educational goal of promoting mature literacy for all our citizens. They all agree that an educational reform is needed to teach more common traditional content apart from the higher-order skills that are commonly emphasized.

Boyer calls for a balance between individual interests and shared concerns while the actual priority is given to the latter. To promote a liberal education, Boyer advocates the "integrated core" or "enriched major"-a programme of general education that introduces students not only to essential knowledge, but also to connections across the disciplines, and, in the end, to the application of knowledge to life beyond the campus.

Boyer points out, knowledge becomes important only when we use it and apply it to humane ends; therefore, the undergraduate experience should not only generate new knowledge, but channel that knowledge to the service of the society. It is a matter of invigorating "the claims of community while protecting with full vigour the dignity and origins of each individual," to use Boyer and Kaplan's words.

In a similar vein, Bloom calls on teachers to look toward the goal of human completeness and to provide students a liberal education, in which learning is both synoptic and precise. To Bloom, liberal education feeds the student's love of truth and passion to live a good life. It also requires that a student's whole life be radically changed by it. Bloom offers an ivory tower vision of the university-"the good old Great

Book approach"-undergraduate students spend four years reading certain generally recognized classic texts for answers to philosophical questions of personal and human identity and aspirations. Bloom thinks that man may live more truly and fully in reading Plato and Shakespeare than at any other time because then they are participating in essential being and are forgetting their accidental lives.

In accordance with Boyer's and Bloom's points of view, Hirsch argues that "the greatest human individuality is developed in response to a tradition, not in response to disorderly, uncertain, and fragmented education" and "only by accumulating shared symbols, and the shared information the symbols represent can we learn to communicate effectively with one another in our national community". However, Hirsch places emphasis more on the content of education, ensuring that students acquire all the "right" elements of knowledge that will enable them to get along in the Real World.

He believes that neither the content-neutral curriculum of Rousseau and Dewey nor the narrowly specified curriculum of Plato is adequate to the needs of a modern nation. Hirsch calls for a curriculum, including extensive curriculum and intensive curriculum with an emphasis on the former, which is traditional in content and provides students with a common core of cultural information. "The conception of a two-part curriculum avoids the idea that all children should study identical materials" Hirsch says.

Based on our literature review, media convergence in our study is defined as the assimilation of media content for multiple media platforms. Media convergence may involve any combination of the convergences of media contents, media forms, media companies, and roles of news practitioners.

Our general research question is how college professors should prepare students to cope with media convergence. To be specific, should college professors prepare generalists who can competently work in multiple media platforms or prepare specialists who know inside out how to work for one particular medium platform? And how should journalism schools balance the teaching of critical thinking and technical skills? Corresponding to these two questions, we also would like to find out if college journalism educators themselves are both theoretically equipped and technologically prepared to teach their students about media convergence. The study serves both as an attitude finder and a fact finder.

We believe that professors, editors, and news professionals are the best candidates to answer these questions. Editors represent the media companies to hire news staffers with news reporting abilities desired by the company. News professionals work in the forefront of news reporting and know best about what news reporting abilities they need.

The attitudes of the editors and the current generation of news professionals toward media convergence will have a great implication on future journalism education. Professors run journalism schools, and they have the final say about where their schools are going. Their attitudes toward journalism education in terms of media convergence will have the most direct influence on the kind of education journalism students will receive and how the students will perform in tomorrow's media.

Editors include daily newspaper editors in charge of newsroom operations or online news operations and news directors in charge of newsroom operations in a commercial TV station with news content, both in the United States. News professionals refer to non-management news staff, such as reporters, anchors, photographers, designers, producers, Web staff, etc., working in American media companies.

Journalism professors are defined as full-time instructors with any academic rankings who teach journalism courses in a U.S. journalism school, department, programme, or division which could be administratively affiliated with an institution with a name like College of Communications or Department of Communications Studies.

To obtain opinions about media convergence, we could

have targeted our survey only at those editors and news professionals in a converged media environment. The opinions obtained from those editors and news professionals, however, could be biased. Those media companies that have not gone through convergence must have a reason for not doing so. We also wanted to find out what they are doing about convergence. Balanced views both from the converged and un-converged media companies will better assist colleges in their strategic planning.

We conducted a national survey among editors, news professionals, and journalism professors with three different versions of online survey questionnaires posted on a school Web site. Respondents were asked to fill out the questionnaire online and submit answers online as well. The answers went through a commercial form handler and reached the primary investigator's email address. By doing so, the primary investigator had no way to detect who answered the questionnaire unless the respondent voluntarily revealed his/ her email address to request the findings from the study.

There were twenty-two questions in each of these three questionnaires. Almost all questions were close-ended. About half of the questions used a 5-point Likert Scale from "Strongly Agree" to "Strongly Disagree." Some questions across the three questionnaires shared similarity, so that comparisons could be made when analyzing data. A text field was created for respondents to provide feedback to the survey freely.

The textual answers in the text field will be reported along with the statistics to illustrate and explain the quantitative findings. All questionnaires went through pilot tests. The unit of analysis was each participant.

In order to conduct a systematic random sampling of editors and news professionals, we needed a list of newspaper editors and TV news directors in the United States and a list of newspaper and TV news staffers. We found that such lists did not exist, though lists of newspapers and lists of TV stations did exist in multiple places online like Editor & Publisher Yearbook and Broadcasting Sr Cable Yearbook.

Therefore, we decided to construct our own. To do so, we went through two steps. First, we constructed a combined list of daily newspapers and TV stations so that we could sample these news institutions. Second, we visited the Web sites of all sampled news institutions to find the email of the editor/news director and the email of one news professional randomly chosen.

In total, 1,190 U.S. daily newspapers with a valid URL were listed alphabetically by state. We sampled one out of every four dailies. Then, we visited each of those Web sites to find the email address of the managing editor, chief editor, online editor, or equivalent in each of those dailies and sent out a survey invitation email to him/her. If an individual email address was not available, we replaced it with a generic email address listed on their Web site and specified that the email was for the editor.

From the list, we removed PBS network companies, which mostly did not provide staff information, companies that did not generate news content such as WB network companies and UPN network companies, religious TV stations, and foreign language stations. In total, we extracted 674 TV stations with a valid URL. Since this population is smaller than that of the newspapers, we over-sampled it. Instead of sampling every other four, we sampled every other station.

Then, we visited each of those Web sites to find the email address of the news director or equivalent in each of those TV stations and sent out a survey invitation email to him/her. If an individual email address was not available, we replaced it with a generic email address and specified that the email was for the news director. In total, we successfully sent out invitation emails to 523 newspaper editors and TV news directors as our sample.

We also sampled one news professional out of each of the sampled U.S. dailies and TV stations for the survey. Since there was always more than one professional in a company, we simply randomly clicked on one name and picked him/her and made sure that s/he was on the news staff. Then, we sent him/her a survey invitation email. If an individual email address was not available, we replaced it with a generic email address and specified whom the email was for. S/he was asked to fill out a questionnaire that was worded in a slightly different manner. In total, we successfully sent out invitation emails to 398 news professionals.

We also needed to conduct a systematic random sampling of college journalism professors, but we were disappointed that all lists we found had many J-schools, even major ones, missing. In total, the new list contains 205 alphabetically ordered U.S. J-schools that contain 2,194 journalism professors.

We sampled one out of every four professors from the virtually running list of all journalism professors across the schools. For instance, if a school had six journalism professors, we picked the fourth one; then, the second journalism professor from next school was picked. We sent an invitation email to every professor in the sample. In total, we successfully sent out 500 emails.

The three samples of editors, news professionals, and professors included 1,421 cases.

We understood that nonresponse had been a serious problem with online surveys in recent years. In order to counter possible low response rates in our survey, we created three samples for editors, news professionals, and professors containing roughly 500 people for each group, which were much larger than the sample sizes for populations recommended by Mildred Patten (2000) in her book Understanding Research Methods: An Overview of the Essentials so that, if low response rates occurred, we could base our confidence limits on the actual number of responses themselves. We also sent out one reminder email to the samples, which drastically boosted the response rates, especially for professors and news professionals.

After two weeks of online data collecting in November 2002, we received 223 responses from professors (a 44% response rate), 151 responses from editors (a 29% response rate), and 142 responses from news professionals (a 35%

response rate). The overall response rate is 36%. As Singletary (1994) notes, returns of 30% to 40% are common in mail surveys.

The response rates of this online survey seem typical. However, the response rates are still comparatively low. A response bias is potentially present. Many respondents (41%) left textual answers to explain and illustrate their answers to the close-ended questions and/or made comments on the topic.

1. What is the status quo of media convergence in the industry?

By the end of 2002, 19% of the newspapers and commercial television stations with news content in the United States had gone through media mergers. Being merged or not has to do with the size of a company. Larger companies tend to have been merged while smaller ones have not. Roughly half of the news professionals surveyed (48%) reported that they produced news content for multiple media platforms on a routine basis; that was true both in merged media (50%) and non-merged media (48%).

In other words, media merger is not the precondition for practicing news for multiple media platforms. The pressure on news professionals to learn to produce multimedia content is also felt in many non-merged media companies. This finding confirms that media convergence is not necessarily related to media merger.

A typical editor or news director was a man (71%) between 36-45 years old (42%) with a bachelor's degree (76%) who had worked for at least two media (57%) for more than 20 years (53%). A typical news professional was either a man (52%) or woman (48%) between 26-35 years old (43%) with a bachelor's degree (84%) who had worked for at least two media (60%) less than ten years (62%).

Editors had generally worked for more years than news professionals, but they did not have more multiplatform experience than news professionals. As more news companies are practicing cross-media reporting with or without their companies being merged, it is important that editors with multi-platforrn experiences are chosen to direct newsroom businesses. Many editors need cross-media training more urgently than news professionals do if the news company they work for produces news contents for multiple media platforms on a daily basis.

2. Should J-schools train specialists or generalists?

Gil Thelen (2002) said that writers should learn how to write for multimedia and still photographers should learn how to shoot videos, but he was not interested in hiring people with multiple sets of skills. We designed four questions to test how popular Thelen's opinion was.

The majority of the respondents (84%) agreed or strongly agreed with Thelen that journalism students should learn how to write for multiple media platforms. One-way ANOVA shows significant difference among the means for professors, professionals, and editors.

Tukey HSD post hoc tests show that professors were more positive on this statement than editors and professionals, while no significant difference existed between editors and professionals.

A similar number of respondents (85%) agreed or strongly agreed with Thelen that journalism students with a visual emphasis should learn how to produce and edit photos, videos, and online interactive images. One-way ANOVA shows significant difference among the means for professors, professionals, and editors. Tukey HSD post hoc tests show that professors were more positive on this statement than professionals, while professionals were more positive than editors.

Most respondents (78%) agreed or strongly agreed that all journalism majors should learn multiple sets of skills, such as writing, editing, TV production, digital photography, newspaper design, and Web publishing.

Oneway ANOVA shows significant differences among the means for professionals, editors, and professors. Tukey HSD post hoc tests show that news professionals who worked in the forefront of news production felt this need more deeply than other respondents. Editors also had such an expectation for them. There is no significant difference between editors and professors.

These findings support the growing evidence that news professionals are being asked to wear multiple hats. The findings also indicate that Thelen's view has its market at this moment when news professionals with multiple sets of skills are highly desirable but not easy to find. Such a view may change as more journalism graduates equipped with multiple sets of skills enter the job market.

The professors' textual answers show that some of the difficulties J-schools have come across include the lack of a friendly curriculum, lack of credit hours to include the components of convergence content, lack of willing cooperation among faculty from different sequences, and lack of expertise, interest, or even time for some professors to develop new courses on convergence.

When asked whether journalism students should still have a specialization, such as writing, photojournalism, broadcasting, and new media, over half (63%) of the respondents agreed or strongly agreed. Over a quarter of the respondents (28%) were negative and 9% were not sure. One-way ANOVA mean comparisons show no significant difference of attitude among professionals, editors, and professors.

Comparing the support rate for this question to those for the first three questions, it is fair to argue that editors, news professionals, and professors emphasized the importance of cross-media training more than that of specialization, though they believed that specialization should not be neglected either.

Currently, students in many J-schools specialize in one area by subscribing to a sequence such as news-editorial, magazine, photojournalism, and broadcast. When asked whether sequences should be reorganized considering the trend of media-platforms merging in the industry, 56% of the professors agreed or strongly agreed, 22% were not sure, and another 22% disagreed or strongly disagreed. The concept of sequences is being shaken among professors though it is still being accepted as a legitimate means of training students in various specialization areas in some J-schools. Speaking on behalf of herself and her colleagues, Professor #93 offered some special insight on this issue:

We can't teach for the "now." We have to prepare students for when they graduate...which in most instances is now five years out. And, we feel a commitment to expose them to all types of writing in all platforms so they can be flexible about their career choice at the front end of their academics. Then, they can apply the skills to a specialty area where they are totally proficient.

"Flexible" is a key term repeatedly seen in editors' and news professionals' textual answers as a suggestion for future journalists. Editors statement is typical:

Our job descriptions are open ended and new hires understand that they are being hired for their skills. They may be hired today to cover the city beat. In six months or in two weeks, if necessary, a person with Quark skills may be asked to fill in or shift duties to include pagination of a particular section. It is important that hires stay flexible.

The new hires, wrote Editor, "need to understand that the information they gather and process can have many different uses, audiences and shelf lives. They need to understand the complexities of the audience mix and be able to respond."

"Those unwilling to be flexible may find themselves in a difficult scenario later in their careers". From a different perspective, Professional concurred: "Students must be flexible, have a vigorous skill set and be prepared to get laid off and move around in the changing media arena." In short, "young journalists must be prepared to fill a variety of roles if they hope to succeed". "The most successful journalists are those that take on assignments willingly, can learn and want to learn".

Specialization in journalistic jobs is still honored, but is losing its favour to cross-media capability in converged media. Today, professionals with different specializations team together to work on multiple media projects. Tomorrow, it is likely that one-man bands will be more and more desired in newsrooms.

3. How should J-schools balance the teaching of critical thinking and that of technical skills?

Most respondents (93%), especially professors, agreed or strongly agreed that journalism students should both learn technical skills, such as online information search and Web design, while learning critical thinking skills in media law, ethics, etc. One-way ANOVA shows significant difference among the means for professionals, editors, and professors. Tukey HSD post hoc tests show that professors were more positive on this point than editors and professionals, while no significant difference existed between editors and professionals.

But, should journalism students spend more time on learning critical thinking skills than on technical skills? Opinions were divided. More than half of the respondents (62%) believed that should be the case, but 19% of the respondents were not sure and another 19% of them did not agree. Oneway ANOVA shows significant difference among the means for professors, professionals, and editors. Tukey HSD post hoc tests show that editors were more positive on this point than professionals, and professionals were more positive than professors.

Throughout all the answers from the three groups of respondents, critical thinking was highly regarded as being more important than technical skills. Editors, news professionals, and professors all liked to see good stories, and good stories come from good thinking ability. An editor said: "Journalism graduates need to have a broad, well-rounded education; be critical thinkers; have the ability to write clearly; have a serious work ethic; and know computer basics - in that order".

"You can teach a monkey to type," echoes a writer. Therefore, he strongly suggested that J-schools "get more critical thinking skills pounded into the skulls of the students". While highly emphasizing the importance of critical thinking ability, editors did not mean to neglect the importance of teaching technical skills in schools. We will develop this point when we discuss the next question. Comparing the professors' highest mean for the first question and their lowest mean for the second question, it is clear that professors saw critical thinking as highly important, but preferred a comparatively balanced approach for the teaching of the two sets of knowledge. One professor's comment illustrated this observation:

Knowing technical skill alone will not make you a "good" journalist. Critical thinking is vital not just to a career but to life itself. Without developing your ability to discern and evaluate, you will become "the prey" of society. Next, a technical skill is critical to a career in journalism today. Even print Journalism is very high tech these days and all electronic media require extensive computer knowledge as well as other technical skills. I would place critical thinking skills first on your list of things to do because a developed mind will make it that much easier to develop a creative and technically sound understanding of the technical side of the business.

From a holistic view, there was no substantial disagreement between classrooms and newsrooms when we examine the issue of teaching critical thinking vs. teaching technical skills. Compared to Terry's 2000 poll, this study shows that professors gave a higher status to technical skills in journalism curricula in 2002 than they did in 2000. This is a period during which media convergence garnered its momentum. In short, all respondents generally agreed that J-schools should place emphasis on teaching critical thinking, but at the same time, should not neglect teaching technical skills.

4. Should technical skills be learned at work or in school?

News professionals were asked, "If you wish to possess the technical skills you don't have now, do you prefer to learn them at work or wish you had learned in school?" Editors were given the same question with a slightly different wording.

Chi-Square test shows that the difference between editors and news professionals is significant. This finding well supplements the findings from the preceding questions. It suggests that editors not only looked at future journalists' critical thinking ability, but also hoped that future journalists would already possess the skills needed in a converged newsroom when they are hired.

On the other hand, most professionals preferred that they spend most of their school time on gaining critical thinking ability and learn skills largely at work. The professionals' general preference, to some extent, also reflected their need for technological update at their current positions, so that they can better qualify for multimedia productions.

Many editors and reporters said that school is the best place for journalism students to explore every facet of the media and acquire basic technical skills, though some advanced skills can only be learned on the job. Learning skills while in school, they said, can build confidence and an expansive and broad understanding of the entire field and help with damage control and communication in newsrooms. "If editing and the technical skills were more prevalent in college courses," wrote a multi-tasking editor, "I think I could stave off a lot of headaches when the students become professionals."

An internship was the news professionals' and editors' most recommended venue for enhancing and learning more technical skills and gaining other practical experience. Reporter said: "While I value my college education, my internship and first job provided me with the most valuable skills today." Another reporter said: "While education is great, students who work in media while in school fare much better in the real world."

Some editors had complaints about graduates with a 3.5 GPA but no practical experience and no published news work. An anchor/reporter said that it is important even "for a freshman or sophomore in college to visit a newsroom and shadow someone. So many students wait until they are juniors and seniors to do this and then they realise they made a mistake in selecting their major. You will learn more by watching and doing". One reporter said, "To remain competitive, education must continue throughout a career".

The implication of the discrepancy from this finding suggests that Jschools should place emphasis on teaching critical thinking, expose students to new technology, and design a comprehensive internship programme for students to gain real-world knowledge and further develop their crossmedia technical skills.

5. What skills do news professionals need to learn most at their current positions?

Both editors and news professionals were given this unstructured question with slightly different wordings. We read through all the answers, and categorized them into the following nine facets in random order:

Multimedia production: producing and editing news stories on video, for the Web, and for print; re-purposing the same story for different media. Editors and news professionals both believed that it is not very important for a newspaper reporter to learn how to talk like an anchor in front of a video camera. This skill was even regarded as being less important than knowing how to speak a second language.

Some editors and news professionals also mentioned learning how to manage time for producing multimedia news stories. Editor hoped that journalists in a converged environment would learn to avoid "extra" work by working "smarter" and with greater awareness of the requirements of the different publishing media.

This finding, again, shows that editors valued critical thinking ability more than news professionals did. Editors wanted news professionals to be good thinkers first, and the latter wanted most to learn how to express their thinking in different media.

6. If news professionals have to re-purpose their work for multiple media platforms, will the quality of their work suffer?

Since some authors such as Haiman expressed the concern about the possible decline of work quality if news professionals have to "re-purpose" stories for multiple media platforms, we tried to find out to what extent this concern was shared by editors and news professionals.

Opinions split. Thirty-eight per cent of the editors and professionals agreed or strongly agreed that the quality would deteriorate, 40% disagreed or strongly disagreed, and the other 22% were not sure. Editors and professionals showed no significant difference on this attitude T-test. Such a concern was not prevalent in the news industry.

In response to such concerns, the news director from a converged media company wrote: "When reporters do cross platforms we give them the time to finish the project for all three platforms.

Quality does not suffer. If we were to try to force reporters to cross platforms while operating under daily deadlines then quality could suffer depending on the nature of the story and the extra time consumed".

Another editor summed up this issue: "Some employees can capably handle multiple media and tell stories effectively. Others cannot. Certainly strong technical skills and training can help, but it's not just dependent on that; it depends more on the attitude and aptitude of the journalist".

Quality multimedia work also involves a solid understanding of different cultures in different media. Editors both for and against media convergence noted the difficulty of merging different media with different cultures, and editors in those merged media called for flexibility in aptitude and willingness to cooperate across platforms. For instance, Editor wrote:

Clarity of what convergence means to the news organization is vital and often lacking. This causes unneeded anxiety. Managers have to realise that each medium has its own culture, language, skill set and timetable and is naturally skeptical of anything unfamiliar. It is also true that these same journalists' stock in trade is learning a new culture, language, skill set and timetable-on a daily basis. Therein lies the hope for an efficient news operation running on all cylinders and an effective -maybe even happy-staff.

If most editors and news professionals are not concerned about the quality of the work prepared for multiple media platforms and if news professionals are given enough time to complete their cross-media work, there is little reason to worry that future journalists, if well trained both theoretically and technologically for multiple media platforms, will produce work of poorer quality. Training students to practice news in multiple media platforms will help bridge newsroom cultures from different media and eventually erase such differences.

We have noticed that no significant statistical differences existed between the editors and news professionals from the converged media companies and their counterparts from the not-yet-converged media companies when they answered the questions reported above.

7. How are J-schools coping with media convergence?

From 1998 to 2002, about 60% of the J-schools in the United States redesigned their curricula or developed new courses to prepare students for practicing news in multiple media platforms.

A typical journalism professor was a man (71%) between 46-55 years old (42%) with a doctoral degree (63%) who worked in news media for one to ten years (48%), may still be practicing news (45%) in one way or another, and conducted academic research (66%).

More professors claimed that they were theoretically equipped (81%) than technologically prepared (53%) to teach students how to report news in multiple media platforms. More than half of the professors (57%) had not taught any journalism courses in the last five years where skill sets were beyond their own expertise; 25% of the professors taught one such course and 11% taught two. Nevertheless, the majority of the professors (84%) added content about media convergence either to their existing courses or to new courses or participated in cross-media team-teaching in the last five years.

Worries, concerns, and, sometimes, misconceptions about media convergence appeared in professors' textual answers. For instance, a professor from Montana said: "convergence is not happening". A professor who no longer practiced news said, "In my judgment, the writing portion of preparing news for print and for the Web is exactly the same". Another professor maintained that it was not necessary to teach cross-media news practicing because "few 'want ads' for newspaper reporter and editor positions specifically listed multimedia platform skills as required or preferred experience for new hires".

Many professors worried that media mergers would restrict the number of voices in a community. They regarded media mergers as a grand experiment in the profession and waited for the FCC's ruling on the cross-ownership of different media in the same market.

Wait-and-see-that was the strategy some universities took for teaching media convergence. One professor said that he needed to see the substantive contribution media convergence could make before he would be more serious about this phenomenon. He said that J-schools should be cautious about embracing convergence. Some other universities didn't have the time and resources to teach convergence courses or make major curriculum changes.

Most professors, however, did believe that media convergence was a reality; and "anybody serious about practicing media needs at minimal an acquaintance with various media and at best multiple competencies," as Professor said. Many professors (and editors and news professionals as well) had a clear opinion as to which comes first, teaching critical thinking or teaching technical skills.

While acknowledging the need for incorporating media convergence content in curricula, especially the technological components, professors cautioned against sacrificing conceptual and theoretical courses such as law, ethics, history, cultural studies, critical perspectives, etc. Professor analogized critical thinking as meat and potatoes and technical skills as dessert and side dishes and argued that "the meat and potatoes need to come before one begins to worry about the dessert and side dishes (or side shows)." This viewpoint was popular. Professor wrote:

It's the message, not the medium, that is of paramount importance. If students cannot understand and appreciate the underlying concepts, principles and ethics of journalism, then they cannot produce the type of content that will be of value to a free society. A thorough grounding in journalism must come before any training in tools. The tools are means to an end, not the end in and of themselves.

Incidentally, a reporter had similar thoughts:

- The medium isn't the message, the message is the message. In short, the fundamental analytic and synthetic skills of the news writer are paramount to the message. The medium does not alter the reporter's craft of interpreting news events in the context of the society in a way that will make sense for the receiver of the information. ... Additional skills may be desirable, but for the most parFinally, my answer on merging media companies... reflects my disdain for the corporatization and concentration of control in the media. I think we ought to train mass communicators for a converged world, but as professors we ought to fight like hell against media mergers.

Very few respondents (19%) believed that media mergers benefit all three parties, the general public, news professionals, and media companies, but about one third of the respondents (35%) believed that media companies are the only beneficiaries to such a practice.

These 35% respondents, who were almost equally proportionally found in editors, news professionals, and professors groups, could be regarded as the most critical toward media mergers. We compared these 35% respondents with the rest of the sample and found no significant difference in their answers concerning the necessity of teaching journalism students cross-media writing and visuals and teaching multiple sets of skills. Always, more respondents believed that professors should teach all those things. In short, the respondents' political view was not directly tied to their views of teaching students cross-media practices.

As an experimental industrial trend, media convergence in the sense of media mergers is still in its formative stage. Whether it will sustain its momentum to reach popularity in the nation and how its advantages balance against disadvantages are yet to be seen. While there seems to be a good deal of support for cross-media education, on some questions, professors are more gung-ho than editors and news professionals about the trend. The legitimacy of media mergers needs repeated tests before such mergers can be truly accepted as a healthy development and a full-force education of media convergence can be seen in many in J-schools.

Media convergence, however, is not tied to media mergers. Media convergence, initiated and made possible by digital technology, is more than media mergers propelled largely by financial considerations. More pervasive is the media convergence in the senses of content convergence, technological convergence, and especially role convergence, which have occurred not only in merged media companies but also more in non-merged ones. No matter whether media mergers will continue, the other three forms of media convergence, which are not subject to the FCC regulations, are likely to continue to develop.

Most editors and news professionals in this survey are not from merged media companies. Many editors, news professionals, and professors do not yet see media mergers as beneficial to the general public and news professionals. But, their backgrounds and political views do not prevent them from sharing with other respondents with different backgrounds and political views many opinions regarding where future college journalism should go. Such common understanding is shaping a force to push forward the education of media convergence in campuses nationwide.

To better direct newsroom businesses in a converged media environment, many editors need cross-media training. Many opportunities are out there for news companies and universities to work together to explore the issue of media convergence and provide mid-career professionals and editors cross-media technological training. It seems sensible that opportunities for learning multimedia skills should be made available both on campus and through off-site continuing education programs that are geared for midcareer news professionals as technological developments continue to evolve.

Multi-dimensional news reporting in multiple media platforms will be tomorrow's way news is presented. Therefore, dealing with media convergence in college journalism education is an urgent necessity. The wait-and-see strategy will place a Jschool in a disadvantaged position over the long run.

These findings tell us that J-schools do need to provide cross-media knowledge and experience to their students, so that the latter can better qualify for cross-media jobs in the future. Media convergence poses both challenge and opportunity to J-schools for them to reconsider their current curriculum design, sequence setting, faculty composition, teaching methods, and internship approaches.

Many professors, editors, and news professionals have expressed concern that media mergers will eliminate voices in a community, thus potentially eroding democracy. However, media mergers did not start only these days. As a TV reporter wrote in the textual answer, when she first went to Philadelphia years ago, there were five daily papers. Now, there are two; and they are both published by the same company.

Philadelphia is not alone in such media reduction. The question is whether the general public feels that it is less well-informed than it was thirty or forty years ago and that democracy has been eroded by such media reduction prior to media convergence. This is a topic for another study. Nevertheless, students should be exposed to such a legitimate concern and learn to take a critical look at the phenomenon of media mergers.

J-schools should continue to teach critical thinking

courses and meld critical thinking components into the teaching of all courses. Critical thinking is the cornerstone of journalism education. However, technology courses or course components should also be given the status they deserve. In other words, there should be a balanced curriculum to include both kinds of courses, and many cross-media related courses should contain both components. An ideal curriculum should balance the load of technical skill-based courses and critical thinking courses, weighting toward the latter.

Critical thinking and technical skills can go hand in hand rather than being competitors for class time. A balanced curriculum can help students better gather, produce, edit, and deliver quality news; more creatively and professionally materialize their ideas; and make them better fit into the market, especially in an economic downturn.

University of Florida professor Melinda McAdams, one of the Washington Post's first online editors, told colleagues that if colleges don't teach journalists the technical skills they will need, no one else is likely to take on the responsibility. "[T]he reality they'll face in the world is they'll have to teach themselves". The classroom should be the first stop for students to at least get exposed to and get familiar with the technology for cross-media practices, though they can become more proficient with such technology through internship and their future jobs.

With all that said, technology courses should not dominate journalism students' education, and technology should not be taught for the sake of technology. Technology must serve the purposes of doing good journalism. Apart from teaching students multimedia productions, new technology, and computer-assisted reporting, J-schools still need to place good writing-the very basics of being a journalist-as the top priority for all journalism students regardless of sequences or specializations.

Many respondents point out that the teaching of technology should not be at the expense of the teaching of critical thinking. Many J-schools have no more elective hours for students to learn cross-media technology within the existing parameter of curriculum. For such schools, curriculum redesign is a necessity.

Though some J-schools such as Indiana University School of Journalism have eliminated sequences to provide a comprehensive education to all journalism students, we expect that sequences will continue to exist for some time in some other J-schools. However, it has become increasingly important to encourage students from all sequences to learn technology and reporting skills from other platforms. Sequences in many J-schools are regarded as dinosaurs because it no longer makes sense to teach broadcast and newspaper, for instance, as two unrelated bodies of knowledge in the era of media convergence and students can opt for a specialization without sequences but with professors' advice.

Most respondents expect that future journalists will be competent in producing news in multiple media platforms while being particularly strong in one area. It appears that students will be prudent to opt to specialize in either print or television and take several electives in a secondary platform, either radio or online journalism. Versatility and specialization should be equally important.

The majority of the editors do expect that future writers will be able to and willing to write for multiple media platforms, and photographers and designers will create multimedia visuals, though such expectations will not be converted into requirements in job ads for a while because "too many newsroom dinosaurs have to die off first," as Editor put it. But chances are they will, as Nelson (2002) predicted. Most editors even expect that new hires will possess multiple sets of skills to become "superhack masters of multimedia," to use Gates's term.

The needs are out there, but whether the training of such superhack masters will become the norm, as Gates questioned, largely depends on whether J-schools are willing and able to develop those "avant-garde" courses. Apart from the technological aspect, students also need to learn to cooperate and collaborate across newsrooms so as to bridge different newsroom-cultures. Students need to be both theoretically and technically prepared for media convergence.

The findings from this study show that more than half of the J-schools in the United States have redesigned their curricula or developed new courses to cope with media convergence, but professors need to be better prepared technologically.

Team-teaching is one approach to solve the problem, but will the teaching of media convergence be more effective if a professor at least knows as much as a student in a convergence class will learn? Does the Gestalt psychological principle "the whole is more than the sum of its parts" also apply in such a context? Professors normally learned little or no technical skills while studying in a J-school doctoral programme.

Their technical knowledge inherited from their previous media experience is easily dated. More than half of the professors (54%) no longer practiced news after they began to teach, as we found out in this study. In some cases, professors know less technical knowledge than their students do.

Therefore, in the middle of heavy teaching and research, updating and learning more technical knowledge for teaching convergence is a big challenge for many professors. Learning from each other during team-teaching is, of course, a good way of learning, but professors also need to find time to do self-teaching to gain more in-depth knowledge. J-schools should provide financial support for professors to attend new technology workshops. Being exposed to or involved in community news reporting in a multiple-media-platform environment, if possible, is an even better way of learning new technology for professors.

Attitude and aptitude, together with time management ability, will be the key to producing quality work in newsrooms. Since editors and news professionals are not prevalently concerned about the quality of work currently re-purposed for multiple media platforms, there is no reason for them or professors to be concerned that students being trained on multiple media platforms will be jacks of all trades but masters of none.

Students need to learn how to re-purpose their work in a timely manner and control the quality of their work in a professional manner. One editor said it best: "To sum things up, journalists need to be prepared to hit the workplace running. With limited resources and cutbacks across the country, the new hire will be the person who is the most skilled, coupled with energy and willing to be flexible as needed."

Media convergence is a comprehensive topic. Many sub-topics related to this study are yet to be explored. For instance, how can the general public benefit from media convergence? Does the general public in markets where media are converged think that they are less well-informed and that democracy has suffered in their areas? How can news professionals benefit from media convergence? What are the typical differences between the career lives of the news professionals in converged media and the career lives the same news professionals led before the media were converged? We call on mass communication scholars to continue to study media convergence to shed more light on this phenomenon that will affect every one of us.

Chapter 7

Newspaper Copy Editors Perceptions

Newspaper copy editors have long been known as "the last line of defence" against errors because they do their work near the end of the production cycle. That also means they have the potential to be a last line of defence against violations of ethical standards. In fact, many editing textbooks say copy editors should be prepared to raise questions about potential ethics-related problems, such as a lack of balance or fairness, and to watch for obvious breaches of ethics like plagiarism. There is anecdotal evidence that many copy editors take this role seriously. In recent years, copy editors have been credited with detecting lifted quotations, plagiarized stories and columns and letters to the editor, and fabricated material.

There is also anecdotal evidence, however, that copy editors' ethics-related concerns are not always taken seriously. For example, a copy editor reportedly raised questions "about the level of truth" in Patricia Smith's Boston Globe columns three years before she was forced to resign under fire for fabrication. Similarly, "growing newsroom unrest" resulted when managers ignored a copy editor's concerns about stereotyping in a Houston Chronicle section on juvenile justice that pictured only minority youths. Articles based on depositions of Atlanta Journal-Constitution copy editors indicate that some tried unsuccessfully to get senior editors to reconsider the fairness of a 1996 column9 likening security guard Richard Jewell-who was never charged with bombing Atlanta's Centennial Olympic Park and was eventually formally cleared10-to Wayne Williams, convicted in 1982 of murdering two people and implicated in the deaths of twenty-two others. The column was published and Jewell filed a 1997 libel suit against the paper that was still pending in late 2005." More recently, John E. McIntyre, managing editor for the copy desk at the Baltimore Sun and former president of the American Copy Editors Society, wrote:

In the endeavor to head off plagiarism and fabrication in news stories, and to ensure the reliability and accuracy of stories . . . the ranking editors and the copy editors are on the same side. The problem is that the ranking editors don't always recognize this. When the American Copy Editors Society presents workshops on structural editing ... a troubling comment keeps surfacing among the participants: "I wouldn't be allowed to raise questions like that at my paper."

Although copy editors' jobs charge them with evaluating stories, their concerns sometimes go unheeded; forces that Shoemaker and Reese identify as stronger "influences on media content" sometimes limit copy editors' authority. Nonetheless, Hank Glamann, former assistant managing editor for editing at the Cleveland Plain Dealer, urged members of the American Society of Newspaper Editors to "create a climate in your newsroom in which any member of the staff can ask any question about any story and expect to be heeded. To restrict who can ask about what is inefficient-and a real waste of talent."

This survey of copy desk workers sought to determine how they perceive their role as "final guardians" of journalistic ethics, and whether there are conflicts between what they think their role should be and what they perceive it actually is. The research is important for two reasons. First, copy editors constitute a significant proportion of the newsroom workforce-nearly 20% in 2005-and are often difficult to hire second, how they see their jobs is important because, as Shoemaker and Reese wrote, journalists' role conceptions affect the content they produce: "[T]hese roles may determine how they define their jobs, the kinds of things they believe should be covered, and the ways in which they cover them." Copy editors do not cover news, of course, but they produce content as they condense news into headlines, elements that can have a bigger impact on readers' impressions of the news than the words written by reporters. In addition, they may select or help select wire stories for publication and help determine story play as they design pages.

Although there has been an explosion of scholarly interest in journalistic ethics during recent decades and much of the resulting literature describes the ethics, values, responsibilities, or roles of particular types of journalists, almost no work has assessed copy editors' values or how they perceive their role in upholding ethics standards. Other research on copy editing, however, suggests that technological innovations, as well as copy editors' perceptions of how others in the newsroom view them, may have implications for how copy editors think of their ethics roles.

During the past half century, newspaper copy desks have coped with at least four job-altering waves of technological innovation, each forcing copy editors to spend time adapting and some permanently reducing the time available for substantive editing. First, during the 1950s, newspapers introduced teletypesetting (TTS) equipment, which transmitted wire-service stories via hole-punched paper tape used to automatically activate linecasting machines. This allowed quicker typesetting but forced some copy desks to adopt new style rules, so that local style would match wire-service stories, and was blamed in one study for an increase in errors. second, during the early 1970s, some newsrooms began using optical character recognition (OCR) equipment to produce perforated tape versions of local stories.

This required copy editors to edit stories with a special pen and have their changes input by a corrections typist, changes that one study found led to an increase in published errors. Then, in the late 1970s and early 1980s, newsrooms introduced video-display terminals, which made updating and comparing stories easier but also introduced physical problems, such as eyestrain and headaches, and, some researchers reported, led to newspaper management devaluing editing in favour of production tasks.

Perhaps the most significant technological change was the introduction in the 1980s and 1990s of electronic pagination, which shifted page makeup responsibilities from composing room staffs to copy editors. It gave editors greater control over page appearance, but also cut into the time copy editors had for substantive editing. In 1994, Russial reported that electronic makeup of a page took on average fifteen minutes more than drawing a paper "dummy."

This time drain, which can be exacerbated by malfunctioning pagination equipment, persisted after newsrooms became familiar with the technology. In many cases, pagination turned the desk "from a centre of editing to a centre of production," and it made some copy editors feel they had become computer technicians or proofreaders.

Meanwhile, there are indications that a significant number of copy editors have felt a lack of respect for their work. A1984 report noted that a survey of forty copy editors had "raised disturbing questions about their treatment by senior editors [and] the lack of respect they got in their newsrooms."

Three years later, a survey of 630 copy editors at fifty newspapers found that although 63% said that their work was supported by senior editors, respondents were evenly split on whether the copy desk had "clout within the newsroom." A 2003 survey found that respect remained a problem, with 47% of 337 responding copy editors disagreeing that "most copy editors feel appreciated at my newspaper" and 40% disagreeing that "copy editors at my paper are held in the same esteem as reporters."

It is understandable, then, that copy editor job satisfaction has lagged behind that of other journalists. In 1989, ASNE reported that 43% of 191 responding copy editors said they would be unhappy if they held the same job in five years, compared with about a third of other journalists. Four years later, Cook, Banks, and Thompson found that 39% of fifty-nine copy editors in a study planned to leave journalism within five years, and Cook and Banks reported that copy editors in a sample of newspaper journalists were more likely to be burned out than reporters.

Similarly, in 1997, Voakes reported that 37% of nearly 200 copy editors in an ASNE-sponsored study thought their current job had not met their expectations, compared with 22% of non-copy editors.

Finally, a survey of copy desk workers conducted in 2002 showed that although more than 70% agreed at least somewhat that they were satisfied with their jobs, fewer than a fourth agreed strongly, this during a year when Weaver et al. found that about a third of U.S. journalists in general were "very satisfied" and 81% were at least "fairly satisfied." Intriguingly, the 2002 copy editor job satisfaction study found satisfaction correlated with copy editors' opinions about the ethics standards of their newspapers.

THEORETICAL PERSPECTIVES

Studies of copy editing have not always made good use of theory, but three perspectives from sociology and mass communication appear useful in considering how copy editors perceive their ethics role. First, as Russial and Brill have proposed, some technological innovations may have resulted in the sort of "de-skilling" of copy editing that sociologist Harry Braverman observed when industrial jobs were routinized by automation. Braverman theorized that the introduction of automation or other technology into an occupation could reduce the number of skills used by workers so much that a job became "de-skilled." That resulted, he suggested, in a loss of power by workers, their supervisors, and the occupation itself.

Although pagination initially required copy editors to learn a new skill, one result of having copy editors paginate "may be a limitation in the discretion journalists have in deciding how much time to spend on traditional [editing] tasks." Thus, some copy desks may have lost, if not the skills of editing, then at least some discretion in how much time they can spend on serious editing concerns, such as story fairness and balance.

Indeed, 53% of copy editors surveyed in 1987 for ASNE perceived they did not have time to edit well. Such changes could also routinize copy editing so much that the job consists of little more than writing headlines, running spell checkers, and moving copy-very nearly what Bleske found copy editors doing at one 60,000-circulation daily. If routinization results in a loss of copy desk power, as Braverman's theory suggests, then it could rob copy editors of the ability to be ethical "backstops."

Power is also a consideration in Shoemaker and Reese's hierarchy of influences. They suggest that content is affected by "environmental factors" or influences, modeled as a series of concentric circles. The media worker at the center is subject to forces in the outer circles-media routines, organizational influences, extramedia influences, and ideology-which are, in turn, subject to the forces in circles beyond them.

Although ethics does not play a large role in the model, the question of whether copy editors can be final guardians of ethical standards can be viewed in terms of the model. According to Shoemaker and Reese, the judgments of an individual journalist possessing sufficient power can influence content if there is no higher-level factor-such as a strong routine or organizational influence-covering the task at hand. As Shoemaker and Reese note, "institutional position greatly determines the power vested in a role," so copy editors may lack the authority to effectively call into question the actions of writers or assigning editors.

Relevant theory also comes from the sociological study of professional ethics, which generally posits that all professions share certain characteristics: a systematic base of knowledge, community sanction, a code of ethics, a distinctive culture maintained by associations, and a high degree of autonomy and authority conferred by clients.

Although some writers have viewed journalism as either a profession or a professionalizing occupation, it has often been seen as lacking several prerequisites of professionalism. For example, Shoemaker and Reese note that journalists are not required to follow specific standards or obtain specific schooling. In addition, their autonomy "is limited by organizational constraints."

Copy editors appear to lack even more of these attributes of professionalism than other journalists. Although copy editors generally possess a broad base of knowledge that is systematic in the sense that it includes detailed information about language, they do not have a great deal of autonomy, they do not have a separate ethics code, and they did not have an association until the American Copy Editors Society was founded in 1996.

Moreover, in many newsrooms, copy editors lack both "community" approval and authority conferred by "clients." The fact that copy editors are hired to be evaluators frequently sets up an adversarial relationship between them and their intra-office "clients," reporters and assigning editors. Copy editors also have external clients, the readers for whom they are pre-publication advocates. However, those reader-clients cannot confer authority upon copy editors, for they generally are not aware that the newsroom's most invisible workers exist.

Even if copy desk workers think they should be guardians of ethics standards, they may not feel support in their newsrooms for such a role. As a result:

H1a: Most respondents will report that identifying and seeking to eliminate potential ethics-related problems in stories should be integral parts of copy editors' jobs.

H1b: Respondents will be significantly more likely to say that finding and eliminating errors and identifying and eliminating potential legal problems, such as libel, should be integral parts of copy editors' jobs than they will be to report that identifying and seeking to eliminate potential ethicsrelated problems in stories should be integral parts of copy editors' jobs.

H2: Respondents will be significantly more likely to perceive that eliminating errors and eliminating legal problems actually are integral parts of their jobs than they will be to say that identifying and seeking to eliminate potential ethics-related problems in stories actually are integral parts of their jobs.

H3: There will be no significant differences between respondents' perceptions of what copy editors' roles in eliminating errors and potential legal problems should be and are, but there will be significant differences between perceptions about what copy editors' ethics roles should be and are.

H4a: Respondents will be more likely to agree that copy editors should be encouraged to take questions to managers than they will be to say that copy editors at their newspapers are encouraged to take questions to managers.

H4b: Respondents will perceive more support for taking potential ethics-related concerns to immediate supervisors or assigning editors than they will for taking unanswered concerns to senior managers.

H5: Respondents who perceive that copy editors' actual ethics role differs from what it should be will report lower levels of job satisfaction than respondents whose ideal and real perceptions of their ethics role match.

H6: Respondents whose perceptions of copy editors' ideal and real ethics role do not match will be less likely than others to rate their newspapers' ethical standards favorably.

Data were gathered via a survey63 sent in fall 2002 to journalists at 105 U.S. daily, English-language newspapers listed in the Editor & Publisher International Yearbook64 as having average weekday circulations greater than 25,000. Because copy editors' names generally do not appear in their newspapers, a two-step process was used to identify recipients.

First, a scientifically selected sample of 105 newspapers was stratified66 into the five largest circulation categories used by ASNE. The names of copy editors were obtained from newspaper Web sites, industry contacts, and the newspapers. Then a random sample of 803 copy desk workers was drawn, using a sampling frame designed to match ASNE's estimates of the distribution of copy / layout editors across the five circulation classes.

The study used multiple contacts to improve response rates, and allowed recipients to fill out the questionnaire on paper or online; 470 usable responses were received from 100 newspapers for a 59% response rate. Nearly 81% of respondents identified themselves as copy editors or copy editor/page designers, though the sample contained copy desk chiefs, page designers, news editors, reporter/copy editors, and others who worked part-time on a copy desk.

H1a, which predicted that most respondents would view seeking to eliminate potential ethics-related problems from stories as an integral part of a copy editor's job, was supported. Nearly 95% of copy desk workers agreed with a statement that made ethics part of copy editors' ideal roles, and more than two-thirds strongly agreed.

Testing other hypotheses involved wading into a long-running methodological debate over how ordinal and quasi-interval data can be analyzed. Ordinal responses to statements about copy editors' roles in eliminating errors, legal problems, and potential ethics-related problems ("strongly agree," "somewhat agree," "undecided," "somewhat disagree," and "strongly disagree") were converted to quasi-interval data by assigning a number to each response so that mean responses could be calculated and compared using f-tests. Although this practice has the support of some scholars, some purists believe that only non-parametric statistics should be used with such ordinal data.

So, while i-test results are reported in the text below, results from the sign test-a conservative, non-parametric test often considered appropriate for non-normal and non-symmetric, paired-measurement data like these-are provided in endnotes.

Both statistical tests offered only partial support for H1b, which held that errors and legal problems in stories would be more likely to be viewed as copy-desk concerns than would ethics-related problems. There was a statistically significant difference between the way respondents viewed copy editors' ideal roles in eliminating errors and potential ethics problems. But there was not a statistically significant difference between support for eliminating potential legal problems and potential ethics-related problems.

H2 predicted greater agreement that eliminating errors and eliminating potential legal problems actually were parts of copy editors' jobs than agreement that seeking to eliminate ethics-related problems was. To test H2, responses to the statements about copy editors' actual roles were compared. H2 was supported. There were statistically significant differences 80 between responses to statements about copy editors' actual roles in eliminating errors and in eliminating ethics-related problems, and between responses to statements about copy editors' actual roles in eliminating potential legal problems and in eliminating potential ethics-related problems.

H3 predicted that respondents would perceive that copy editors' ideal roles matched their actual roles when it came to eliminating errors and potential legal problems but not when it came to identifying and seeking to eliminate potential ethics-related problems. Contrary to expectations, there were statistically significant differences in respondents' perceptions of what copy editors' roles should be and what they are related to all three tasks: identifying and eliminating errors identifying and eliminating legal problems and identifying and seeking to eliminate potential ethics-related problems.

H4a, which predicted that respondents would be more likely to agree that copy editors should be encouraged to take ethics-related concerns to managers than to say that they actually are encouraged, was supported.

First, there was a significant difference between responses to statements, suggesting copy editors should be and are encouraged to bring concerns about ethics-related problems to their supervisors and/or assigning editors. Second, there was a significant difference between responses to statements about whether copy editors dissatisfied with those front-line managers' responses to potential ethics related problems in stories should be encouraged and are encouraged to carry the concerns to senior editors.

H4b, which asserted that respondents would be less likely to support and perceive encouragement for raising questions about ethics-related problems with senior managers than immediate supervisors or assigning editors, was supported.

Respondents were significantly more likely to agree that copy editors should be encouraged to take ethics-related concerns to their immediate supervisors or the assigning editor for the story than they were to support taking subsequently unresolved concerns to senior managers. Respondents were also significantly more likely to say encouragement actually existed in their newsrooms for approaching immediate supervisors or assigning editors than for carrying concerns to senior managers.

H5, that copy desk workers would be less satisfied if they thought their ideal and real ethics roles differed, was supported. Independent samples f-tests showed that among respondents with opinions, those who perceived their ideal and actual ethics roles differed were significantly less likely to agree with five of seven statements about job satisfaction. The editors whose responses revealed a disconnect had significantly lower mean scores on statements about overall satisfaction, the prospect of doing the same work in five years, their prospects for advancement, and satisfaction with supervisors.

In addition, respondents whose responses showed the disconnect had significantly lower scores on intending to remain at their newspapers for the next two years.

H6, predicting that respondents whose perceptions of copy editors' ideal and real ethics roles did not match would be less likely than others to rate their newspapers' ethical standards favorably, was supported. Respondents rated the ethics standards of their newspapers lower if their ideas of what copy editors' ethics roles should be did not match their perceptions of reality. The copy editors think they should be the final guardians of journalistic ethics but perceive little newsroom support for that role.

For example, almost three-fourths strongly agreed that addressing ethicsrelated problems in stories should be part of copy editors' jobs, but only about 40% said that was the case in their newsrooms.

Similarly, although all but three respondents agreed copy editors should be encouraged to take concerns about ethics problems to their immediate supervisors and/or the assigning editors, only about 55% said such a simple step was "always" encouraged in their newsrooms.

There was even less perceived support for pursuing ethics-related discussions to a higher level: 90% agreed copy editors should be encouraged to take unresolved concerns to senior managers, but fewer than 15% said such encouragement is "always" given. This suggests that newsrooms are constraining employees willing to serve as ethical backstops from using their niche in the production process to do so.

Constrained Copy Editors. Comments written in the margins of some returned questionnaires or in answer to two open-ended questions90 suggested how these constraints may be working: some come from deadlines, workload, and technological pressures. For example, a news copy editor at a newspaper with 500,000+ average weekday circulation wrote:

If for example there are 35 stories appearing in the paper, more likely than not, 25 of the stories move to the copydesk in the last 45 minutes before the paper is slated to lock upeverything (or much of it) pops near deadline. That puts a strain on the ability to check facts, weigh fairness, check spelling & grammar, rectify inconsistencies, write a good headline and trim the story to fit the hole.

A features/lifestyle copy editor at a major metropolitan newspaper echoed Braverman's de-skilling theory, writing that with the [newspaper's] conversion to CCI [a proprietary electronic editing and pagination system sold by CCI Europe] the "art" of copy editing is being overtaken by the need for copy editors to act as typographers. This is compounded by a recent redesign that is adding a layer of mumbo-jumbo. It's less and less about journalism and more and more about production.

That copy editor's concern may be telling: 58% of respondents designed pages using electronic software; 28% worked for newspapers that changed editing or design software during the previous year; and 52% worked for newspapers or sections that had been redesigned during the previous year.

At Issue: Power. Other comments suggested that the issue is power, a central notion in Braverman's de-skilling theory and Shoemaker and Reese's theory of influences on media content. A copy editor at a newspaper in the 25,001-50,000 weekday circulation group wrote: "We're grammarians and headline writers and only rarely deal with the substance of a story except to return it to [the assigning editors] if there's a problem in that area."

A copy editor/page designer at another small newspaper described a similar situation: "The way our system is set up, the city desk determines content and balance on stories, and we merely lay out the pages, write headlines, and edit for AP style. We are not allowed to cut local stories, and not encouraged to question content and balance." Another wrote, "We're not allowed to change local copy."

In those cases-which may be particularly representative of small dailies with beginner copy editors, a powerful city editor, and no highly placed advocate for copy editors (e.g., an assistant managing editor for copy desks)-the ability of copy editors to be ethics advocates may be constrained by their place in the newsroom hierarchy.

Shoemaker and Reese suggest that media routines trump the individual's ability to influence media content, except in areas where there is no established routine. At some newspapers, not only is the routine for dealing with potential ethics-related problems in stories well established, but it also ends at the assigning desk. As a result, assigning editors do not grant to copy editors the sanction or approval they need to serve as even backup guardians of ethics standards.

Constraints on copy editors extend beyond ethics-related concerns. Although the largest difference between copy editors' views of their ideal and actual roles involved identifying and eliminating potential ethics-related problems, there were also significant differences between their ideal and real roles in eliminating errors and potential legal problems. Newspapers may also be wasting the talents of key employees by not supporting their efforts to find and eliminate errors and potential legal problems, such as libel. An assistant copy desk chief at a small daily wrote:

The other departments sometimes forget that we are not trained monkeys drawing boxes on the computer. We sift through wire copy and photos to select the most relevant and compelling items for our readers.

When it comes to decisions about local copy and photos, however, comments from the copy desk are often pushed aside. The next afternoon we are the ones questioned about any confusing information, mistakes or questionable remarks. "Why didn't the desk change that?" "How did that get by the desk?" Limits have been placed on our authority as copy editors, yet we are still held responsible for the decisions we cannot make.

One effect of a disconnect between ideal and real roles is a lack of job satisfaction. The nearly one in five respondents reporting that disconnect was more likely to be dissatisfied with aspects of his/her job and to have a lower opinion of the ethics standards of his/her newspaper. However, it is impossible to tell which came first, the disconnect or the discontent.

How should newspapers tackle this situation? If newspapers want to enlist all journalists to help preserve ethical standards and, thus, credibility, managers should encourage copy editors to raise questions when stories with potential ethics-related problems reach them. This encouragement should be delivered in a public way so that newsroom staffers who have traditionally controlled the routine of dealing with substantive questions can see that newsroom policymakers want those routines to include copy editors.

In addition, copy editors who still have concerns after talking with their supervisors and/or assigning editors should be encouraged to approach senior editors. A procedure for doing this should be made public, which could help reduce the perception that copy editors who take concerns to senior editors are acting maliciously, rather than merely doing their jobs.

Meanwhile, both copy editors and senior managers should make increased efforts to get to know each other. As The Poynter Institute's Karen Brown Dunlap has noted, one factor that can make copy editors' position in the newsroom precarious is that "their day begins as many reporters and editors prepare to end the day, keeping copy editors out of the flow of newsroom conversation."

Greater connections between copy editors and senior editors would give the former access they need to raise concerns informally and offer the latter a better sense of what is going on in the trenches. It also might introduce senior editors to copy editors with reporting experience (of which there were many in this study) who would be good candidates for assigning editor positions. Considering them would help address two problems reported by this study: a perception that copy editors are not respected and the dissatisfaction of more than half with their prospects for advancement.

Further research might look beyond the copy desk to consider what reporters, midlevel managers, and senior managers consider their ideal ethics roles to be and how those stack up against what newsroom routines allow them to question or take responsibility for. Although media ethics research has often asked journalists "What behavior do you consider ethical?" it has less often asked "What part of ethical journalism do you consider yourself responsible for?"

A large body of work has tried to determine what

influences the behavior of journalists and other media practitioners. Those studies generally have assumed, though, that media workers will do what they think they should do. This study revealed a disconnect between the "ethics backstop" role some copy editors thought they should have and the roles they perceived they did have. Other journalists may similarly be disconnected from roles they believe they should fulfill.

Chapter 8

Perceptions of Newsroom Cultural Change

Less than a decade ago, there was a growing concern among corporate executives, scholars, and even many editors about the future of the newspaper industry. Newspapers faced stiff challenges on every horizon: circulation was stagnant, and a smaller percentage of the public was reading newspapers than at any time in the past half-century; the Internet was competing for the populace's time and advertisers' money; the costs of doing business were rising and unpredictable; and, for public companies, profit pressures were increasing as corporate managers sought to maintain control over their companies amidst waves of hostile buyouts and takeovers. The message to those leading the industry was clear: change or fall victim to the forces redefining your environment.

There were also rumblings within the industry for change. Some influential editors and journalists became outspoken critics of how newspapers had lost sight of their public service mission and lost touch with their communities. These critiques often focused on the insular nature of journalism, emphasizing that journalists are "insider-oriented" elitists.

This inner directedness could be understood in at least two ways: first, journalists tended to assess the value of their work in relation to how it is viewed by other journalists, not the public; second, working close to politicians and other powerful sources resulted in reporting more focused on power struggles and personal political battles than the issues that affect the daily lives of average citizens. Some editors - buoyed by support from scholars, a small body of research, and philanthropic organizations - became convinced that if journalists were able to get closer to readers, reconnect with their democratic mission, and begin framing stories from the centre of their communities, then newspapers would reclaim their relevance.

It is within this framework that newspaper executives - addressing both internal and external issues - re-evaluated the goals and practices of the industry and set out to put it back on course. In 1994, the American Society of Newspaper Editors created a Change Committee, a group of editors given a 5-year period to develop and experiment with initiatives that would ensure the long-term viability of the industry. Founded on the heels of a recession that had lingered since the late 1980s and resulted in smaller newsroom staffs and budgets, the committee focused its attention on exploring ways to: (1) reorganize newsrooms for better efficiency and (2) realign journalists' values more closely with those of readers and citizens.

Change initiatives emerged that attempted to transform the culture of the newsroom, making it more externally focused on markets and readers, while internally changing the nature of work by abandoning the century-old beat system of news coverage and replacing it with collaborative teams. "Change" became the mantra of many leading editors and executives, and the new, restructured approach to producing newspapers was labeled "strategic," "reader-driven," or "market-driven" journalism.

Newsroom managers, recognizing that they lacked the organizational background to plan, execute, and monitor fundamental change, increasingly looked to outside consultants to guide their efforts and alleviate employee resistance. The process of change, seldom easy in any organization, became a target of skepticism for journalists, who worried that initiatives jeopardized core journalism values and credibility.

Organizational development (OD) is the study of how organizations evolve, learn, and adapt. This line of inquiry is well suited, although it lies been rarely used, to explore and understand the process of change in the newspaper industry.

The research reported in this monograph uses OD theory as a framework for assessing the perceptions and attitudes that top newsroom managers and rank-and-file journalists have about initiatives aimed at changing the newsroom culture.

This study also explores the impact of two newer, largely unstudied variables that have been a part of change initiatives - newsroom restructuring and the reader-oriented redefinition of news values - to better understand how journalists perceive change and its impact.

Organizational development scholarship is rooted in social psychology and management. OD scholars concede that because organizations vary in size and resources and have different goals, OD research has generally focused on one organization at a time. Argyris acknowledges that this situation-by-situation approach, which relies on on-site observations, in-depth interviews, and situation-specific variables, makes the task of generalizing results and theory building more difficult.

This study takes a different approach than most OD research and attempts to advance OD theory building and the practical understanding of ongoing newspaper change by surveying a relatively large probability sample of rank-and-file journalists and a census of top newsroom managers from 17 newspapers most experienced in ASNE-sanctioned change initiatives.

The logic of the approach is that journalists working at newspapers that have experimented with similar change initiatives create a population of cohorts who have clear perceptions regarding change based on their common experiences. This commonality should permit valid research that extends beyond single organizations and site-specific variables, producing results that can benefit newsrooms embarking on change initiatives. Accordingly, this study extends newspaper change research by addressing the problem differently, both in terms of its theoretical framework and methodological design.

The extent to which change initiatives can be tied to economics is uncertain. By 2001, a recessionary national economy led the nation's largest public newspaper companies to downsize their workforces between 5 and 10% to maintain profit levels attractive to investors.

However, the late 1990s, a period of a strong economy and fast and furious change, saw the same high profits that had characterized the industry a decade earlier. Publicly owned companies, which account for nearly half the nation's daily circulation, returned an average profit of 20.7% in 1998 and 22.2% in 1999.

Advertising revenue was also at record levels, reaching $46.3 billion in 1999, the eighth consecutive year of record highs, casting doubt on prognosticators who only a half-decade earlier had predicted the Internet would spell doom for newspapers.

CHANGING NEWS VALUES

Aware that their readership is stagnant and influence declining, newspaper managers and journalists have been reexamining their news values. This introspection has manifested itself in several ways: an increased marketing consciousness, a desire for more credibility, the involvement of readers in deciding news and how it should be reported, and a sense the media are failing to live up to their historic democratic role of informing people of issues important to successful governance.

American Journalism Review, in a 2000 cover story titled "Reader Friendly," reported that the emerging culture of restructured newsrooms around the country is characterized by:

- Enthroning readers as the "invisible giants," elevating them to near equal partners in decision making;

- Erring on the side of caution rather than aggressiveness, rejecting stories that might offend readers as lacking compassion or sensitivity;
- Promoting cooperation with everyone, from City Hall to the paper's advertising departments.

The long-time taboo of "pandering" to readers has been swept away by an attempt to reverse what some editors have called a "disconnection" between newspapers and the public. Following a series of meetings called the Journalism Values Institute in which 30 editors from around the country debated the problems of the industry, Peck (1996) wrote, "The essence of these evaluations comes down to this: American journalists continue to say they practice good journalism in the public's interest - but the public doesn't believe we deliver".

Editors left the meetings agreeing that newspaper content includes too much gossip, not enough substance, bias but no balance, and a preoccupation with conflict and few solutions. The Oregonian's Bhatia summed up the problems: "Our comfort zones are painting the world in black and white. And our comfort zones are seeing the traditional good side and evil side of whatever issue it might be. We've got to blow that up".

Many of the editors most active in the ASNE Change Committee borrowed ideas from and adopted the language of civic (or public) journalism. Civic journalism broadens the concept of journalistic social responsibility into a more active role, with the goal of journalism becoming a catalyst for the revival of civic life by promoting citizen engagement and dialogue.

Merritt insists the practice of civic journalism requires journalists to abandon several common and traditional practices, including: valuing conflict as the primary narrative device, framing issues at extremes, maintaining an adversarial role with institutions, treating the readers as audiences rather than participants, and insisting that journalism credibility arises from detachment.

Stopp wrote that a cross-country tour of newsrooms

left him impressed by how many newsrooms were using the language and techniques of civic journalism. he notes that when he raised this issue many editors and journalists dismissed it, suggesting civic journalism is a project-driven formula that they don't understand.

Stepp, however, concluded: "Perhaps the resistance to the civic journalism label simply underlines how much some of the techniques have seeped into the newsroom groundwater".

CHANGING THE NEWSROOM CULTURE

Nearly all editors who have involved their newsrooms in change initiatives have suggested the key to making change work is to create a new culture. Weaver said changing the newsroom culture requires "getting the staff to think of the whole paper, as opposed to their own story or small piece they contributed." She said that reporters need to be trained to work in a new system, as many lack the editing, headline writing, and design skills required in the team structure.

Managers, too, have more pressure, as the staff is often competing for the attention of fewer bosses. And, because of the changing nature of journalism work, job performance evaluations need revision to reflect the standards and goals of a new system. She admits that "newsroom stars" under the old system often fool stifled by the team structure. Teams require a "new breed" of journalist with different personality traits and skills than the "lone wolf" who worked well alone and often produced breakthrough stories.

Sue Deans, editor of The Sun News, said for change initiatives to work staff members need to understand that change is a constant; it will not go away after a short time or a few experiments.

The two "core issues" of change are continuous product improvement, and keeping aware of what readers want and the market demands. She said changing the newsroom culture requires emphasizing "passion" for the newspaper business and:

- Impressing on people who do not want change that they must change or leave;
- Eliminating "silo" thinking by creating cross-departmental approaches to work and evaluating work quality;
- Staying focused on strategy and on the market.

Campbell, who resigned in April 2000 as Si. Louis Post-Dispatch editor after a stormy 3 1/2 years, had embarked on an ambitious attempt at "cultural transformation" at the paper. He claims the existing newsroom "judgmental culture" is part of the problem with American journalism, and he attempted to change the Post-Dispatch's culture from one based on "judgmentalism" to one based on "collaboration."

By the millennium, the ideas for change that began in a couple dozen newsrooms in the mid-1990s were becoming the industry norm. Stepp (2000) wrote:

"From civic journalism to New Directions for News, from credibility reforms to the Committee of Concerned Journalists, a host of foundations, trade groups and other forces have been pouring millions of dollars into attempts to remodel how journalists think and act".

IMPACT OF CHANGE ON MORALE

Change initiatives have required journalists to rethink some fundamental principles of their work: their sense of news, audience, organization, and even the purpose of journalism. Signs of eroding morale were present before change began in the mid-1990s, and morale problems in relation to change initiatives have been reported in trade journals.

Gassaway used observation and survey to study the social construction of a journalist's reality. he found news judgment decisions were most often the result of "preordained news," determined by coverage beats and how editors decide to use their resources. Editors and reporters struggle for control of information because they often disagree on what should be communicated to the public. Editors' authority is derived from organizational hierarchies, but reporters can deny editors' authority by controlling information obtained in iiewsgathoriiig. Gassaway concluded editors and reporters negotiate for control to prevent confrontations and reduce resorting to power.

Jeffers and Lewis studied organizational communication at a midsized newspaper and found rank-and-file journalists perceived their communication with their immediate supervisor and publisher as poor.

They suggested the organizational climate could be improved by increasing the amount and frequency of communication at all levels. The authors concluded their study supported the findings of Pincuss, Knipp, and Rayfield, who found rank-and-file employees' communication relationship with their immediate supervisor is a predictor of job satisfaction; however, employees' sense of having meaningful communication with top-level managers was as strong a predictor of satisfaction as immediate-supervisor communication.

In the mid-1990s, several scholars began to assess organizational structure and goals, often considering profit motive and its impact on normative journalism values. Deniers integrated organizational and economic theory in his book, The Menace of the Corporate Newspaper: Fact or Fiction?, to define the corporate newspaper, its characteristics, and organizational dynamics. Demers asserted that corporate newspapers are complex bureaucracies controlled by trained managers, not owners.

These managers are best understood as innovative professionals or "technocrats" who are morn interested in professional, organizational, and technical goals than profit goals. Demers juxtaposed the roles of managers to those of owners, defining the latter as "capitalists" most interested in returns on their investments. In the 20th century, managers replaced owners as the driving force; in corporations because the organizations had become complex bureaucracies that required professional management.

Further aiding the transition was the death of the original owners, whose influence was dispersed over time and divided among heirs. Deniers wrote the result is that corporate newspapers are efficiently managed and structured to maximize profits, but they place less emphasis on profit than non-corporate newspapers, which tend to be family-owned, less bureaucratic organizations. In two studies, his results indicate that newspapers become more rigorous editorially as they become larger, more complex organizations.

In studies that both support and refute Deniers' work, Beam studied the conditions that influence newspapers' market orientation and whether market orientation affects content. To define and measure market orientation, Beam explored the extent that newspapers: (l) have one or more departments active in understanding customer needs and the factors affecting the needs, (2) share this information across departments, and (3) have various departments engaged in meeting select customer needs. He found that ownership by a large group is the most important predictor of a newspaper's market orientation, suggesting the corporate parent may not be involved in specific content decisions but is more likely to require certain general processes be followed in making content decisions.

He concluded that traditional journalistic values are important at market-oriented papers, and while more market-oriented newsrooms are more committed to special interest and visual content, they are not less committed to traditional content, including public affairs. Beam (2000) has also found that newspapers that are part of privately owned companies are more market oriented than those of public companies. Using his survey data, Beam (2001) then chose 10 newspapers for a content analysis - 5 papers with strong market orientation and 5 papers with weak market orientation.

He found the majority of items on page one of both orientations was "public sphere" content, which includes government affairs; however, the percentage of public sphere items on page one for weak market orientation newspapers was significantly higher (65.6%) than for strong market orientation papers (54.9%). Overall, Beam analysed the display pages (section front or topic lead page) and found papers with strong market orientation have proportionately more items devoted to private life, coping, and sports, while proportionately fewer items about government and public life.

Martin compared profits earned by 15 public newspaper companies to profits of publishing companies and yields from corporate and government bonds over an 11-year period. For the entire period, newspaper profits averaged 90% higher than publishing companies, 78% higher than government bond yields, and 54% higher than interest payments from corporate bonds.

Using a scale created by an economist that labels profits 50% above those of comparable measures as "excessive," Martin found that in 23 of 33 annual comparative indices (70%) the newspaper companies in the sample earned excessive profits.

In some cases, these excessive comparative profits occurred in the early 1990s during what an analyst called "the biggest advertising recession since World War II".

After newspapers embarked on broad, and in some cases bold, change initiatives in the 1990s, a few researchers began to study these initiatives through the lens of organizational development.

Gentry observed while a small California daily embarked on several change initiatives aimed at better aligning its content with community interests. The year-long efforts, orchestrated by New Directions for News, led Gentry to conclude the following elements were essential for successful newspaper organizational change: (1) strong leadership; (2) management communication about: why change is needed, management's vision, and new performance standards; (3) staff involvement in the change process; (4) management rewarding correct behaviour and extinguishing improper behaviour; and (5) anticipating problems of acceptance and implementation.

Working a few years later with the American Press Institute, Gentry developed a model he calls "A Roadmap for Change" that added several variables, including: (1) prechange analysis of the current culture to determine the extent and types of changes needed; (2) use of mission statements to clarify core values for employees; (3) flexible management strategies and putting people in the proper roles to execute them; (4) enabling structures, such as job training; and (5) creating visible symbols of the new culture.

Testing the model, Gentry (1997) surveyed management and rank-and-file at six newspapers and found management thought it was doing a better job than the staff thought it was doing on all 10 elements of change the study addressed.

In a longitudinal case study, Gade and Perry measured newsroom employees' perceptions of change initiatives led by editor Cole Campbell from 1996-2000 at the Si. LOUJS Post-Dispatch. Over 4 years, Campbell, known as an industry innovator, had some success making news values more reader driven, but the 1999 reorganization of newsroom coverage from beats to teams left much of the staff confused about their roles and job responsibilities.

Campbell's embrace of public journalism did not resonate with a majority of the staff. Morale declined and was lowest among respondents with management duties. Respondents consistently indicated they wern open minded toward change until after reorganization, which apparently was the last straw in a series of changes that underscored Campbell's tenure as editor (he resigned under pressure in April 2000). Over the course of the study, respondents consistently indicated that they failed to see how change initiatives contributed to better journalism.

At a time when cross-departmental teams were still new to the industry, Sylvie studied how department heads of news, advertising, and circulation perceived their identity and ability to cooperate with each other. News managers named advertising as the most difficult department, while the advertising directors named the news editors as least cooperative. Newsroom managers were the only department heads of rank their respective department's concerns as most important, ranking circulation success the most important.

News editors showed a significantly greater tendency to say more cooperation between departments is needed. Sylvie concluded the news managers exhibit a "surprising sensitivity" to market-oriented concepts, which gives credibility to journalists' anecdotal claims that the newspaper industry is moving toward a greater market orientation.

A meager amount of research exists on newspaper team performance. Russial studied changes in health and science content at The Oregonian after that paper created a Health and Science team. He found that the team produced more coverage that received better play (Al or Metro section front) than before the team was created. Russial suggested that although his study did not measure coverage quality, the creation of a team-based system represents a realignment in the use of newsroom resources that may have important consequences on news content.

Neuzil, Hansen, and Ward surveyed Minneapolis Star Tribune and St. Paul Pioneer Press journalists working in teams and found most thought they had less authority and less success getting story ideas in the paper than before teams were created. Those who thought they had less authority also said they were unsure of the chain of command, worked on larger teams, and wore reporters more than editors. The researchers concluded if a goal of team work was to "empower" journalists by granting them more autonomy to be innovative, this goal was not being met.

In sum, trade journals and a developing body of research provide evidence that newspapers are changing in some fundamental ways: flattening organizational structures, replacing traditional beats with teams, revising job descriptions and required skills, rethinking organizational values, and redefining news judgment.

USING ORGANIZATIONAL THEORY TO MAKE SENSE OF CHANGE

The study of "organizations" is a relatively new discipline. Drucker wrote that "no one in the United States - or anyplace else - talked of Organizations' until after World

War ?" Drucker said that the modern idea of an organization - as a purposely designed and specialized entity that is defined by its task and is distinct from society's other institutions - emerged in the second half of the 20th century with what he calls the "management revolution." Initial theoretical assumptions of this revolution were largely shaped by turn-of-the-century scholars: Taylor's views on "scientific management" and Weber's ideas on the rational and specialized bureaucracy.

This organizational model is characterized by a hierarchical division of labor where managers are the "thinkers" and laborers are the "doers". Employees develop highly specialized skills that increase performance and productivity, while management's job is to ensure the conditions exist for the organizational "machine" to run smoothly. Recognizing that organizations must evolve and adapt to survive in changing environments, Lewin suggested a "natural" (as opposed to mechanical) metaphor to explain organizational dynamics; change, he wrote, can be best understood and managed through a process of "unfreeze, change, refreeze."

These early attempts to understand organizations and their dynamics prepared the intellectual soil for the growth of organizational development, which attracted the interest of U.S. scholars and corporate managers in the last quarter of the 20th century as the changing global marketplace threatened U.S. dominance.

Although Taylor's and Weber's (and to a lesser extent Lewin's) ideas are considered outdated, they have proven resilient and modest adaptations of them are still very much alive in both theory and practice. Bergquist wrote that most organizational theorists have conceived organizations as pendulum-like mechanisms, which value "simplicity in motion" and homeostasis. When organizations experience turbulent times, they tend to seek equilibrium by returning to their previous form and function.

However, the structured and predictable environment in which U.S. companies once thrived no longer exists, and

Bergquist contends a more accurate metaphor in the postmodern world is that of the organization as a liquid, "poised on the edge of order and chaos". The liquid system, he wrote, contains at the same time both elements of stability and change, especially along the edges, or shifting boundaries.

In an organizational sense, it is the shifting boundaries that offer potential for understanding the change process. It is these places on the "edge" where innovation occurs and where organizational traits such as mission, communication, and leadership become integral to success.

In perhaps the seminal book on organizational change and development, Kanter wrote American companies that value "innovation" are better placed to use their employees' creative capacities and stay ahead in changing environments. Interviews with 65 corporate executives led Kanter to conclude the innovative companies are integrated (my italics); they grant power to individuals to encourage fresh thinking and create opportunities for new ideas to cross organizational boundaries.

She juxtaposed integrated companies with "segmented" companies, which are characterized by an "ovorspecification" of resources and consider themselves successful when every segment works well independently, without much need for communication. Segmented companies, Kanter wrote, seek stasis, because they are constantly looking to the past to define the future; accordingly, habits and routines that maintain the course are valued.

Kanter identified five major building blocks in change initiatives that increase the company's capacity to meet new challenges:

- Departures from tradition: activities or ideas that require the organization to think and behave in new ways.
- Crisis or galvanizing event: a critical event that cannot be solved by traditional means. This allows a non-traditional idea to be pushed forward.
- Strategic decisions: the opportunity for management

to create a vision by articulating a deliberate and conscious direction.

- Individual "prime movers": people who push the innovative strategy through the organization by communicating strategic decisions and manipulating the symbols of the organizational culture toward the direction of change.
- Action vehicles: mechanisms that allow new action. These include training programs, successful results for people using new practices, new organizational rewards that support new practices, and ongoing messages of the benefits experienced by individuals using the now practices.

Kanter wrote that managers need three new sets of skills to operate effectively in integrated, innovative environments: "power skills" used to persuade others to invest in new initiatives; ability to manage problems associated with teams and greater employee participation; and understanding of how organizational change is designed and constructed. She concluded that "the art and architecture of change" requires managers to abandon their reliance on traditional analytical tools, which measure what already exists or has occurred.

"Change efforts have to mobilize people around what is not yet known, not yet experienced ... they require a leap of faith that cannot be eliminated by presentation of all the forecasts, figures, and advance guarantees that can be accumulated". Accordingly, the paradox of managing changes, she wrote, is "there needs to be a plan, and the plan has to acknowledge that it will be departed from".

Most attempts at organizational development involve efforts to transform an organization's culture. Schneider, Brief, and Guzzo wrote that the values and beliefs that are the foundation of an organization's culture can be changed by focusing on the tangible things - such as practices, policies, and procedures - that define daily life in the organization.

It is these tangible phenomena that comprise an organization's climate, and for real cultural change to occur, management must change the climate in which the employees exist.

The authors contend that many efforts at cultural change are focused on "macro" issues such as values and beliefs, while overlooking the more tangible issues that create the organizational climate in which employees experience everyday life.

They wrote: "Sustainable organizational change is most assured when both the climate - what the organization's members experience - and the culture - what the members believe the organization values - change".

Successful companies have increasingly educated workforces, and they are creating cultures that are more innovative and flexible. The new, desired culture is one in which power and accountability are shared between managers and employees in a manner that allows companies to respond quickly to challenges and opportunities. The goal of these efforts is to unleash and channel the power of employees' knowledge in an organizational "culture of contribution."

Fisher acknowledges that this is a major cultural shift for most U.S. companies because - unlike the Japanese, whose collective society adapted easily to a team-building, egalitarian corporate model - "America's professional workers value their individualism and often express it in counterproductive ways". Corporate America also clings to some values that work against creating a culture of contribution; most prominent among these, Fisher wrote, is the corporate view on job attachment. Workers are expected to accept such surprises as downsizing, job reclassification, or relocation with quiet stoicism, which contradicts companies' claims they are striving to empower employees as co-partners with management.

Fisher contends that U.S. managers need to be aware that there is no single ideal corporate culture; rather, corporate culture is better understood as a combination of macro and micro cultures. Many senior managers claim to embrace a culture of contribution, but Fisher contends that few have ideas about how to put a programme or process in place to let the transformation occur.

On the other hand, the changing nature of professional work, driven by new technology, has organizations acting as though they are horizontally constructed even though most corporate organizational charts still reflect a vertical hierarchy.

If management is to be successful creating the culture of contribution, it must cede some of its "span of control" and forge a "span of relationships," with workers and managers acting more as "learners than knowers, listeners than tellers, partners than adversaries".

Fisher cautions that management should not be too optimistic that a reorganization into teams will solve the ills of the company; rather, a culture of contribution is more likely to develop in a climate where workers are trusted and have the freedom to think and act like owners.

At the core of many organizational development efforts over the past two decades has been the restructuring of organizations from vertical hierarchies into more horizontal, "flattened" designs where most of the work is done by self-directed teams.

In theory, teams "empower" employees by giving team members more decision-making authority and eliminating vertical chains of command. However, empowerment efforts not only require management to share power, they also demand that individual team members think differently about the nature of work. Labianca, Gray, and Brass (2000) found that empowerment efforts require a change in "schemas" - cognitive frameworks that give meaning to experience - for both management and lower level employees.

The authors analysed a 2-year organizational development project involving team building and increased participation of lower level employees in decision making. Before the project, the "schema-in-use" for organizational decision making was that management should maintain control of events and decision making, and this schema was understood by both management and employees. The expected new schema for management included: making the organization more team oriented and collaborative, empowering lower level employees, aligning organizational structure effectively, and keeping current workers.

For the ruiik-aiid-filu, the expected new schema was characterized by working on team building, creating more avenues of communication, and encouraging employees to air their "beefs."

The authors found: a great amount of employee skepticism at the outset about the likelihood of real change; despite a series of organization-wide meetings, interviews revealed both managers and nonmanagers were unclear about the project's goals; resistance was heightened when managerial behaviour failed to conform with its stated expectations; and management incorrectly assumed that employees would postpone judgment of the reorganization plan until after it was implemented.

Randolph (2000) wrote that few managers or employees fully understand how empowerment affects traditional patterns of corporate hierarchy and behaviour. Management confuses empowerment as "giving people the power to make decisions," and this perception misses the essential notion of empowerment, that a great amount of power already exists in employees' knowledge, experience, and motivation.

Rank-and-file perceive empowerment to mean they will be given the freedom to make all major decisions about their jobs. Randolph wrote that empowerment efforts do require a cultural shift; however, the shift is from one person making decisions to team-based shared decision making.

He asserts that empowerment makes employees more accountable than the older, hierarchical culture, and it is best understood as a strange combination of opportunity and risk.

An organization moves toward team-based empowered culture through three stages: (1) starting and orienting the process of change, (2) making changes and dealing with discouragement, and (3) adopting and refining empowerment to fit the organization.

Each stage utilizes three "interlocking tools" - sharing information, creating autonomy through boundaries, and replacing the hierarchy with self-directed teams.

Hirschhorn, a management scholar whose work focuses on team-based organizations, wrote that the entire philosophy of management is changing as corporations flatten hierarchies and adopt new team environments. Successful managers develop roles for team members and "manage the boundary," communicating the company's needs to the team and the team's needs to the company. Managers lead by creating a structure in which the team can be successful and by positioning themselves to defend the team's efforts.

Managers must realise they are both cause of and solution to many team problems. To be successful, managers must show their vulnerability (a traditional management faux pas) and willingness to learn from team members. Exhibiting these traits shows that managers are open to new ways to solve problems and encourages team members to respond to challenges that can enhance team performance.

Although development efforts are characterized by dispersing power throughout an organization, management's ability to provide leadership remains a key to organizational success. Kets de Vries, a psychologist who focuses on the "psychodynamics of organizations," wrote that organizational culture depends on the psychological contract that exists between its leaders and followers.

Effective leaders need to: articulate a vision of the future; create symbolic impressions to communicate the vision; build networks; empower followers; make choices (often painful ones); and keep perspectives of the followers based in reality. he wrote that the leader/follower relationship a process of social comparison that involves power, authority, hero worship, flattery, ambition, and attention seeking - provides tremendous opportunities for distorted management reasoning.

The key is for managers to "preserve their hold on reality." Trust is essential for a healthy organization, and trust is dependent upon communication, support, respect, fairness, competence, and consistency on the part of the leaders. he concluded, "In order for the leader to understand the meaning of these words, it is important that he or she realise what it means to be a follower, how it feels to be in that position".

The importance of communication in organizations, especially during times of change, has spawned its own discipline of study. Lewis wrote that a growing body of empirical research indicates that the communication process and organizational change efforts are "inextricably linked processes".

Communication plays an important role in several aspects of the change process, including: creating and articulating a vision; soliciting input and channeling feedback to and from all levels of the organizational hierarchy; and propelling and altering the paths of change.

The organizational communication literature reveals that communication has been shown to reduce uncertainty associated with change efforts, increase accuracy in perceptions about the reasons and goals of change, and increase willingness to participate in planned change.

Studying the methods and channels organizations use to communicate change, Lewis found change agents consider themselves to be the primary sources of change-related information, and they solicit input much less frequently than they disseminate information.

She suggests that management's lack of use of channels of communication, especially upward channels, limits feedback from lower level employees who do the work of the organization.

This approach can affect the success of change efforts, as "changes in status, reward structures, job descriptions, roles, work methods, work relationships, and procedures bring significant organizational issues to the surface" that increase rank-and-file employees' need to communicate with their supervisors.

There is a small body of literature; on organizational

attempts to initiate market-oriented cultural change. Narver and Slater described a market-oriented culture as one that most effectively and efficiently creates superior customer value. Harris defined a market-oriented culture as "the dominant, dynamic segment of an organization whoso orientation, attitudes and actions are geared towards the market".

Harris contends that most reseachers err when they assume an organization has a single, unitary culture. This approach ignores the dynamic interaction of many aspects of an organization's culture and denies the possibility of the existence of multiple cultures. Generally, developing a market-oriented culture can be understood as a means to improve organizational efficiency and effectiveness. However, Piercy maintains the success of developing such a culture is largely dependent on internal power relationships and organizational politics, which - at least in the short term - do not necessarily lead to high levels of organization-wide motivation, commitment, or satisfaction.

When understood in this context, developing a market-oriented culture can be seen as one of many ways that an organization can impose cultural control over the attitudes, actions, and behaviors of its members. Overall, Harris and Ogbonna wrote that the literature on the effects of developing market-oriented cultures is inconsistent, with some stüdies suggesting that the new culture improves employee satisfaction and commitment and others indicating this is not the case.

However, researchers tend to agree that the success of any attempt at creating a market-oriented culture is contingent on employees who have to implement it. In nearly all cases, this is the front-line employees who are the primary link between an organization and its customers. The authors also contend that developing a market-oriented culture should be concerned with the long-term generation of values, attitudes, and behaviors, but the underlying assumption of the market culture is continuing responsiveness to customer needs.

The dilemma for organizations is how they can craft short-term responses to "increasingly fickle" customer needs in a manner that does not conflict with long-term organizational objectives. Harris and Ogbonna concluded that this condition is "a contradiction yet to be resolved or fully understood".

Change, because it requires giving up what is known and routine for something new that may not be understood, is often met with resistance. De Jager (2001) wrote that many managers perceive employees who resist change as a problem. he contends this a short-sighted view that fundamentally misunderstands the causes of resistance and the potential benefits resistance can exert on an organization.

De Jager wrote that businesses today acknowledge the need to change, but there is so much change that employees become confused and see themselves pushed in conflicting directions. Management is wise to understand that resistance to change is a tool that can be used to guide an organization. "Another way of looking at resistance is as a gateway or filter. Resistance to change helps us select from all possible changes the one that is most appropriate to the current situation". Because change involves replacing old organizational routines and values with new ones, managers must be able to provide answers for employees to some fundamental questions:

- Why is the old status quo no longer sufficient?
- What will it cost to make the transition from the old to new ways of doing things? De Jager identified several likely costs: disruption of routines, training, temporary low morale, new hires, people leaving, and the emotional cost of destroying what was.
- Is the cost of change justified by the incremental benefits of the change proposed?
- Does the proposed change support and reinforce existing core values?

As the millennium approached, the newspaper industry faced imposing, concurrent challenges on several fronts: stagnant circulation and a slowly dwindling base of readers;

a fragmenting mass modin market; new electronic media that are changing the way people access and use information; threats to traditional sources of advertising; and unpredictable but rising costs of production.

In the wake of a mid-1990s recession that saw significant cutbacks, layoffs, and downsizings, newsrooms were restructured and reorganized. Hierarchical newsroom designs were flattened, and the beat system of coverage centered on social institutions was replaced by a team system that defined coverage areas by topics believed of greater interest to readers and consumers. What becomes apparent from the industry trade journals is that "change" became the guiding light of the industry in the late 1990s.

Feeling out of step with the social patterns and interests of the public, the industry questioned its news values and management has focused on changing the culture of the newsroom to include greater marketing awareness and knowledge.

Editors are increasingly taking on marketing duties, working in cross-departmental teams with advertising, circulation, and marketing directors to create strategies to attract readers, often in specific demographic groups that advertisers are willing to pay to reach. Rank-and-file journalists are expected to accept restructuring, redefined news values, and a greater sensitivity to marketing as part of a larger cultural change process that is redefining their jobs and norms as journalists.

Organizational theory suggests that integrated organizations are more innovative and flexible and respond more quickly to opportunities and challenges. The basis of power and decision making in integrated organizations shifts from being solely in the hands of management to a shared arrangement that empowers employees to use their knowledge and skills in team-based systems.

Teams, and their individual members, respond to more decision-making power and autonomy by taking more responsibility for the quality of their work and becoming more productive. Organizational change and development is understood as a process with several stages, including planning, executing, and monitoring the progress and results.

Because organizations have different values and goals, the study of OD has usually focused on one organization at a time, identifying the impact of site-specific variables on organizational development. This approach, while making theory building more difficult, has, however, led to researchers identifying several variables that impact the success of OD efforts.

These variables include an organization having a clear mission, employees who understand the mission and organization's core values, effective organizational communication, employee participation in Grafting and implementing change initiatives, strong leadership, trust, flexibility, and mechanisms that monitor the progress of change initiatives and reward desired behaviour. The effect of successful OD efforts should be empowered employees who, in self-directed work teams, are more motivated, productive, and responsible for their work. In theory, at least, successful OD efforts should in the long term improve employee morale.

However, change is also understood as a difficult and risky process. It requires employees (both management and rank-and-file) to embrace new values, to alter routines, and to think differently about their organizational roles and the nature of their work. It requires greater accountability from empowered rank-and-file and a new, less autocratic style from management. Accordingly, resistance to change should be expected, and in some cases is rational. For management, successful OD includes understanding the reasons for resistance and having the flexibility to find ways of working through resistance.

In short, the challenge of conceiving and leading change falls on management, while rank-and-file are expected to enact and embrace change initiatives that affect many of their conventions and values.

Management perceives it is initiating change in the best

interests of the organization and industry, while rank-and-file ponder the reasons for change and are sensitive to how it is implemented.

Organizational theory and change models provide conceptual guidelines that should help predict effective organizational development (OD) initiatives. Given the vast amount of change in the newspaper industry and the relative dearth of research studying these OD initiatives, this study of top newsroom managers and rank-and-file journalists at newspapers leading industry change explores the following research questions and tests three hypotheses.

RQl: What are the attitudes and opinions of management and rank-and-file journalists toward organizational change?

RQ2: How do management and rank-and-file perceive the change process in relation to organizational development theory?

RQ3: How do management and rank-and-file perceive organizational change in relation to the normative values of journalism and marketing?

RQ4: Have change efforts affected rank-and-file perceptions of news values and organizational structure?

RQ5: Have change efforts affected rank-and-file morale?

RQ6: Does organization size (measured by circulation) affect how rank-and-file perceive change?

H1: Management will perceive it has done significantly better at organizational development than rank-and-file.

H2: Morale among rank-and-file will be low.

H3: Rank-and-file perceptions of organizational development will predict morale.

This study used two survey instruments: a 62-statement survey sent to a sample of rank-and-file at 17 newspapers that have been engaged in change initiatives and a 20-statement survey sent to a census of top newsroom managers at the same papers. The rank-and-file survey was designed to explore respondents' attitudes toward concepts important to all newspapers experimenting with change: news values, organizational structure, and morale. The survey included statements that allowed measuring the degree to which the newsroom change process has adhered to organizational development theory.

There were also statements asking rank-and-file to assess the relationship of change with journalistic and marketing goals. The 20-statement management survey focused primarily on issues of organizational development, asking managers to assess the change process and their leadership of it.

These 20 statements also appeared on the rank-and-file survey, allowing for a comparison between managers and rank-and-file on issues important to successful organization development. On both surveys, respondents were asked to record their level of agreement or disagreement to stimulus statements along a 5-point Likert-like intensity scale.

VARIABLE MEASURES

Most of the 62 rank-and-file survey statements were written to probe change initiatives in relation to news values, organizational structure, organizational development, and morale. The statements exploring news values incorporate ideas from trade journals about the changing nature of news, but also reflect norms articulated in the Libertarian and Social Responsibility theories of the press.

The statements that construct the organizational structure variable were taken from trade journal and organizational development literature. The statements in the organizational development construct were all derived from the OD literature.

Morale statements were written to explore both individual respondents' attitudes about their own morale and their perceptions of morale in the newsroom. Factor analysis of the rank-and-file data assisted construction of the four concepts: 14 statements measure news values; 12 statements measure organizational structure; 14 statements measure organizational development; 6 statements measure morale.

Statement responses - on a 5-point scale with 1 strongly agree, 5 strongly disagree, and 3 neutral - were coded so that a positive response indicated support for the concept (i.e., positive response indicated high morale). Conceptual quotients were created by calculating the mean response to the set of statements measuring the concepts. Accordingly, a quotient significantly below 3.0 (the assumed population mean on the 5-point scale) indicates positive agreement with the concept, and a quotient significantly above 3.0 indicates that respondents disagree with the concept (i.e., disagree with statements suggesting high morale).

Comparisons between Management and Rank-and-File

Organizational Development. The literature indicates that cultural change is difficult, requiring management and rank-and-file to adapt to new values, structures, routines, and goals. However, management and rank-and-file have different roles in the change process. Management is responsible for conceiving, guiding, and monitoring change, while rank-and-file must execute management's vision and live with the new roles and values associated with change.

Management is expected to perceive OD initiatives more broadly, in concert with strategic organizational goals, and guide and assess the change process from a position of leadership and accountability. It is expected that management will perceive that its OD initiatives are rooted in sound strategies and practices, while rank-and-file will question the reasons for change and be sensitive to how it is implemented. This logic is the basis of the following hypothesis:

Hl: Management will perceive it has done significantly better at OD than rank-and-file.

At test of independent samples was used to compare the OD quotients (mean value of the 14 statements in the construct) of management and rank-and-file. This hypothesis is supported.

The data indicate that management believes OD initiatives have generally followed theoretical guidelines, as the OD quotient for management shows modest overall agreement with the statements (quotient is less than 3.0). Conversely, the rank-and-file OD quotient shows general disagreement that change initiatives are in accordance with the parameters defined by OD theory. Thus, there is not only a significant difference between the OD quotients, there is also a clear difference of attitudes: management perceives it has generally implemented change in accordance with OD, while rank-and-file think the process of change has not adhered to ideas and practices consistent with successful OD. This finding is further reinforced by looking at the pattern of responses to the variable statements. Of the 14 OD statements, management agrees with 9 and rank-and-file agree with only 3.

T tests wore also used to compare individual statement means, and there are significant differences on 11 of the 14 statements. Because the OD variable is a broad measure of change, with survey statements addressing planning, training, commitment, leadership, communication, participation, and a system of rewards, the significant differences on so many OD aspects reflect both the intensity and broad-based nature of the differences between the groups.

Six of the statistically significant OD statements show a clear difference of attitudes, with management agreeing with the statement and rank-and-file disagreeing. The two groups have differing opinions on some of the most basic aspects of change (means noted parenthetically).

Management believes the newspaper's mission and core values are understood by newsroom employees, while rank-and-file are apparently unsure about their paper's mission and values. Management believes the staff has participated in drafting change, while rank-and-file disagree; and management says that it has asked for staff feedback about change, while rank-and-file apparently think management is not interested in feedback, or at least not interested enough to ask.

The importance of communication in the change process is also shown, as management agrees that change initiatives and the reasons for change have been continually communicated, while rank-and-file disagree.

Most telling about communication is the large difference of opinion concerning honesty. Management shows quite strong agreement that it has been open and honest with staff about the reasons for change, but rank-and-file exhibit equally strong disagreement. This .8 mean difference on honesty (on a 5-point scale) is the largest gap between the groups' responses to any of the 14 statements in the OD variable.

Even on the eight statements where the groups tend to agree, there are significant differences in their intensity of agreement on five statements. Although rank-and-file credit management for its strong leadership role and unified commitment to change, management assesses its leadership role and commitment in significantly more optimistic terms. In those areas where management is relatively self-critical, rank-and-file tend to be more critical.

Management concedes it has not thought through the long-term implications of change, but rank-and-file take a harsher view; the scenario is similar concerning a system of rewards for work that meets the goals of change, with management disagreeing that such a system is in place, but rank-and-file disagreeing significantly more. This trend might be best shown with management's relatively strong disagreement to the statement that change initiatives have helped build stronger trust between management and rank-and-file.

Management's response is a candid assessment of an unpleasant reality and a subtle admission of a failure of change; yet, rank-and-file are significantly harsher in their assessment, with their strongest level of disagreement to any of the 14 statements. These differences underscore that even when management and rank-and-file find areas of common ground, they still tend to disagree.

Of the 14 OD statements, management has a stronger level of disagreement to only 2, and these 2 statements are among the 3 statements that do not have significant mean differences. Management disagrees that it has overestimated resistance to change, while rank-and-file are neutral; and managers disagree that the staff is open-minded toward change marginally more than rank-and-file.

Although not significant, taken together, the ideas that management perceives more resistance and less open-mindedness suggest that management believes their staffs are generally resistant to change initiatives. This perception is likely to influence how managers approach leading change. Managers would be likely to view with more optimism the task of managing a staff that is open to new ideas and practices. Conversely, managers who perceive a resistant and inflexible staff are more likely to judge the task of leading change as more difficult.

COMPARISONS OF STATEMENTS NOT IN THE OD VARIABLE

There were six statements appearing on both surveys that were not part of the OD variable. T tests were performed on the responses, and significant differences were found on four of the statements.

Two of the significant statements show a clear difference of attitudes. Management, consistent with other responses that show more optimism about change than rank-and-file, agrees that there has been a noticeable change in the newsroom culture that has improved the organization, while rank-and-file disagree quite strongly. This large difference of opinion (.82 on a 5-point scale) underscores the different experiences and perceptions the two groups have about the impact of change on the newsroom culture. But the pattern of management optimism is reversed when the groups are asked about an indicator of journalism quality. In this case, rank-and-file agree that newspapers arc doing a boiler job portraying a representative picture of society than in the past, while management is significantly more pessimistic, disagreeing with the statement. This finding could help explain why management sees a need to get closer to readers and redefine news to be more aligned with the lives of people in a changing and diverse marketplace.

Management concedes it has not thought through the long-term implications of change, but rank-and-file take a harsher view; the scenario is similar concerning a system of rewards for work that meets the goals of change, with management disagreeing that such a system is in place, but rank-and-file disagreeing significantly more.

This trend might be best shown with management's relatively strong disagreement to the statement that change initiatives have helped build stronger trust between management and rank-and-file. Management's response is a candid assessment of an unpleasant reality and a subtle admission of a failure of change; yet, rank-and-file are significantly harsher in their assessment, with their strongest level of disagreement to any of the 14 statements. These differences underscore that even when management and rank-and-file find areas of common ground, they still tend to disagree.

Of the 14 OD statements, management has a stronger level of disagreement to only 2, and these 2 statements are among the 3 statements that do not have significant mean differences. Management disagrees that it has overestimated resistance to change, while rank-and-file are neutral; and managers disagree that the staff is open-minded toward change marginally more than rank-and-file. Although not significant, taken together, the ideas that management perceives more resistance and less open-mindedness suggest that management believes their staffs are generally resistant to change initiatives.

This perception is likely to influence how managers approach leading change. Managers would be likely to self-critical, rank-and-file tend to be more critical. Management concedes it has not thought through the long-term implications of change, but rank-and-file take a harsher view; the scenario is similar concerning a system of rewards for work that meets the goals of change, with management disagreeing that such a system is in place, but rank-and-file disagreeing significantly more.

This trend might be best shown with management's relatively strong disagreement to the statement that change initiatives have helped build stronger trust between management and rank-and-file.

Management's response is a candid assessment of an unpleasant reality and a subtle admission of a failure of change; yet, rank-and-file are significantly harsher in their assessment, with their strongest level of disagreement to any of the 14 statements. These differences underscore that even when management and rank-and-file find areas of common ground, they still tend to disagree.

Of the 14 OD statements, management has a stronger level of disagreement to only 2, and these 2 statements are among the 3 statements that do not have significant mean differences. Management disagrees that it has overestimated resistance to change, while rank-and-file are neutral; and managers disagree that the staff is open-minded toward change marginally more than rank-and-file. Although not significant, taken together, the ideas that management perceives more resistance and less open-mindedness suggest that management believes their staffs are generally resistant to change initiatives.

This perception is likely to influence how managers approach leading change. A one-sample t test indicates the quotient mean is significantly higher than the assumed population mean. Accordingly, rank-and-file have a negative attitude about changes in news values. In general, respondents think they are doing what they can to preserve some traditional journalism values in an era when newspapers are more market driven.

Responses to the individual statements shed some light on specific news value issues that shape respondents' attitudes (statement means noted parenthetically). Journalists agree that newspapers are doing a better job portraying a representative picture of society than in the past, but they are neutral about whether papers are doing better at providing a truthful account of the day's events in a meaningful context than in the past.

The rank-and-file journalists do not believe that content decisions are based solely on journalism criteria, as they agree strongly that more gossip, trivia, and non-news features are used to fill the paper and recent changes in design stress style over substance to the point that look and feel of the paper are more important to editors than the depth of the news.

They have slight agreement that their newspaper has less breaking news than before change initiatives, and significant disagreement that changes in the industry have made papers more thoughtful and provocative. Journalists feel the impact of new methods and structures on their news values.

They agree focus groups, surveys, and community meetings are good methods to generate ideas for news coverage, but they acknowledge an impact of organizational integration, showing strong agreement that journalists working at papers that have eliminated divisions between news and business are more likely to engage in self-censorship when writing about issues important to advertisers.

And they disagree that change has increased resources for practicing journalism and led to more investigative reporting. This point is underscored by journalists' agreement that an important issue is less likely to become news if it takes a great deal of time to uncover and report. The respondents see journalism independence, a traditional benchmark of news values and credibility, as on the road to obsolescence. Journalists agree that the opportunity for independent-minded publishers or editors to run their own newsrooms is coming to an end and are neutral when asked whether the role models for today's managers are those editors and publishers who in the past told the truth when it was not popular or profitable to do so.

ORGANIZATIONAL STRUCTURE

The quotient for the 12 statements that construct this variable is 3.55, which a one-sample t test shows is significant to the assumed population mean. This finding suggests that journalists generally responded negatively to the impact of changing newsroom structures. When viewed individually, the statement means indicate that journalists recognize that changes in structure (the most common being from beats to teams) have impacted their work, but seldom in ways theory would predict nor management would desire.

Journalists indicate modest (but significant) agreement that they work more closely with their colleagues than in the past, but they agree much more strongly that newsroom changes have too often meant attending meetings that cut into time spent on journalism. Contrary to theory, rank-and-file don't see that restructuring the newsroom has flattened the hierarchy, disagreeing strongly that the number of layers of management has decreased. This finding is reinforced by nearly equally strong agreement that newsroom restructuring seems to require more editors who send out memos about the new goals of restructuring. The journalists in this sample are still wary of the impact of cross-departmental teams, indicating strong disagreement that directors of advertising, circulation, and marketing should participate in news planning.

Also, they do not see a connection between the team structure and better journalism, disagreeing that reorganization has helped the staff better understand readers and that work teams have improved product quality. Moreover, the rank-and-file see media executives as having different values than they do, with executives more focused on market and strategy than on the experiences of their employees; respondents also disagree strongly that structural changes place more emphasis on nonprofit goals (organizational efficiency, the latest technology, product quality, and worker autonomy and creativity) than profit goals.

VARIABLES AFFECTING MORALE

Considering the vast amount of change being implemented at newspapers in the sample and the difficulties associated with OD in general, a particular interest of this research project was to measure the impact of change initiatives on morale. Toward this end, the variables constructed to measure the three concepts common to change efforts at newspapers - OD, news values, and organizational structure - were used as independent variables in a regression model to assess their relative impact on morale.

Because OD is a broad measure of change and OD initiatives impact an organization's structure and values, it was expected that the 4 variables (OD, news values, structure, and morale) would be highly correlated. This was indeed what occurred, as the correlations were all significant at the $p < .001$ level. A colinearity test for tolerance showed these correlations did not violate the assumptions of multiple regression. A multiple regression model was then built to test:

H3: Rank-and-file perceptions of organizational development will predict morale.

To control for the demographic variables of age, ethnicity, gender, experience, and duties, these variables were entered as a block into the regression model before the three independent variables. Experience, duties ("some managerial duties" or "no managerial duties"), and age were significant predictors in the block. Together, the demographic variables accounted for 5.77% of the variance.

H3 is supported. Organizational development, entered as the second block in the model, explained 45.8% of the variance after controlling for demographies. OD is clearly the strongest predictor of morale among all the independent variables. Accordingly, the data indicate that as rank-and-file's attitudes toward OD become more positive their morale increases; or, as rank-and-file's attitudes toward OD become more negative their morale decreases.

After all the independent variables were entered in the regression model, OD, structure, and news values are significant predictors of morale. However, after controlling for demographics, the explained variance each variable adds differs notably. OD explains 45.8% of the variance, organizational structure accounts for 7.8% of the variance and news values accounts for 2.0%. What is interesting is that news values, so basic to journalists' jobs and how they perceive their roles, explains a relatively small amount of the variance. Perhaps this is because in the midst of organizational changes that affect the most basic elements of work - schedules and routines - journalists continue to see the basic elements of news as information gathering, interviewing, writing, and editing.

It is logical that news values impact morale, but change initiatives that require training and re-ordering of work priorities, as well as newsroom restructuring, are tangible symbols of a new culture. Because they are the most easily identified signs of change, they are the most likely targets for acceptance or resistance. Thus, it appears that changes most affecting morale are those OD and restructuring initiatives that management believes will eventually reconstitute news. News values are changing, but the results suggest that among the types of change, rank-and-file see changing news values as having a smaller impact on their morale.

After all the variables were entered in the model, duties were also shown to be a significant predictor of morale. A dichotomous variable (0 = no managerial duties, 1 = some managerial duties), the negative beta weight indicates an inverse relationship.

In other words, journalists who have some managerial duties have significantly lower morale than those who have no managerial duties; or, those with no managerial duties have higher morale than those with some managerial duties. This result supports anecdotal evidence that change has been most difficult for low- and mid-level managers. These managers tend to get "squeezed" by change, expected to execute the change initiatives of top management while working most closely with non-managers.

Statements Not Part of Variables. The statements not part of variables also provide some useful insights. One of the research questions in this study was whether newsroom employees think the direction of change better fits the goals of journalism or marketing. As noted in the comparative results, of the 62 statements in the survey, rank-and-file's strongest agreement was with the statement: "There is more emphasis on maintaining or increasing the paper's profits than there used to be".

There was also strong agreement that newsroom managers have become increasingly aware of the concerns of stockholders and capital investors. Respondents think this increased awareness or pressure created by financial performance does not need to be expanded, as there is significant disagreement to the statement that the newspaper industry needs a culture that requires greater marketing intelligence in the newsroom. Taken together, these statements indicate rank-and-file journalists believe newspapers are becoming more sensitive to marketing and this movement has gone far enough.

There is also a concern about the ethical issues and threats to journalism independence that removing the wall between the news and business may initiate. There is strong agreement that ethical committees are needed to draft guidelines for editorial staff participation in promotional events and significant agreement that journalistic independence has helped establish newspapers as credible. The journalists in this sample still use journalism excellence as the standard for quality, and they like competition. Even in the era of increased profit pressures, there is significant disagreement that most newspaper companies would trade Pulitzer Prizes for consistently high profits, and, in an apparent longing for days past, respondents show strong agreement that journalism has suffered in the era of one-newspaper towns.

There is additional evidence that rank-and-file do not perceive OD as progressing in accordance with theory. Rank-and-file disagree that management has done a good job preparing employees for change, and they disagree that management has done a good job measuring the results of change. Respondents have even stronger beliefs that management is ego driven and inflexible. Rank-and-file agree that some managers have embraced formulas of change because they have invested so much money, time, and ego in them that they can't admit their lack of success. And there is a similar strong agreement to the idea that managers who have found resistance to change have responded by saying in effect, "The train is leaving the station, you can get on or get off".

Furthermore, journalists don't see change meeting its stated objectives, as they show strong agreement there is little evidence that common changes (i.e., redefining of news, newsroom restructuring, and use of emerging technologies) are attracting more readers and advertisers.

The data also lend support to the idea that news managers and the growing number of consultants employed in newsrooms misunderstand journalists' resistance to change. The journalists in this study do not see themselves as opposed to change; in fact, they show significant disagreement to the statement that they look forward to when change is no longer such a large part of work. But journalists tend to like to be left alone to do their jobs which runs counter to theory that predicts workers are happier when they collaborate and more productive in teams. The more than 450 rank-and-file in this sample significantly agree with the statement: "I am happier when I can work alone".

ANALYSIS BY CIRCULATION

Because organizational resources are determined in part by an organization's size and group dynamics can be impacted by group size, this study explored whether newspaper size (measured by circulation) impacted respondents' attitudes toward change. To test for differences by circulation, means for each variable were calculated by circulation size.

The data show that small newspapers are having more difficulty with change as it relates to two variables: OD and morale. A one-way analysis-of-variance test indicates that morale is significantly lower at small papers; also, small paper respondents indicate significantly higher disagreement that OD initiatives have been in accordance with theory. It is worth noting that the means for all four variables are higher for small papers.

These results also reveal no significant differences between mid-size and large papers. But perhaps more telling about this analysis is that there is not a positive attitude toward any of the variables at any size paper. In other words, even though some aspects of change are more difficult at small papers, these strata show that respondents do not believe change has gone well (or in accordance with theory) on any of the measures, regardless of newspaper size.

The challenge of change from the standpoint of management is getting rank-and-file to accept the core values that embody management's vision for a transformed newsroom culture. The data provide strong evidence that management's OD initiatives are failing to win rank-and-file support - regardless of whether the initiatives are in concert with theory. What is surprising in these findings is the extent to which management and rank-and-file disagree and how often.

Of the 20 statements that appeared on both surveys, there are significant differences on 15 of them. Of these 15, the responses to 9 statements indicate clear differences of attitudes, with one group agreeing and the other disagreeing. Of the 14 statements that construct the OD variable, there are significant differences on responses to 11 statements. Taken as a whole, the responses show that many important divisions exist between management and rank-and-file, and even when the groups can agree, they often disagree on their level of agreement. In many instances the gap between responses is so large that it is hard to understand the two groups are sharing the same experiences, and perhaps they are not. The groups' roles in the change process differ.

The sample of newsroom managers in this study is comprised of many of the nation's leading editors. Their involvement in the ASNE Change Committee reflects their interests beyond the walls of their newsrooms, and suggests they positioned themselves as leaders in an industry-wide effort to respond to the forces mandating change.

The rank-and-file in this sample must adapt to management's vision by executing their jobs in accordance with the new procedures and goals of change. Despite these different roles, however, as part of the same organizations, management and rank-and-file should share similar values. Both groups are journalists.

Management's self-assessment may be a bit optimistic, but it is grounded in reality and is at times unflatteringly candid. Managers have a great deal invested in change initiatives, both in terms of organizational resources and their individual careers. A role of management is to "see the big picture," which suggests that management should be able to assess the process and progress of change within its overall strategic goals better than rank-and-file.

Thus, management's general optimism regarding change may be a reflection that the broader process is proceeding in the right direction, even if certain aspects tend to get off course. The data support this. Management gives itself high marks for leadership and generally following the prescriptions for change articulated in OD models and theory. Management views itself as trying to do what should be done to enable change to succeed.

Yet, as Kanter suggests, change requires a "leap of faith" to get people to embrace an organizational reality that is not yet known. And on this issue, the data show management to be quite honest, admitting the entire change formula has not been worked out. Even more candid, however, is management's admission that certain parts of the process that it can control have not been well-managed. Management concedes that it has not adequately thought through the long-term implications of change, and it acknowledges there is not a system of rewards for work that meets the goals of change initiatives.

Accordingly, it is not surprising that management recognizes that its short-comings have contributed to a breakdown of trust with rank-and-file, while at the same time perceiving a cultural change that has improved the organization. This apparent contradiction must be perplexing and difficult for newsroom managers. There is some evidence in the data that managers are a bit frustrated, placing the "blame" for a lack of success on rank-and-file, who are perceived as close minded and resistant to change.

However, the results from the rank-and-file survey suggest it is not accurate to simply dismiss journalists as resistant to change. Rank-and-file indicate they accept change as a part of work and are personally committed to their paper's change efforts.

They credit their managers for taking leadership roles and being committed to change. However, they question the factors motivating change and are able to distinguish between intentions and results. In brief, while management says it has articulated a vision, included employees in creating changes, been flexible, and sought feedback about the change process, rank-and-file respond that they are confused about the vision, fool loft out of the process, and perceive their managers as inflexible.

Rank-and-file also sense management's vulnerability and frustration in leading change, showing strong agreement that change is ego driven by inflexible managers who, refusing to recognize its lack of success, resort to authoritarian measures to counter pockets of resistance. Rank-and-file's perception that management has failed at nearly every step of the process, combined with their sense that profit is increasingly important to newsroom managers, further explains the low level of trust rank-and-file express toward their managers.

Numerous scholars cite trust as a prerequisite condition for successful OD initiatives. Thus, despite management's general optimism about an improving newsroom culture, the breakdown of trust that both management and rank-and-file acknowledge does not bode well for continuing efforts at change, as theory suggests and common sense reveals that people do not readily accept the ideas of those whom they do not trust.

Beyond the organizational development issues associated with change, rank-and-file's skepticism about change can be understood by an apparent lack of producing successful results. Change initiatives are not only failing to create more efficient, productive, and happier newsrooms, they are also falling short on their stated goals. Journalists don't perceive changes as attracting more readers and advertisers, or helping to produce better newspapers. Instead, rank-and-file connect change initiatives with fewer resources for journalism in a more market-driven culture and industry.

Kanter, Drucker, Bergquist, and many organizational scholars would suggest that "breaking down the wall" between the newsroom and other departments in the news organization is an important step toward creating the "integrated" and "innovative" organizational culture required to meet challenges swiftly and capitalize on opportunities in the postmodern business world.

The data in this study suggest that rank-and-file perceive the new, integrated culture as a threat to their values, most of which are rooted in journalism.

Much of rank-and-file's resistance to change is related to a sense that the "journalism-based" culture of their newsrooms is being replaced with a culture that places less value on journalism norms. In this way, there is a cultural "battle" unfolding in news organizations as they become more integrated.

Harris, writing about the clash that occurs when an organization attempts to create a market-oriented culture, asserts that the market-oriented values that define the culture must come to dominate the existing cultures for the transformation to succeed.

This study indicates that this type of cultural struggle is being waged in newsrooms experimenting with change. When viewed in this regard, resistance to change can be understood as both rational and part of a cultural conflict. However, if cultural change is achieved through a combination of macro (values and beliefs) and micro forces (the tangible things such as practices, policies, and procedures that define daily life in the organization), then management's attempt to change the newsroom culture by changing the organization's structure and work routines appears to be well-advised and well under way.

This study also opens for re-examination several theoretical assumptions. The idea that modern newspaper organizations are characterized by complex, hierarchical bureaucracies and specialized labor appears to be less accurate today than it was before "change" became an industry buzzword and organizational goal. Media corporations, no doubt large bureaucracies, can however be understood to be "disassembling the assembly line." The goals of OD and change most often focus on creating flatter corporate flowcharts with the expectation that employees need to be more versatile and multiskilled.

Clearly, this is the opposite of labor specialization. Furthermore, the empowerment assumptions of restructuring hierarchical organizations into flatter, team-based units have not materialized for the rank-and-file journalists in this sample.

Rank-and-file understand restructuring as a mechanism that affords them fewer resources to practice journalism, and, contrary to theory, rank-and-file perceive restructuring has created more layers of managers and a more "managed" newsroom. The journalists in this sample say that the team-based structure has not brought them more autonomy, nor has it provided more decision-making authority.

It is possible that the empowerment expected to result from restructured newsrooms is misconceived. A primary rationale for less hierarchical organizations is the team-based structure unleashes the knowledge and creativity of lower level employees. This view presupposes that management, under the hierarchical structure, has not previously afforded employees the power to effectively utilize these assets. However, this assumption seems to neglect the nature of newspaper work, which has traditionally afforded rank-and-file a great deal of latitude, encouraging journalists to apply their knowledge and be creative.

Long before empowerment became a management cliche, Gassaway's 1984 social construction work found that rank-and-file journalists and newspaper managers negotiate for power, with rank-and-file having considerable leverage, because as newsgatherers they control the initial flow of information.

Furthermore, journalism is one of the few occupations where employees at the bottom of the corporate ladder consider themselves professionals. Valuable newsroom employees have long been those who could work well on their own, digging for stories and building relationships with sources. Interviewing is a craft, writing and design are forms of self-expression, and editing is a skill built on an individual's grasp of language and professional values.

To require journalists to give up the individual nature of their work asks them to sacrifice some of the skills that have become a part of their professional identities. There is strong evidence in this study that journalists have not accepted the idea that team-based newsrooms empower them or better utilize their skills.

This finding supports previous research and reinforces the idea that the organizational theory that managers are using to empower their employees and restructure their newsrooms could be misapplied, as it misunderstands the nature of newspaper journalism work.

The assumptions about the organizational role of management are changing, too. This study finds little support that newsroom managers are "technocrats" who value organizational and technical development more than the profit goals of their "capitalist" owners. The data indicate it is more accurate, as Kanter and others suggest, to understand change as a process of integration, where the marketing goals of the traditional "business side" of the news organization have become more apparent to journalists and more valued by management throughout the organization.

Galbraith's "approved contradiction" concept - that innovative managers will focus on professional and organizational goals while returning just enough profit to keep their capitalist owners satisfied - is a core assumption of Demers'research on the corporate newspaper. This study found little support for the existence of an approved contradiction; rather, managers and rank-and-file perceive change as both market and profit driven at the expense of organizational issues thought to be of prime concern to professional managers (product quality, technology, and employee development).

These findings suggest that modern news executives are no longer "technocrats" in the sense Galbraith defined them, but are closer to the "capitalists" who sought maximum financial return on their investments. The practice of offering newsroom managers incentives (salary bonuses or stock options) tied to the financial performance of the company is one way corporations subtly "disapprove" of the approved contradiction.

LIMITATIONS OF THE STUDY

An obvious shortcoming of this survey method is that it can only provide a "snapshot" of attitudes at the time of the study. Change is an ongoing process, and the instruments used can only provide a one-time glimpso of the process. As the change process unfolds in newsrooms across the country, it would be wise to continue to monitor change initiatives and journalists' attitudes toward them. Also, this study did not attempt to measure the amount of change orthe phases of the change process. Thus, while all the respondents have a commonality of change experiences, it is not clear if attitudes toward change differ based on the amount of change or stages in the change process.

There is also a chance to refine the instruments and measures of change used in this study. Organizational development research has generally focused on one organization at a time, using site-specific variables. By taking a different approach, there were very few established measures. Accordingly, the attempt here was to create "tools" from which scholars can begin to empirically assess change.

Suggestions for future research. The findings in this study point to several theoretical areas that should prove fertile ground for exploration. This study adds to the small amount ol research thai suggests restructuring newsrooms into team-based systems does not "empower" journalists in the manner theory predicts. If team-based newsrooms are the future of the industry, then changing organizational relationships spawned by restructuring offer interesting opportunities for study. Among some of the questions these changes suggest: Do team-based structures impact the ways journalists work with one another? Do teams impact the ways journalists develop relationships and interact with their sources?

Do teams require and reward different personality traits? How does the resourceful journalist, the "gumshoe" who worked well alone, often producing front page stories in the beat system, perform in the team structure?

Do team-based newsrooms produce different content than the beat system does? And possibly most important to understanding the values that will drive the industry in the future are the questions of management influence and power. Do newsroom managers and editors see themselves as the innovative "technocrats" that theory presupposes?

How much influence do newsroom managers have when it comes to setting the vision for change? To what extent do newsroom managers embrace the changes they are expected to lead? These questions, along with the need to develop better change-related measures over time (throughout the process of change], provide an abundance of directions for research.

This study surveyed a purposive sample of the nation's newspaper managers most experienced in industry-wide change initiatives; it also surveyed a much larger sample of rank-and-file from those same papers. The managers in this study have, in effect, used their newsrooms as laboratories to experiment with new and far-reaching change initiatives. These changes have become - depending on whom you ask - new standards of excellence or points of controversy and resistance.

Although the results from this purposive sample cannot be generalized to the entire industry, the relatively large sample gives a good indication of what change has meant to journalists at newspapers on the cutting edge of industry-wide change. These findings should prove useful for the many news managers and editors who find their newsrooms embarking on or considering similar change initiatives. This study has also tested the key concepts of organizational development, making it one of only a few attempts to understand the complexities of newspaper industry change through the lens of organizational theory.

Given the size of the sample and the scope of the newspapers (circulations ranging from 5,000 to more than 1,000,000, including public, private, and family-owned papers that are located in every major geographic region of the country), this study represents one of the largest scale attempts to date to assess journalists' perceptions about change initiatives that are sweeping through newsrooms nationwide.

Management, despite some res- ervations about the market-driven nature of change, thinks it is doing reasonably well following the guidelines of organizational development in a manner consistent with creating a more outer-directed and reader-driven newsroom culture. In short, management believes it has "managed" the change process in general accordance with theory.

Rank-and-file, on the other hand, feel more victims of change than participants in it. The gulf between management and rank-and-file experiences with change has facilitated a breakdown in trust that could seriously hamper ongoing change initiatives. Morale among rank-and-file is low, and data suggest it is getting worse.

The newspaper industry finds itself in the throes of a cultural revolution precipitated by internal and external forces. Yet, the industry remains highly profitable and has shown resiliency in the information age, remaining a respected and widely utilized source of news and information. The predictions of doom are far from materializing, but many of the challenges that served as catalysts for cultural change remain. The findings of this study suggest there is a struggle unfolding between the core values of two cultures - marketing and journalism - and rank-and-file perceive organizational development efforts are focused on creating a more dominant marketing culture, often at the expense of journalistic norms.

This study has extended previous change research by approaching the problem differently. Organizational research has seldom been conducted on more than one organization at a time, and its methods are usually qualitative. The constructs in this study held up quite well to tests of reliability and statistical analysis, showing the depth of common experiences of journalists at newspapers implementing change. An important methodological finding of this study is that change can be studied at more than one newspaper at a time. Studies that go beyond site-specific variables are possible, which should encourage more research using larger, representative samples with the goal of testing and building theory.

Chapter 9

Principles in the basic News Reporting Classroom

Basic news reporting classes offer us an excellent opportunity to alert future journalists to important aspects of human perception such as those studied in the field of general semantics. Reporting required identifying and discovering enormously complex events and responsibly representing them in summary form. Even the most energetic and capable reporter, however, cannot discover all the complexity and detail available in a single observation of a single event, and describe it while still meeting deadlines. Scholars in the field of general semantics have made the study of perception central to their discipline, and acquainting novice reporting students with some of their findings can help students understand the role perception plays in reporting.

Journalism scholarship includes perception among its many areas of investigation, but the articles that focuc on perception tend to primarily identify examples of differences in the way people perceive and how these differences contribute to interpretation of events.

Eberhard demonstrates that "news value" treatments differ among newswriting texts; Van Ommeren shows that knowing reporters' backgrounds changed student views about published stories; McAdams examines relationships between psycholinguistics and perception; Allen shows that journalists often do not explain how disparate pieces of information fit together; Stocking and Gross establish that people make errors in assessing risks; and Abbott and Slattery explore topics like "intuitive goods ears." Journalism scholarship does not appear to have directly focused on examining and explaining human perception as it relates to observing and interpreting human behaviors and world events.

Allen perhaps comes closer to recognizing a need for specific focus on perception than most scholars when she observes that we need to be "...more aware of culture as a blueprint for perception..." and suggests "But neither anthropologists nor journalists nor educators nor anyone else is assuming the responsibility for sharing the contextual frameword necessary for interpreting this morass of data..." Stocking and Gross suggest we may be "unknowingly failing our students and profession" not only in failing to point out common perception errors, but also in not developing exercises that "...will provide opportunities for learning about cognitive distortions without sacrificing the basics." We propose the field of general semantics and specific focus on human perception as one contribution to meeting Stocking and Gross' requesting.

If you ask basic news reporting students (or even experienced reporters for that matter) if their stories accurately represent what actually happened in a given instance, they are likely to say yes. They are used to relying on the fact that as humans they have sophisticated powers of observation and are able to quickly process large amounts of stimuli. They might readily accept the analogy that they record events much like a camera.

Korzybski, the founder of the general semantics movement, suggested even the mosot careful observer is unable to observe all stimuli within range. Bois offered an extension of Korzybski's work in a somewhat more understandable form. Both authors offered models that explained how perception necessarily differs from a given stimulus field. The models also show how perception may even result in reports that add up to more, or in some cases less, than the sum of the stimuli observed. Russell has adapted these earlier perception models and added to their range. This modified model may help basic news writing students understand that, much like a camera, their perception is limited and subject to distortion.

AVAILABLE STIMULI

This human perception model illustrates how perception is incomplete and how it always differs from the observed stimulus field. The open-sided box on the left represents the infinite stimulus field containing all individual stimuli potentially observable (dots). Some of the stimuli are in free space and others are within contained areas labeled Remembered Past, Attended to Present and Anticipated Future.

The Remembered Past box represents our ability to recall some, but not all, of the events from our past. We can recall events in varying degrees of completeness, but never completely. Our recall of these events can serve as a filter of present and future events. For example, previous deception by an assumed reputable source can influence belief in a present source.

The Attended to Present box represents stimuli available for detection in the present. Again, these stimuli are not all of the stimuli available. Fewer stimuli are attended to than are available. Psychological experiments show only a few of any available stimuli may be attended to by the senses and consciously registered at any one time. Magicians and three-card monte players know this principle well, as do sources who mislead by answering with an avalanche of irrelevant facts instead of those few facts which would answer a question.

The Anticipated Future box represents stimuli thought to be probable in the future. Those things, which are inconceivable to the subject simply do not exist in this perceptual frame. But items in an anticipated future can filter both present and remembered stimuli. For example, suddenly realizing that a source, caught in a compromising position, plans to lie to protect his reputation, could contribute to reconsideration of his previous comments and also the conclusion that his present comments may be untrue.

The model presumes a balanced individual in whom the Attended to Present is larger than the other two areas. Healthy observers pay more attention to the present than to their Remembered Past or Anticipated Future. This apparent contradiction must be perplexing and difficult for newsroom managers. There is some evidence in the data that managers are a bit frustrated, placing the "blame" for a lack of success on rank-and-file, who are perceived as close minded and resistant to change.

However, the results from the rank-and-file survey suggest it is not accurate to simply dismiss journalists as resistant to change. Rank-and-file indicate they accept change as a part of work and are personally committed to their paper's change efforts. They credit their managers for taking leadership roles and being committed to change. However, they question the factors motivating change and are able to distinguish between intentions and results. In brief, while management says it has articulated a vision, included employees in creating changes, been flexible, and sought feedback about the change process, rank-and-file respond that they are confused about the vision, fool loft out of the process, and perceive their managers as inflexible.

Rank-and-file also sense management's vulnerability and frustration in leading change, showing strong agreement that change is ego driven by inflexible managers who, refusing to recognize its lack of success, resort to authoritarian measures to counter pockets of resistance. Rank-and-file's perception that management has failed at nearly every step of the process, combined with their sense that profit is increasingly important to newsroom managers, further explains the low level of trust rank-and-file express toward their managers. Numerous scholars cite trust as a prerequisite condition for successful OD initiatives. Thus, despite management's general optimism about an improving newsroom culture, the breakdown of trust that both management and rank-and-file acknowledge does not bode well for continuing efforts at change, as theory suggests and common sense reveals that people do not readily accept the ideas of those whom they do not trust.

Beyond the organizational development issues associated with change, rank-and-file's skepticism about change can be understood by an apparent lack of producing successful results. Change initiatives are not only failing to create more efficient, productive, and happier newsrooms, they are also falling short on their stated goals. Journalists don't perceive changes as attracting more readers and advertisers, or helping to produce better newspapers.

Instead, rank-and-file connect change initiatives with fewer resources for journalism in a more market than they disseminate information. She suggests that management's lack of use of channels of communication, especially upward channels, limits feedback from lower level employees who do the work of the organization. This approach can affect the success of change efforts, as "changes in status, reward structures, job descriptions, roles, work methods, work relationships, and procedures bring significant organizational issues to the surface" that increase rank-and-file employees' need to communicate with their supervisors.

Other influences, such as physical condition and competing stimuli can also serve to filter perceptions, of course, but the five offered above can begin to help students in recognizing human perception is more complex than a simple stimulus-response act.

CLASSIFY

This box only has only one dot in it which represents the tendency in human perception to think in terms of classes and thereby reduce something complex into something overly simple. Classification encourage equating the characteristics of new members of a class, with characteristics of established members of the class. Perhaps, the intent is to help understand the world, but the outcome is more often to ignore important differences among members of the class. Making the comparison with known members of the class can contribute to assuming the new member is "exactly like" the known members. For example, knowing that a source is a Catholic could contribute to assuming she is opposed to abortion "because Catholics oppose abortion."

NAME

The box also only has one dot in it to represent yet an additional reduction of stimuli that are attended to. In naming, something complex is overly simplified. For example, a complex and unique individual can be reduced to "politician," or a thousand separate activities can become "war." Names represent on enormous reduction of available and observed stimuli.

MEANING

This box represents an expansion of the reduction process that has occurred in the first three boxes. At this stage of perception, individuals begin to determine the meaning of their experiences. Scholars in the field of general semantics hold that meaning is something created by an interaction between the individual and stimuli. The increased number of dots in the meaning box represents the capacity of expand what was previously reduced.

The additional dots in the box do not mean the available stimuli, or only those attended to have been faithfully reproduced. For example, a police officer could primarily attend to the reflection of light in a suspect's hand, and conclude the reflecting object is a gun. The officer may then assign this perceived stimuli to mean danger and that he must therefore protect himself.

Meaning is a very private construct and the meanings of stimuli are not necessarily universally shared. Assuming they are may lead to misunderstanding. Determining that a public official is acting out of caution or weakness can be as much the consequence o the observer's assigning meaning as the official's actions.

The final box represents an additional reduction inthe perception process. The fewer dots in this box compared to the meaning box suggests we are unable to share all of our private meanings. This is particularly important for reporters since time and space constraints alone will always limit their ability to offer all that they know.

The lines going out of the What We Can Share box enter the available stimuli for others. This area is represented by a question mark because we have no way to be sure what others do with our stimuli. The number and nature of dots in their perceptual field is subject to their control and limits, not to the journalist's.

As a result of long experience in assigning meaning in particular situations, a reporter may understand the implications in a political candidate's refusing to debate an oppenent. Merely reporting the action, however, does not mean the reader will automatically grasp these implications.

Exposing news reporting students to the models of human perception suggested by general semanticists may help students appreciate what Harrison Salisbury (1988) recognized after many years of reporting.

[The war in Vietnam] was the first of the separating images which, as time went on, showed me that in war, as in the simplest things in life, truth is multifaceted, a crystal that refracts light in many forms and many shapes, the quicksilver of the mind.

Basic news reporting students who can understand and appreciate that human preception is not a simple stimulus-response act, and is always incomplete can perhaps begin to demonstrate what has been called maturity and good news judgement. If they can be taught their observations are by definition incomplete, perhaps they will learn to ask even more questions and search for more sources and vantage points before concluding they have observed and reported everything.

Admission criteria for journalism and mass communications programs vary, ranging from a GPA requirement, to satisfactory completion of an introductory course, to use of language skills examinations. Concerns about admission requirements surfaced in the mid-1970s when enrollment growth began to exceed programme resources and was accompanied by a decline in scores on national standardized college entrance tests, especially in verbal scores reflecting writing achievement.

Results of a 2003 ACT National Curriculum Survey of high school and college instructors found that while college instructors believe grammar and usage skills are important skills for entering college students, high school teachers ranked these skills as least important. However, writing for the National Review Online, Ridgley (2003) laid the blame for declining writing skills on universities that fail to teach writing basics and place a misdirected focus on "strange literary theories."

Ridgley, a former executive director of the Collegiate Network, a national association of college newspapers, and a Duke University instructor, lamented that too many college students graduate "without the ability to express themselves with the written word".

For graduates of mass communications programs, such inability threatens the very core of a profession that depends upon communications skills. This concern about students' weak writing skills has been echoed by many, including Maxwell (2002), who in an article in the Alameda Times-Star wrote: "They [students] need to learn the craft and art of writing.

Unfortunately, most writing-across-the-curriculum programs are too hit-and-miss to inculcate a love of writing or even an attitude of appreciating the importance of writing".

This chapter examines one department of journalism's efforts to identify, address, and correct basic writing deficiencies for students seeking a journalism degree with a concentration in news-editorial, broadcast, or public relations.

Northwestern State University's (NSU) Department of Journalism, located in a mid-sized, open-admissions university in the rural South, initiated a writing diagnostic test as a prerequisite for admission to the gateway media writing course required of all majors. To assist students failing the test, the department created a new elective course, "Literacy Skills for Journalists".

This preliminary report presents the findings and discussion based on initial data collection and instructor observations.

These results provided a platform for discussing the efficacy of requiring diagnostic writing tests for admission into a journalism programme and the most effective methods to remediate poor writing, to teach writing basics, to focus students' attention on the importance of good writing, and, ultimately, to develop writing skills acceptable for entry-level mass communications positions.

Bissell and Collins found in their research that writing deficiencies have not gone unnoticed at the college level. However, the issue remains: what are universities doing to correct students' writing deficiencies?

For journalism programs, corrective action is critical because writing remains at the profession's core. Kunkel, dean of the Merrill College of Journalism at the University of Maryland, stated succinctly, "Writing instructors are obligated to teach the fundamentals of media writing". Calling journalism writing "part skill, part craft and part art" he said that students should have a solid foundation in reporting, writing, and editing.

The LSDT was administered to 175 students between spring 2001 and 2003. While some quantitative figures for the LSDT pass-fail rates and for successful completion of the basic media writing course were identified, both the data and faculty member observations, at this point, are more qualitative in nature.

The database used for this study includes LSDT test data, ACT scores, and grades in prerequisite English and journalism courses. Additionally, identification of effective methods for data collection and analysis are ongoing. The initial findings and conclusions presented in this chapter represent efforts to address a curriculum problem through an action research project.

The Unit's diagnostic assessment and foundations course were created with the following beliefs:

1. Many students enter the programme with weak writing skills;
2. The results of the LSDT will alert students and faculty to writing deficiencies;
3. Poor writing skills can be improved with added emphasis and through curriculum offerings;
4. Students who pass the LSDT and the literacy skills course will successfully complete the basic media writing course; and
5. A writing diagnostic requirement will emphasize the importance of writing skills for journalism majors.

THE FINDINGS

Data for this study were gathered over five fall and spring semesters during the 2001-2003 academic years. Basic descriptive statistics were calculated based on this data. Since the initial data were sparse, findings are reported below as frequencies and as percentages.

1. As of spring 2003, 175 students have taken the LSDT. Of these, 100 students (57%) failed to perform at the expected level.
2. Of those who took the LSDT, 29 students (91%) having ACT-English scores requiring a developmental English placement (ACT 0-17) did not meet minimum scores on the LSDT. Of those students having ACT-English scores not requiring a developmental placement (ACT 18-27), 66 students (49%) failed to meet the minimum score requirement on the LSDT.
3. All students who initially did not meet minimum scores on the LSDT, took the JOUR 1010, and afterward met minimum score requirements on the LSDT earned average final grades of"B" and "C" in the gateway media writing course (JOUR 2510). None, however, earned a final grade of "A."
4. Of those 100 students who did not meet minimum

scores on the LSDT, 55 students (55%) have not yet taken JOUR 1010 and have not been admitted to the gateway course;

5. Students who took the gateway course after successfully completing the remedial course and passing the LSDT (38) earned grades of "B" and "C" in the gateway course.
6. An analysis of English course placement indicated that 19 students (21%) who obtained three hours of credit in freshman English (ENGL 1010) based on ACT scores (28-31) passed the LSDT. All seven students who received six hours of credit in freshman English (ENGL 1010, 1020) based on ACT scores (32 and higher) passed the LSDT.
7. Not enough evidence was available to determine the significant effects of successful completion of ENGL 1010 and 1020 on the pass rate of the LSDT. However, an analysis of grades in freshman English reveals that students who received a grade of "C" or higher in the prerequisite freshman English courses experienced equal success in the gateway media writing course.

Since the implementation of the prerequisite diagnostic test, faculty members have noted three major outcomes: (1) more instruction and activities have focused on media writing principles and techniques, rather than writing remediation; (2) grades averages have improved; and (3) students' confidence in their writing abilities and awareness of the importance of these skills for the profession have lessened the complaints (whining) about instructor emphasis on correct language usage.

Students' increased confidence correlates to the importance of student self-efficacy in a media writing course, as described by Collins and Bissell (2002).

This study, based on a pilot diagnostic and basic writing skills course, validated faculty members' beliefs and the literature that addresses poor preparation for college-level writing. Specifically, findings from this study indicated that a majority (57%) of those students taking the LSDT did not meet minimum requirements for success. Of this group, those having developmental English placements based on ACT-English test scores constituted the largest non-success rate on the LSDT (91%). Of note, however, is the significant number of students with no developmental English course placements (49%) who failed to meet the minimum score requirement on the LSDT.

One of the more important findings was that all students who initially did not meet minimum score requirements on the LSDT, who successfully completed JOUR 1010, and afterward passed the LSDT earned passing grades in the gateway media writing course.

The study also found that earned credit in the first English course only does not provide the adequate preparation needed to meet the requirements of the LSDT. However, credit in both ENGL 1010 and 1020 yielded a 100% pass rate.

Lack of sufficient evidence precludes determining the significant effects of successful completion of ENGL 1010 and 1020 on the pass rate of the LSDT as well as precluding determining the significant effect of "C" or higher grades in the prerequisite freshman English courses on success in the gateway media writing course.

The findings, though sketchy, warrant future investigation into the efficacy of diagnostic tests likes the LSDT and basic writing skills coursework for journalism majors.

Continued collection of data will allow for more significant data interpretation. Additionally, a more in-depth look at the basic writing skills course and its effect on improved writing skills is needed. Nonetheless, the findings to date have validated the need for assessing writing skills and providing corrective programs.

Faculty members in this department have commented on students' general poor preparation for college-level writing and the lack of student interest or motivation to write well and often, or both.

Writing, like any skill, takes practice. The best can take that skill from a craft to an art. One challenge is to have journalism majors meet basic skill requirements and be able to advance academically and professionally based on their studies, talents, and desires. The second challenge will be to better understand how best to teach writing and motivate students. The LSDT and literacy skills course are efforts to remediate weak writing and position students for curriculum and career success.

Chapter 10

Civic Utility of the News

All three publics for the news intuitively grasp the idea of civic utility, and among all three publics there are strong beliefs that much of what one finds in the daily news lacks relevance.

Public opinion polls and focus groups can detail these views with considerable specificity—whether ascertaining overall evaluations of news media performance or evaluations of the coverage about individual issues, public figures and other topics.

This kind of research is needed on a continuing basis to measure exactly how effective the news media are as public communicators, to measure how relevant citizens find the content of the news media, and how much the public has learned from this content.

Moreover, this research should go beyond general descriptions of how the public responds to the daily news and measure the performance of the news media against some very specific criteria. One source for these criteria is the venerable Hutchins Commission report, "A *Free and Responsible Press.*" However, before reviewing the criteria for media performance advanced by that commission, some important aspects of its background need to be noted.

Although this report is most frequently discussed in the idealistic context of social responsibility theory—one of the grand macrotheories, along with the libertarian and authoritarian theories, of how the mass media are organized in various societies—the origins of this report were imminently practical.

The commission was suggested to University of Chicago Chancellor Robert Hutchins by *Time* magazine founder and publisher Henry Luce and substantially funded by Time Inc. However, the members of the commission, distinguished academics and public officials of their day, enjoyed complete freedom in their deliberations.

Their comprehensive analysis of the mass media, not just the news media of their day but also movies and books, identified five requirements for a free and responsible press in a democratic society:

- A truthful, comprehensive, and intelligent account of each day's events in a context that brings out their full meaning. There is already enough in this initial criterion of media performance to fill the questionnaire of a public opinion poll or discussion guide for focus groups. And numerous examples already have been offered here of gaps and irrelevancies in daily news coverage. But there is more to consider.
- A forum for the exchange of comment and criticism, a requirement that advocates of public journalism contend goes considerably beyond letters to the editor, op-ed pieces and occasional news reports on public hearings, civic debates and other incidental public affairs events.
- A representative picture of the various social groups that constitute American society, a requirement that has taken on considerable significance since September 11th. The importance of understanding people who trace their ethnic and cultural background to the Middle East, other parts of Asia, and to Latin America was further underscored by the 2000 Census with its detailed findings on the substantial immigrant population of the United States. It is also particularly important to take note of the long history of public reports

seeking better understanding of racial relations and tensions in our country.

- Presentation and clarification of our country's goals and values, a requirement inextricably linked with the previous requirement because of the increasing cultural complexity of the country as a whole and its individual cities, towns and neighborhoods. Noting that the mass media are "an educational instrument, perhaps the most powerful there is, " the Commission also observed, "The mass media, whether or not they wish to do so, blur or clarify these ideals as they report the failings and achievements of every day. "
- Facilitation of citizens' full access to information about the current state of public affairs. Facilitating full access does not ignore differences in an individual citizen's need for orientation or the existence of multiple publics for the day's news.

We do not assume that all citizens at all times will actually use all the material they receive. By necessity or choice large numbers of people voluntarily delegate analysis and decision to leaders who they trust. Such leadership in our society is freely chosen and constantly changing; it is informal, unofficial, and flexible. Any citizen may at any time assume the power of decision.

In this way, the government is carried on by consent. To paraphrase a more recent *New York Times* advertising campaign touting that newspaper's extensive news coverage, "You may not read it all, but isn't it comforting to know that it is there." Especially in a time of declining political participation, maintaining the option for every citizen to participate in a knowledgeable way is critical.

There are three publics for the daily news, and news media have a responsibility to be effective communicators to all three. This requires careful professional reflection about the choices made each day for the media agenda. It also requires precise measurement of the public's response to this agenda, explicit feedback that measures the effectiveness of journalists as public communicators with a vital social role.

Much like those swelling waves that can move across the vast reaches of the Pacific Ocean, steadily growing in size and momentum until their gigantic flood engulfs some isolated island, a vast technological wave moved relentlessly across the 20th century and pounded onto our shores in this new millennium.

Early in that century, radio—the first of the electronic mass media— supplemented the hundreds of newspapers and magazines. By midcentury, television added to the reach and power of mass communication, soon augmented by ever expanding cable television channels.

As the century moved toward its close, the personal computer and the Internet opened a vast new universe of information, a combination of an international yellow pages targeted at specific individual needs and an international newsstand offering mass media from every corner of the world with every perspective on the day's news. Technological marvels—the gee-whiz stuff of feature stories— had created a gigantic wave of information.

Although there always has been a tendency to view new communication technologies as unmitigated blessings, as a panacea for our social problems, it also always has been the case that reality soon provides a corrective discount. This already is apparent in regard to the flood of information chan nels now available to us. The lessons to be learned from Postman and Thoreau in this regard were cited at the very beginning of this book. More is not necessarily better.

MEDIA COMPETITION AND DIVERSITY

In elaborating why more is not automatically better, we preface our discussion of the situation here in the new millennium by reviewing a widely shared belief about mass communication, the belief that competition creates diversity.

As the number of daily newspapers in the United States receded from 1,772 morning and evening papers in 1950 to

1,480 dailies at the end of the century, leaving more and more cities with a single newspaper voice and an ever-smaller number of companies owning a larger and larger proportion of the newspapers still publishing, critics viewed these trends with great alarm.

In their view, the marketplace of ideas—the supply of news and opinion— became significantly less diverse when a competitor disappeared from the market and left a city with only a single daily newspaper.

In those earlier times when daily newspapers were the dominant mass media, the presence of competing daily newspapers in a community was taken as prima facie evidence of diversity in the supply of news and opinion. But was that true? Or, alternatively, is the menu of news and opinion available to the audience largely determined by the traditions and practices of journalists regardless of the ownership structure?

The traditions of journalism centre on news values and ethical standards, such as balance and fairness, and the homogenizing influence of these traditions on news content have been traced as far back as the 19th century. The routines of news gathering—for example, the organization of news beats, reliance on press releases, and covering events, many of which are staged specifically to attract press attention—further define the homogenous behaviour of journalists across news organizations. The social perspectives of journalism are a centripetal force for a centrist convergence on social and political issues.

In short, this body of evidence on the sociology of news collectively predicts that news media competing in the same geographic and demographic markets will produce highly similar, not diverse, products. Back in the time when there were competing newspapers in many cities, a detailed content analysis of the situation in 23 cities across the United States found minor differences at best between the "leaders" and "trailers" in 22 categories of content.

Nor was there any difference in the proportion of the newshole that was devoted to news and editorial content.

This null relationship between competition and diversity of content is succinctly summed up by the title of another article on this topic, Rivals in Conformity.

Further perspective on this question is gained from a comparison of competing newspapers in Cleveland, Ohio, Winnipeg, Manitoba, and Montreal, Quebec prior to the end of competition in those cities and a further comparison of the surviving newspaper before and after the suspension of its competitor. Detailed comparisons of general content categories for the entire newspaper, of more specific categories for the news of the day appearing in the front section of the newspaper, and of the geography of the news coverage essentially produced portraits of rivals in conformity.

An additional qualitative analysis of the Montreal newspapers' coverage of an extensive regional power blackout indicates that the readers of both Montreal papers received virtually the same facts from the same sources over a three-day period. Nor were there any major changes for better or worse in these three surviving newspapers a year after the disappearance of their competitors.

A comprehensive look at the broad mix of nine news media available to Chapel Hill, N. C., voters during the 1972 presidential election is compelling testimony about the homogeneous nature of the marketplace of ideas. There was no local daily in Chapel Hill, but voters used four dailies from nearby cities, the *New York Times*, two television networks, and two newsmagazines as major sources of information about the issues in the campaign.

Comparisons of the pattern of news coverage among these nine news media can be summarized by correlation coefficients in which 1.0 is a perfect match and 0.0 is no match at all. Among the four local newspapers, the median correlation is +.90. Across this entire mix of news media the median correlation is a hearty +.78.

Despite the technological diversity of these media of communication and the significant diversity in the geography spread and demography of their audiences, when these news organizations look out at the issues of the day, their observations are virtually identical. A multiplicity of media voice is no guarantee of diversity in content.

There is a tremendous amount of redundancy across the news media. More frequently means more of the same. Professional norms of journalism, more than the presence of competition from other news media, determine the range of content available to the audience.

As to the quality of that content, little seems to have changed since Raymond Nixon and Robert Jones drew this prescient conclusion after an extensive mid-20th-century examination of 420 competitive and noncompetitive U. S. daily dailies:

Differences in quality seem to hinge upon the "social responsibility and professional competence" of those who own and operate the papers, irrespective of whether they have competition.

At the time of this observation, a media company typically was a corporation that owned a large number of newspapers and perhaps a scattering of broadcast properties. Over the last half of the 20th century the media companies grew ever larger, frequently buying smaller groups of newspapers and adding a variety of other communication operations ranging from cable television franchises to outdoor billboards.

By the new millennium, the reach of the major media companies included various mixes of newspapers, magazines, broadcasting, cable television, book publishing, television and feature film production, and dot-corn ventures on the Internet. In this setting, the magic word was *synergy*, the business world's equivalent of "the whole is greater than the sum of its parts."

It was anticipated that the presence of so many outlets under a single umbrella would generate greater momentum and excitement. But in many cases the result was no more than the redundancy of existing material across more outlets. In the case of the online versions of many daily newspapers, the jargon for the software used to transfer this material to the Web was "shovelware."

Just shovel the stuff from the newspaper onto the Web. For the producers of media content, particularly news, there are now more outlets for the distribution of this news. More channels create greater convenience for the public, but not necessarily any greater diversity in the availability of useful content.

From another perspective, more channels create greater inconvenience both for the public and for journalists and other producers of media content. For journalists, the basic problem is that by traditional definitions of what is news there is only a limited supply of news most days. How to fill all these outlets—and attempt to maintain some appearance of differentiation among them to attract an audience—is a major problem.

Contemporary solutions to this problem have produced two trends: fragmentation and the blurring of the line between news and entertainment. The news cycle—once a relatively clean dichotomy between morning and evening newspapers and a distinct set of television news programs spaced across the day—has grown ever shorter for all the electronic media.

To reduce the sheer repetition of the same news over and over, new stories often are rushed onto the air or onto the web site in rudimentary outline on the flimsiest of sourcing. Audiences are bombarded with scattered fragments, many of which are later retracted. This approach to news reporting is more likely to produce bewildered citizens who are not sure how to assemble these scattered fragments into any meaningful mosaic.

But even this strategy is dependent on the existence of real news, which is a relatively scarce commodity. So the set of acceptable stories for the news report has expanded, a strategy that helps solve the problem of how to fill voracious newsholes and that offers the potential of creating synergy between the news report and other media products produced by the same corporation.

In practice, the frequent result has been a blurring of the line between news and entertainment. The focus of the synergy often is a new television programme or feature film that receives a level of attention far beyond any thing that press agents or publicists of past decades would have imagined in their wildest fantasies.

There is, of course, another form of entertainment that is wholly journalistic in its origin— scandals and sensational behaviour. Once virtually the exclusive province of the supermarket tabloids, the last decade has seen a running catalog of these stories. O. J. Simpson and Monica Lewinsky were just the most visible tips of an ever growing iceberg.

Journalists have always sought good stories to attract the interest of an audience. But in recent times this narrative imperative—the urge to tell a good story—has taken on startling dimensions. Is it possible that the deluge of these salacious tidbits from running stories that offer little more that the satisfaction of curiosity— some would say prurient interest—are linked to the steady decline in the news audiences for all media and in the continuing decline of public trust in the news media?

THE END OF MEDIA AGENDA SETTING

A vast array of agendas are now readily available to the public, leading some social observers to predict the end of agenda setting as audiences fragment and virtually everyone has a unique media agenda that is a highly individualized composite constructed from a vast wealth of news and information sources.

The result of these idiosyncratic personal agendas will be a public agenda characterized by diversity and the scattering of attention, some observers predict. Perhaps it is even incorrect to speak of a public agenda in these circumstances, they suggest.

This perspective on the future is the antithesis of the long-standing situation in mass communication characterized by large audiences receiving highly redundant agendas from the media. As previously noted, the initial observations in Chapel Hill, NC, of the agenda-setting influence of the news found substantial similarity—a median correlation of +.78—

among the nine media agendas that were the dominant sources of news and information for voters.

Obviously, this degree of similarity is not found across the total array of Web sites on the Internet, leading to the prediction that the era of agenda setting is coming to an end. But like so many prognostications about the magic of a new technology as the source of radical change, these predictions about the disappearance of any substantial agenda-setting influence simply may be wrong.

Predictions about the disappearance of agenda setting as a potent social force are grounded in a broad assumption that audiences will fragment and avail themselves of vastly different media agendas. Corollary to this assumption is the expectation that the redundancy across outlets characteristic of mass communication for many decades will be greatly reduced as niche media offer very different agendas.

Moreover, there is the expectation that a substantial number of individuals will use a significant number of these multiple sources of news and information, patterns of behaviour that will result in a large number of highly idiosyncratic personal agendas. At present, there is little evidence to sustain these assumptions.

Most of the news sites on the Internet are subsidiaries of traditional media, the online versions of newspapers, magazines and cable TV news channels. In this setting, it already has been noted that the popular buzzword synergy means amortizing the costs and increasing the profits of news by distributing the same basic content through numerous channels.

It also is the case that, currently, the audiences for all Internet sites are very small. In short, the redundancy in the media agenda to which most of the public is exposed is likely to continue for at least the near future.

An additional major constraint on exposure to the agendas of multiple Web sites is time and effort. Few people have the time or wish to expend the effort to explore this virtual library in any depth except under extraordinary circumstances.

Despite the plethora of sites that could be accessed, there already are suggestions of the existence of a news and information oligopoly in which a small number of sites command the largest proportion of the Internet users. Even when software allows members of the public to specify their categories of interest in advance, most people also want to know about the day's most important events regardless of the category in which they fall.

Under these circumstances, editors will continue to edit—that is select and summarize from the vast daily array of news. The fundamental nature of the front pages of newspapers and the opening segments of TV newscasts as a showcase for the day's most important events is likely to remain largely the same.

There still will be a relatively homogenous media agenda, at least until someone invents a new kind of news that eclipses the traditional news audience. If that happens, it will be the result of journalistic creativity, not technology, and it will shift the agenda-setting influence of the news media to a new source.

New technologies offer vast new opportunities. But technology is only a means of distribution, not a substitution for content that citizens find compelling in their personal and civic lives. Success in the new millennium will be measured by the quality of journalists' daily response to the question, "Why do we do journalism?"

For 60 years, the prevailing model of public affairs journalism in the United States has been one in which reporters and editors "cover" people and events that they deem to be important or newsworthy. They write about those people and events with the aim of informing citizens about public matters.

The flow is from source through journalist to citizen. Reporters and editors assume the posture of neutral observers, detached conveyors of information. Sometimes because of the complexity of events, they become analysts and interpreters, but only out of the necessity of helping people understand, not out of any admitted desire to affect the flow of events. The goal is to present information in a "journalistically objective" way—that is, fairly, honestly and accurately, with proper balance—and let citizens make of it what they will, do with it what they will, or ignore it altogether.

Limiting the role to neutral observer and conduit is both compelling and convenient. It allows journalists to focus on the singular task of transmitting information and absolves them of any other responsibility. The simple, straight-line model is based on several assumptions:

- Those citizens are, or at least should be, intensely interested in being well-informed about public affairs and thus are eager receptors of what journalists consider important.
- That "truth" put to the test in fair contest will always prevail over "untruth."
- That new information has intrinsic, utilitarian value simply because it is new.
- Those governments and other institutions are inevitably the "actors" and citizens the "acted on" and therefore the journalistic conduit need only be one-way in design.
- That "giving people what they need" and "giving people what they want" are distinct functions, and the former is far more important and valuable than the latter, which is somehow seen as fundamentally threatening to journalism's foundations.
- That the public sphere, the private sphere and the journalistic sphere are necessarily separate, like atoms held in eternal stasis by immutable natural forces and connected only by the flow of information.

These assumptions, each of which is arguable in today's world, form the basis for journalistic reliance on the model of detached observer and transmitter of information from source to citizen.

That efficient though simplistic model has ceased to well

serve either public life or journalism, and a more sophisticated model is needed. The new model challenges the dynamics of the old one and involves two fundamental shifts: repositioning journalists and repositioning citizens, that is, challenging the stastis model of the three spheres. "Positioning" in this usage is not a mechanical event; it is a conceptual one. It is the picture in the journalist's mind of the relationship among citizens, journalism and public life; conceiving of those spheres not as in stastis but as a dynamic.

Nothing in this model suggests that journalists abandon what is commonly called journalistic objectivity, that is to say, the imperative to be fair, honest, accurate, and clear-eyed about facts. It does suggest that journalists move away from the idea of detachment, that is, the mistaken notion that journalists are and necessarily must be separate from the consequences of their decisions.

While the terms *objectivity* and *detachment* are often used interchangeably and sometimes in the same sentence, as in "detachment and objectivity are fundamental to good journalism," our model makes a distinction between the two. That distinction is best illustrated this way. Jonas Salk discovered a vaccine for polio.

As a professional scientist, he had to be objective about the facts of his research, if for no other reason than those scientific protocols require that other scientists be able to replicate his results.

But he was not detached. He did not enter the lab willy-nilly, wondering what he might find. He had a purpose: finding a cure for a dread disease. And he cared very much whether or not he discovered it.

Another way of thinking about the difference between objectivity and detachment is this. You want your doctor or lawyer to be objective. That is, you want her or him to be clear-eyed and clear-minded about the facts of your case, to be truthful with you about it, to be fair in the way your case is treated. But you do not want him to be detached. You want her to care very much about a successful resolution of your situation.

Likewise with professional journalists, it is both possible and desirable to be objective without being detached. Objectivity reflects intellectual and professional honesty; detachment reflects a lack of concern.

Moving away from DE-tachment does not mean moving to full AT-tachment; for instance, caring about whether a problem is solved does not mean dictating how it is resolved. Detachment-attachment do not lie on separate sides of a single, fine, bright line; they constitute a continuum. Imagine two vertical lines, one to the left of this page, the other to the right.

The one on the left represents the pole of total detachment that positions journalists at a far remove from the events they cover, free from all consequences of their decisions, able to say, "We just tell the news and have no responsibility for anything other than doing that fully and honestly."

The other line represents total attachment, which positions journalists as fully engaged in the events they cover. Just as full engagement by journalists is obviously unacceptable, so is the other position. Journalists in today's world necessarily must operate somewhere in that middle ground between the poles, for reasons that have to do with the preservation of both the profession and democracy.

The paraphrase from John Dewey at the opening of this chapter reflects a concern about the usefulness of the profession of journalism. Dewey's original comment was about his profession, philosophy.

As a pragmatist, Dewey was interested in having the work of philosophy resonate in society in a useful and important way. It cannot be influential if the central concern of philosophers is insular—the problems of philosophy. What is necessary is to address, among other things, the concerns of democracy and its people, Dewey felt.

Traditional journalism can sometimes slip into insularity, in part because journalists fail to distinguish between objectivity and detachment. Defining and operating within that middle ground between dangerous total detachment and equally dangerous total attachment is what the balance of this book is about.

Only a limited number of journalists are available to monitor daily life. Even if there were an infinite supply of journalists, the capacity of the various news media could not accommodate all their reports. This is true even though with Web sites and all the other new technologies, there is far more capacity than at any time in the past.

Even this enlarged capacity poses a problem for the public, whose available time, range of interests, and span of attention are limited. Of necessity, the reported and received news is a tiny sample of all the daily happenings in the world.

More important, the news is a highly idiosyncratic sample of each day's events and situations. A grab bag of professional routines and traditions largely inherited from the past define how journalists sample the world around them—what they pay close attention to and what they ignore as they prepare their news report for the public.

More than 75 years ago, Walter Lippmann talked about the beat system and its dominant underlying rationale that news is not a mirror of social conditions but the report of an aspect that has obtruded itself. Good sources for information about situations in which daily life departs from its normal, mundane channels include the police station, fire department and court house.

The contemporary expression, "If it bleeds it leads, " is a culmination of this perspective about news that results in some local television news relying on a heavy diet of stories about accidents, crimes and fires. In less spectacular fashion, the beat system expanded to include a wide variety of officials at all levels of government—everything from the local zoning board to the White House—is a productive source of reports and statistics about non routine events that are grist for the journalistic mill.

Of course, not everything that occurs at these locations or that is reported by these routine sources of news is sampled by journalists, only those occurrences that pass muster in terms of the traditional litany of news values. The resulting sample of the day's happenings that is presented to the public is a highly peculiar one, a set of events mostly involving government officials in some role and heavily weighted toward conflict and bad news.

Nowhere is this latter aspect of the sample—conflict and bad news—more obvious than in the reporting of presidential campaigns over recent decades. Think about the total set of events that make up a presidential campaign each day or each week. Then compare the sample presented in the news. To use the language of mathematics and polling, it is not a representative sample.

In public opinion polls, which have become a staple of both the news media and political campaigns, achieving a representative sample of the public is the central goal. The core idea is to convey an accurate picture of the prevailing views among the public.

To achieve this representative sample of the public, pollsters utilize the technique of random sampling, a procedure in which at the outset of the selection of persons to be interviewed for the poll, every person in the relevant population has an equal opportunity to be selected.

Obviously, this kind of random sampling would not work for observing the occurrences of each day. The vast majority of these occurrences are of no interest to the general public. Who cares that Fred had a beer after work and talked sports with his friend, Bob; that 86 people renewed their drivers' licenses that day in Austin, Texas; or that Amtrak Train 27 arrived in Chicago five minutes ahead of schedule?

Actually, there are a few people who care about each of these things, but these people are not a very large proportion of the public. So, to use the technical language of sampling, journalists employ the technique of stratified sampling. That is, they divide the events of the day up into various categories or strata. To use Lippmann's term, a simple, first cut at sampling the day's events is to group them into two strata, the obtrusive and the unobtrusive.

The latter strata, the unobtrusive and routine, are deleted

from any further consideration, just as many political pollsters define persons not registered to vote out of their picture of political trends. One of the purposes of stratification is to focus attention on particular kinds of events or persons.

A major part of the problem with existing definitions of news, which fewer and fewer members of the public find relevant, is that the strata of daily occurrences defined as newsworthy are too narrowly focused. Put the other way, too many strata are defined out of the picture. First, consider the sampling of obtrusive events from a limited set of news beats. This yields a considerable amount of news. But many times the public—and investigative journalists—are interested in an overall situation, not just the obtrusive events that are the latest aspect of the larger situation.

The news about the rapid growth of Austin, Texas, is more than the latest zoning controversy or the month-long detours on the interstate highway. These are small bits in the larger mosaic of urban growth. On a broader scale, the information collected in the national census every 10 years provides a wealth of news stories that detail not just how many of us there are in the United States, in each state, and in each community, but what kinds of people live in what kinds of homes and how all this differs from 10 years earlier.

This is one example of news stories about who we are and how we live our lives. There are many others that present the full picture, not just the obtrusive events. Our stratified samples of life in the world around us need to encompass general situations as well as obtrusive events.

These stratified samples of events and situations also need to extend beyond the traditional journalistic strata of government, sports, finance and entertainment. Even in the unfamiliar language of sampling theory, the names of these strata sound familiar because these are the typical sections and topics of most daily newspapers.

Those are the strata routinely sampled each day by journalists. But there are many other strata that could be sampled to provide the public with news that it finds newsworthy and relevant.

Until very recently, religion was one of those strata defined out of the news picture. Some years ago, a public opinion survey asked Maryland residents in the area adjacent to Washington, D. C., who were the important community leaders in their area. This roster of leaders was compared with the sources quoted in the Maryland section of the *Washington Post.* You can guess the results. Clergy were high on the public's list of leaders, but seldom quoted in the newspaper. There were numerous other disparities. Many strata of activities that are relevant and interesting to the public are ignored by most news organizations.

STRATIFIED SAMPLES OF REALITY

Because the tradition of news beats and news values is so familiar and so entrenched in the thinking of journalists and because the concept of stratified sampling is so unfamiliar, we review the basic outlines of the idea of stratified sampling before discussing some creative ways to apply this idea to gathering the news. Pollsters divide people into groups—in other words, they stratify society into two or more groups—for two basic reasons.

One of the reasons already mentioned is that it makes no sense to interview certain kinds of people. In an election poll, only the opinions of persons eligible to vote are meaningful. In a survey of what people watch on cable TV or how people use the Internet, only the responses of those who actually subscribe to cable or who have access to a computer and use the Internet are meaningful. Stratification is used on many occasions to exclude some people and narrow the focus to others whose behaviour is more relevant.

At other times, the reason for stratification is to emphasize the focus on certain kinds of people, usually people characterized by some relatively rare trait or pattern of behaviour.

If you want an accurate assessment of the political views of American Indians in North Carolina or of persons who contribute money to political candidates, a stratified sample is needed to find enough of these people who are relatively rare in the population in order to make any accurate assessment of their views or behaviour.

In sum, we as journalists stratify to sharpen our focus, sometimes to exclude those in whom we are not interested so we can attend to the others, sometimes to ensure that we have an accurate picture of an important group.

Sampling people, even in strata that are defined by some very rare trait, is much simpler than that the task that faces journalists; sampling all the happenings in the world. There are a lot of people in the world, even in the United States or even in a single community. But it is a finite number. In contrast, the number of happenings in the world each day, even the number of happenings in a single community in a single day, is essentially infinite.

There are many, many ways to define and describe the happenings of the day. Identifying the relevant ones—defining and sampling the key strata of happenings—is the creative aspect of journalism.

Of course, journalists have been constructing stratified samples that included some of the happenings of the day for decades. News beats and the various sections of the newspaper are one way of stratifying the happenings of the day. Each is an outcropping of some aspect of life in the nation or community. But the traditional set of news beats and newspaper sections aren't the only—or even the best—way to find news that is meaningful to the public, even with some of the new wrinkles added in recent years such as religion, shopping malls and high-tech.

In the face of yawning disinterest among large segments of the public, especially among young adults, journalists need to understand two fundamental points. First, any plan of news coverage is, in the abstract and of necessity, a stratified sample of the day's happenings.

Most aspects of reality are ignored; a few are heavily sampled. Second, there are many ways to construct a stratified sample of reality, many interesting and useful ways to define the newsworthy strata of your community. Creative journalists will identify these strata in innovative ways to produce stories that an audience will consider as important news, something that involves more of their life than just passing the time.

There are no fixed or magic answers to the question of how to sample the day's happenings. But there are some very familiar starting points for thinking creatively about how to sample the important realities of everyday life and how to develop new kinds of content and insight to the public.

Probably near you at this moment is a highly detailed catalog of the activities in your city that occupy a substantial part of everyone's time every day—the yellow pages. All those classifications tell you how most people spend most of their week, either as the providers of those different kinds of goods and services or as the consumers of them.

To sharpen the focus on what is important to people in your city, compare the yellow pages in your town with those of other cities and towns. Social scientists have done that as a way of profiling the differences among communities. You also can compare the current yellow pages with editions from previous years to track key changes in the community.

In Austin, Texas, the yellow pages reveal that there is not a major bank in town today with the same name as any bank doing business here a decade ago.

What are the implications of this upheaval in the financial community? At the same time, the continuing growth of the metropolitan area is indexed by a significant increase in the number of retail outlets listed for the two major grocery chains and two major drugstores, a quick indicator of how much growth there has been and in which parts of town the growth has occurred.

For another slice of daily life in Austin (pun intended), the four largest pizza companies now have more than 60 locations spread across the metropolitan area. Even a yellow pages-based stratified sample can provide insight into a community's dynamics and suggest trends that can be pursued with more detailed reporting.

OTHER GUIDES TO IMPORTANT ACTIVITIES

There are many other readily available guides to the activities that engage major segments of people's lives every day and thus provide clues about their interests. These range from time-use studies on how people carve up each 24 hours into a variety of activities to the economic analyses of each state's gross domestic product, the total dollar value of the goods and services produced.

Of course, at the individual level there also are numerous analyses of how consumers spend their money. In the hands of creative journalists, these statistics become the indicators and the foundation for news stories that address key aspects of daily life, news stories that will resonate with readers and viewers because they describe and explain important parts of people's lives.

Another key indicator of events and situations that resonate with the public because they impact daily life are occupational surveys, both those indicating major shifts and those indicating stagnation. A computer company that didn't exist 20 years ago now employs 21,000 people in central Texas. Investigating and explaining the implications of that for life in that metropolitan area—daily life for everyone, not just those 21,000—can keep a newsroom full of journalists busy for years.

At the other end of the spectrum, there also are major implications for daily life in communities where the mix of occupations shows little change over time. This situation often indicates current or impending economic and civic stagnation.

And, of course, in both changing and unchanging situations, there is likely to be major news about the dominant occupational groups in the community, whether they are government workers, low-level service providers or high-profile professionals. What people do for a living tells you a lot about a community and can be important clues to news about the activities that engage people every day.

In a similar fashion, the way that land is used—and how that may have changed over the past decade—also tells a lot about a community and points the way to news that resonates with the public. Nearly half of the land in downtown Los Angeles is dedicated to automobiles in the form of streets and parking facilities and about half of the land in downtown Syracuse, N. Y., is tax exempt because it is the site of various governmental and religious facilities.

These facts are the opening gambit to major analyses about life in these cities. Every county has extensive property tax records, most urban areas have detailed zoning maps, and many areas have extensive urban development plans. These lead to news stories ranging from the fifth generation family farm about to become part of the new expressway to how much money people pay—and are likely to pay in the future—in property taxes.

CURIOSITY AND UNDERSTANDING

If telephone books, compilations of economic statistics, and zoning maps seem mundane, it is because they are. These are the detailed maps of everyday life in the community, the state, and the nation, much of which is mundane and ordinary. But there are leads to many fascinating individual stories in these sources, and in the aggregate they trace the trends that impact people's lives in very significant ways every day.

These trends are the stuff of compelling news stories that resonate with readers and viewers and engage their close attention. To characterize these sources and many similar ones as unproductive lodes of journalistic ore is to commit two fallacies.

The first fallacy, which already has been discussed, is to miss the opportunity to broaden the sampling of events and situations in the local community and to retreat into narrow, shopworn definitions of news that engage fewer and fewer members of the public each year. The second fallacy is to miss the critical distinction between curiosity and understanding. Both are innate, embedded psychological characteristics.

Most people are curious, and most people seek to

understand significant segments of the world around them. Last year, the short three-block-long street that loops into our immediate neighborhood from the main thoroughfare suddenly filled with fire trucks and police cars, lights flashing and sirens blaring. About as many neighbors turned out on the street that evening as turn out for the annual neighborhood picnic. People were very curious about what emergency might account for the sudden appearance of all these vehicles.

The explanation—a high intensity lamp had overturned and set a rug on fire in the living room of a neighbor's home—satisfied their curiosity. The crowd quickly melted away, and the incident was largely forgotten.

Do a simple experiment. Park a police car, or some other emergency vehicle with flashing lights on top, in front of some commercial establishment. A crowd is likely to quickly gather. People are curious. There are many journalistic examples, of course, and the most famous of recent times may be the OJ. Simpson "chase" in Los Angeles in which TV news helicopters followed O. J. and his friend for miles as they drove along the freeways.

In subsequent weeks, both television and newspapers continued to feed this curiosity with dozens and dozens of news reports. People are curious and these kinds of news reports do draw an audience. But in the long run, do people really care? People slow down to stare at automobile accidents along the highway.

They are curious, but this is not an endorsement for more automobile accidents or more coverage of fender benders. People are curious about many things, but most of these are not things that they really desire to understand. Why? Because these things have little or no bearing on their personal lives.

For a brief time, people were curious about Monica Lewinsky. Her misadventures had all the elements of superlative gossip. But most people quickly grasped the essentials, including the fact that this sex scandal had little or nothing to do with President Clinton's governance of our nation. The press' persistent salacious framing of the scandal guaranteed both its short-term appeal to curiosity and the lack of any long-term link with the need to understand the political environment.

Many topics can briefly arouse people's curiosity, but individuals are highly selective about the topics that they seek to understand. This desire to understand significant aspects of the surrounding environment is innate within humans—and is quite distinct from mere curiosity. But unless the content of the news media satisfies this basic need for orientation, these audiences will continue to shrink.

The news media are frequently described as people's windows on the world. But to what extent does the view through this window provide personally relevant surveillance of the world around us? This is a key ethical question and organizing principle for journalists' techniques of sampling the news.

Beyond this question about the topics that the news media offer for public attention and scrutiny, there is the critical follow-up question of how well the public understands these topics. Recall that attention and comprehension are the two aspects of the communication process involved in the agenda-setting role of the news media. In this chapter, we have talked about focusing journalists' attention on topics that the public finds relevant. Extending this discussion to comprehension, we talk about framing news stories in ways that engage and inform citizens.

Chapter 11

Positioning as Journalists

The purpose of democracy is to answer the question, "What shall we do?" In a representative democracy such as that in the United States, an important subsidiary question is "Who should decide what we shall do?" Thoughtful people can disagree about the role the average citizen can or should play in answering those core questions. Walter Lippmann insisted that the average citizen was capable of playing only an oversight role: voting representatives in or out on the basis of self-interest and the level of personal comfort he or she felt. John Dewey argued that the average citizen could be and needed to be much more directly engaged in instructing those representatives.

Michael Schudson and Robert Putnam extended the discussion in relation to today's society. One need not decide whose ideas are closer to reality to think about possible roles for citizens and journalists in public life. Where should journalists imagine themselves positioned in the democratic equation?

The traditional position, that of the detached observer, reflects Lippmann's views that democracy functions best when left to experts and elites; the modern world is far too complex for average citizens who are not capable of absorbing and putting to effective use the information that floods in on them. Therefore, the reporter's role is to expedite the conversation among decision makers and support the exchange of information about events.

Newspapers, the medium that dominated news gathering when Lippmann was expressing his philosophy, need relate to average citizens only on matters of procedure such as voting, and, as noted earlier, Lippmann's minimal expectation was that citizens would vote for the "ins" if they felt things were going pretty well and for the "outs" if they felt things were not going well.

Lippmann's philosophy, then, positions journalists as potentially among the elites and apart from citizens. It requires little of journalists in relation to average citizens except to act as an effective conduit to citizens on the limited occasions when that seem necessary and appropriate.

This positioning immediately causes problems, as is readily seen in the disconnect between journalists and average citizens. Detached, elite observers quickly lose touch with the people they seek to serve and are seen by those people as part of "them" instead of "us." As a result, journalists have little regard for the citizens or confidence in their abilities, and citizens, in turn, view journalists with suspicion and invest little credibility in what they say.

Other positionings are possible, desirable and more useful to the ends of democracy. If journalists believe that citizens are capable of active participation in governing themselves beyond casting an occasional vote, then they must adopt a position that allows the voices of citizens to come through to them and through them into their work. Jay Rosen expressed this as "starting where citizens start."

The traditional view of the journalist as conduit between decision makers and from them to citizens is immediately changed when journalists start where citizens start. Now the journalist has additional conductive roles: from citizens to decision makers and from citizens to citizens. This positioning makes a broader democracy more likely but does not entirely solve the problem.

It is not possible for journalists to act merely as conduits, for there is far too much information to pass along. Therefore, journalists necessarily become selective in what they pass along, and it is in the act of selecting that the journalist's values and worldview are unavoidably applied. So positioning oneself as a journalist in a democracy that works requires an additional calculation: deciding what values or beliefs one will bring to the task of filtering information. We suggest four.

- Democracy works best when people are broadly engaged in it.
- Average citizens, given information and a way to discuss its implications, are in fact capable of reaching sound public judgment.
- Representative government does not mean that citizens surrender their authority to those they elect; they place them in office as instruments of the public's will. The fact that elected representatives can nevertheless, at least between elections, override the will of the public is an important safeguard against the potential tyranny of the majority.

EFFECTIVE LISTENING

At the heart of the disconnect between journalists and citizens is a learned disregard on the part of journalists for the opinions and desires of ordinary people. Much of our routine experience as journalists feeds that disregard. After all, traditional journalistic practice deals primarily with the people and institutions that need to be covered, that is, watched and written about: public officials, institutional leaders and experts in various fields.

Little time is left to hear from ordinary people whose views and desires at any rate are often wildly out of touch with "factual reality" as journalists understand it. Journalists interpret this as an information gap caused by ordinary people's ignorance or lack of interest when in fact the gap can also be the result of differing values, differing rates of information absorption and varying levels of interest.

When traditional journalism wants to get the views of the people, it almost always seeks them en masse, with surveys, or anecdotally, with random interviews. In both cases, the brief questions asked are answered off the top of the head, and the responses usually reflect under informed, knee-jerk opinion. Certainly they do not reflect judgments based in deliberation. Journalistic judgment about the value of ordinary citizens' opinions is also influenced by repeated tests of the public's level of information recall: Name your city council member. Who is the chief justice? Who was the second U. S. president? The results are almost always distressing and lead to the conclusion that ordinary people are hopelessly ignorant and certainly unworthy of much attention, if not downright dangerous.

Such experiences, however, can be misleading because those traditional reporting devices are shortcuts designed to turn around stories or get quotes in a hurry; that is, they reflect something *journalists* are trying to demonstrate rather than a true exploration of what's in peoples' minds and hearts. Discovering that requires conversation, including different ways of listening.

When journalistic interest in public opinion stops at that level, a great deal is missed that can inform journalistic practice. Not recognizing and doing something about that disconnect leads to errors in story framing, news judgment and overall focus that can make the journalistic product seem, to ordinary people, wildly out of touch with *their* factual reality.

People interpret this as a credibility gap caused by what they see as journalists' elitism or lack of interest in the real world as citizens see it. One way to begin to repair the mutual disconnect and play a more useful role in the democratic equation is to become better listeners and to cultivate the habits of what can be called public listening.

The pressures of daily journalism, the 24-hour nature of news and most journalists' instincts invite, perhaps demand, a particular way of listening to the world: Our ears are open for stories, for good quotes, for conflict, for the unusual.

This necessarily means that the usual, the routine, the mundane interests and concerns of most people are neither sought nor heard and being unheard, do not become part of the calculation when decisions about news and story content and framing are made.

The result is a fatal disconnect; a mutual dissonance that makes the journalistic product less useful than it could be. Cultivating the habits of public listening requires deliberate effort, either organized or informal, either as a staff or as individuals.

ONE FORMAL PROCESS

Beginning in 1995, The Pew Centre for Civic Journalism and The Harwood Group experimented with methods of public listening involving the staff of *The Wichita Eagle*. The result was a model that offers both a way of organized listening and a way to know more about how issues move within a given community. The results were published in a booklet called *Tapping Civic Life: How To Report First, and Best, What's Happening In Your Community*.

Out of the experiment, Richard C. Harwood and his staff developed two key concepts: layers of civic life and types of community leaders. The researchers identified five layers of civic life where very different kinds of civic conversation occur: official, quasi-official, third places, incidental and private. Each has its own unique qualities and each offers unique challenges and opportunities for journalists, particularly third places and incidental places.

Official spaces include such things as city council meetings where the formal business of politics and civic life occur. These are familiar and comfortable to most journalists, less well-known and comfortable for citizens.

Quasi-official spaces are such things as neighborhood associations, civic groups, and nonprofit, grassroots organizations in which meetings are held, leaders designated and agendas are prepared. Both journalists and citizens move fairly easily in those spaces.

Third places is the name given to public gathering places, rooted in daily life, where people choose to spend their free time: barbershops, churches, coffee shops, bookstores, recreation centers. These places are not expressly political, but conversation about challenges, concerns and ideas is common and informal.

The *incidental* layer of civic life results from random, everyday encounters among friends and acquaintances in which gossip, chitchat, storytelling and idea exchanges occur on sidewalks, front porches, in the school parking lot, at the soccer game. It is "the swamp" of public life. *Private* spaces are inside the home where conversation is limited to those who live there.

As the objective of public listening is to hear real conversations not affected by the trappings of formality, the third place and incidental conversations are of the most interest and potential use for journalists. They are also the most difficult to access. The primary difficulty, but one that can be overcome, is that a journalist who goes into those places as a journalist immediately changes them. Going into those places in search of stories or quotes simply frustrates both the participants and the journalist and changes the nature of the conversations.

The Wichita, Kan., experiment involved reporters identifying third places in various parts of the city and going into them as committed observers interested in finding out how the people and places work and why people talk and believe as they do (as opposed to going in search of stories.)

Succeeding at that obviously requires both time and good will, but the results can be important: a fuller, more intimate knowledge of the community and its people; a common perspective on events to balance the official perspective that most reportorial practice provides; insights into issues and concerns before they reach the official layer; and, importantly, a perception on the part of citizens that reporters and their institutions are honestly interested in them.

Reaping these benefits can require some trade-offs on the reporter's part. The notebook stays in the pocket and the camera is left at the office: The reporter is there to learn and understand, not to grab a quick story or a quote. Sometimes, particularly in the early stages of developing the rapport, reaping the long-term benefit means passing over a potential story in favour of learning things much more valuable. Good reporters do that with their normal, official sources, sometimes deciding that a continuing relationship built on mutual trust is more important over time than ripping off a small story.

Sometimes the reporter needs to become part of the conversation rather than merely acting as an observer to encourage and stimulate the conversation (without directing it) and to build trust and a human connection with the people there. Such participation does not violate the journalistic principle of not becoming a part of the story because reporters are not there to get a story.

Reporters are there to learn about civic life in their community and use that to better inform their work. They are there to gain knowledge and insight, not information.

Another important advantage of moving in those third and incidental places is that the reporter learns who the leaders are in that segment of the community: the thought leaders who stimulate conversation and know what is going on. Those people, outside of those places, can be cultivated as sources of information, insights and ideas.

Harwood's framework helps to identify different types of leaders, including two types—catalysts and connectors—who, unlike elected leaders and civic leaders, are not usually known to reporters yet who play important roles in community life. The publication *Tapping Civic Life* contains rich detail about how to take advantage of the process and turn it into better journalism.

CIVIC MAPPING AND THE SWAMP

Some newspapers and broadcast outlets, with help from the Pew Centre and the Harwood Group, have taken the listening process a step further by experimenting in what is called "civic mapping."

The origins of the concept lie in remarks made in 1993 by David Mathews, president of the Kettering Foundation of Dayton, Ohio. He compared the most fundamental and essential processes of civic life to the swamps of his native South.

The swamps, he said, were viewed for decades as places of little value, a region of snakes and 'gators, strange noises, mosquitos, and bad smells. When waterside property became scarce, it occurred to some people to fill in the swamps and build condominiums, shopping centers and housing developments, superimposing their notion of usefulness on what they felt were a useless, smelly mess.

Of course, the inevitable happened. The fish in the bays began to disappear, the shrimp became scarce and the water turned foul. A fundamental and microbiologically crucial process that humans could not see and would not have found very attractive had been going on in the swamp, and we had interfered with it. We began to learn the lessons of ecology.

Mathews drew the comparison with the cultural ecology of civic life that has a swamp of its own, a fundamental place where public issues first arise and brew in a conversational stewpot of opinion, rumor, fact and conjecture.

It exists out of sight of journalists who are either ignorant of its importance or fastidious about its messiness and therefore avoid that cultural swamp. Instead, we as journalists focus coverage of public affairs on formal, safe, visible governmental and civic structures and easy-to-reach experts, superimposing our notions of public life on the reality of the swamp.

This avoidance of or ignorance about the swamp creates two dangers for journalists: We don't really know what is going on, why issues are arising and how they move, and that lack of understanding leads us to reflect, in our reporting, a process of civic life that simply does not ring true with the people in the swamp.

And it creates a danger for the cultural swamp itself, as, like the developers of the natural swamp, we run the risk, through our ignoring it or our lack of interest, of damaging the process itself and losing its benefits.

The Harwood idea is to make a map of that cultural swamp and help journalists learn how to operate within it without, as the developers did with Mathews' biological swamp, destroying it.

Rebecca Allen, an editor at *The Orange County Register*, helped lead about 100 members of that California newspaper's staff through the learning process in 1998 to 1999. The process was not an easy one and required commitment, she said, but immediately began to pay off because, "I began to see stories get better." Here's how she characterized her newspaper's venture into the swamp.

When I was first introduced to the concepts of civic mapping, I was very put off by what seemed like a lot of empty jargon to me. It felt as if I was in a blizzard *of connectors, catalysts, essences and frames.* But I learned as we studied the concepts that they can be very helpful for journalists. I came to this realization when I started seeing stories get better.

For example, the idea of *connectors* (people who connect and spread ideas and norms among various organizations or groups) in the community and *cata*lysts (unofficial experts who spark change) is useful.

For years we talked about officials and "real people" but reporters were reluctant to quote anyone without a title. Now it seems very clear that there are many people with vast amounts of knowledge and expertise on their neighborhoods or on an issue who should be in stories to help the reader understand and work through the issues.

AN INFORMAL PROCESS

Listening differently need not involve a formal process, although both the learning curve and results are accelerated when the formal commitment is made. The key to better listening in either environment is, again, one of positioning on the part of the reporter.

Traditional journalistic training, the dogma of the profession, insists that we as journalists act at all times as detached observers, as recorders of a passing scene. When we listen only from that position, we miss a great deal. Having a useful conversation aimed at discovery rather than reporting a specific story requires that we participate also as a citizen. The important content of such a conversation is often not in the questions we ask and the responses received so much as it is in the give-and-take, the sharing of thoughts and ideas.

Absent an organized process that involves many members of a staff, individuals can develop their own routines for listening in a different way. It may be as simple as deciding that you as a journalist will engage two or three people a week in a conversation aimed not at "getting news" but at gathering understanding.

Initiating such conversations requires that the person being engaged believes that you value his or her words for their own sake and not as ammunition for some journalistic act.

"I want to understand about. ..."

"Tell me why you feel as you do about. ..."

"Have you always felt that way, and if not, what changed your mind?"

"If you need something done in your neighborhood, who do you call? And who would he or she then call?"

"What things are you most concerned about?"

"What concerns you about that?"

"What are the arguments for the other side of the question?"

These are the kinds of questions that can lead to understanding. All of the foregoing—the four values, the tools of positioning and public listening, understanding public judgment—will be essential as journalism seeks to define a more useful role for itself in the complex, relentlessly changing environment of 21st century democratic life. They are neither, however, a quick fix for public malaise nor an easy device for propping up stories.

The objective of journalists positioning themselves to hear the public voice is twofold: first, to make their stories more authentic and thus more resonant with readers, who can then begin to see themselves as a public capable of action; and second, to communicate those voices to decision makers and leaders. Moving to this dual role completes the change of journalists from Lippmann's conduit between decision makers and from them to citizens by also making journalists conduits from citizens to decision makers and from citizens to other citizens.

Finding and communicating public voices does not guarantee, of course, that the voices will be immediately heard by those directly responsible for conducting the public's business. Often, in fact, rigidly structured government processes—public hearings, committee hearings, closed discussions by officials—fail to invite or recognize more than limited public participation. Worse, such processes do invite and recognize the voices of organized interests that have the time and resources to closely track government and political activities and influence them.

But, as readers will see, even the most arcane and distant processes (setting energy policy, for example) can be penetrated by public voices when media or academia or citizen groups combine relevant information with opportunity. The mechanism that organizes those voices is deliberation.

Their action came naturally to them because they shared at least one important value, in this case their mutual desire for a good relationship. That value and how they acted to maintain it differentiated what they did from other forms of talk: debate, discussion and dialogue. Without the shared value of a desire for the relationship, they might well have merely discussed or debated their choices.

The difference is important to our understanding as journalists of the various kinds of public talk that goes into our politics. The words for four common kinds of talk—debate, discussion, dialogue and deliberation—are often, and improperly, used interchangeably.

Specialists in public talk recognize distinct differences in both the tone and content of the four and understand that they often have different objectives. Specialists do not always agree, however, on the particulars of some distinctions, so for our purposes, we define the modes of talk (and, in the case of deliberation, thought) this way.

Discussion is a conversation among two or more people in which ideas are exchanged. It may or may not involve disagreement and thus can be the simplest kind of talk beyond casual conversation.

Debate is a discussion aimed at persuading others to your point of view; the objective of debate is to win, to have your ideas prevail. It is characterized by some level of combativeness, challenging the arguments of others, defending your assumptions as truths and demonstrating the falsity of others' assumptions.

It thus has many of the qualities of a competition and, in politics, is often seen as a useful way of winning votes for a candidate or a policy. Debate is an effective way of testing ideas in the caldron of competitiveness, but it is not useful as a way of resolving things because its purpose is just the opposite—to turn away opposition, to prevail rather than to embrace another's ideas.

Dialogue is a word that has suffered through many abuses in recent years, but is gradually finding an understood and respected place. In contrast to debate, it is characterized by collaboration in thought and objective, listening to understand the arguments of others, expressing your assumptions so that they may be tested and reevaluated, and seeking to grasp the strengths of others' assumptions. The objective of dialogue is to reach an understanding and, perhaps, define a course of action.

Even failing that, it at least preserves the possibility of future agreement. Daniel Yankelovich, in *"The Magic of Dialogue"* identified three distinctive and essential attributes of dialogue. If any of these are lacking, dialogue is not occurring: equality and the absence of coercive influences, listening with empathy, and bringing assumptions into the open.

Deliberation, for our purposes, is discussion and/or dialogue aimed at making choices among courses of action. Deliberation cannot occur without the involvement of dialogue and its attributes at some point in the conversation. David Mathews, whose Kettering Foundation and National

Issues Forum have spent decades studying and encouraging deliberation, defined it as:

A vehicle for making tough choices about basic purposes and directions.... To deliberate is not just to "talk about" problems. To deliberate means to weigh carefully both the consequences of various options for action and the views of others.... Without the discipline of serious deliberation, it is impossible for a body of people to articulate what they believe to be in the best interest of all—in the "public" interest.... Without deliberation, governments are left without direction and legitimacy....

So citizens struggle with how they can take action as individuals or as members of interested groups. Deliberation invariably requires a reference to deeply held principles, one's own and those of others. Unlike debate, deliberation is not aimed at changing anyone's mind. Its goal is that through talking about various approaches to a problem, hearing the deeply-held beliefs of others and considering the consequences of various courses of action, people will discover areas and ideas that they can agree about and see new possibilities for acting in at least complementary ways rather than competing ones.

The most common example of deliberation occurs in courtrooms. A jury of ordinary people is supplied, not coincidentally, with the same three elements that are required for democracy:

- Shared, relevant information: that is, facts that are found to be relevant through the process of give-and-take among the two sides and the judge.
- A forum for discussing the implications of those facts: the court process and the jury room.

And talk they did, for hours. As is typical and necessary in deliberation, knee-jerk opinions, fondly held assumptions (and misconceptions) and misinformation emerged first. These were quickly challenged, as, for instance, when a remark about welfare mothers was greeted with, "Yes, that's me," from the person in the next chair. Second thoughts began to emerge, as people actually faced the flesh-and-blood embodiments of the images and assumptions in their heads.

Facts were brought to bear on misinformation. A statement such as, "We could solve the problems of education if we wouldn't spend all that money on foreign aid" was faced with the budget reality that foreign aid is less than 2 per cent of federal spending, hardly enough to "fix" public education.

At the end of the convention, the delegates were given the same opinion survey they had responded to three months earlier. Had their discussions changed anything? Yes. The delegates' attitude, knowledge and opinions all changed at statistically significant levels on a number of key items. In describing their own roles, delegates were more likely to agree with the statement "I have worthy political opinions" after the convention than before.

Likewise, fewer agreed with the statements, "I have no say in government," and "politicians are out of touch." Not surprisingly, because they were given factual information, delegates' knowledge about the issues improved. Perhaps most significantly, their opinions on several parts of the three issues changed in statistically significant ways.

The National Issues Convention experiment thus demonstrates that deliberation is a tool for developing sounder, more thoughtful public judgments and that average citizens are capable of participating at a high level given the resources and the opportunity. The National Issues Convention did not, of course, reflect the real world of public life and politics. It was a limited demonstration of deliberation. The process we think about next moves citizen deliberation a step closer to that real world.

NATIONAL ISSUES FORUMS

The idea of people getting together to address the question, "What shall we do?" is rooted in the concept of democracy and has found various forms of expression over the centuries, from the early Greek republics to the town meetings of the colonial United States. Its forms reflect the practicalities of the times, but the objective remains constant: seeking common ground for resolving public issues.

In *"Politics for people,"* David Mathews described the development, over nearly two decades, of one broad-based process of deliberation: National Is sues Forums that began in 1981 when several civic and educational organizations began to coordinate their efforts under the National Issues Forums umbrella. They annually take on three policy questions—such as crime or drugs or health care.

The Kettering Foundation and Public Agenda, another nonpartisan research organization, prepare issues books providing relevant, shared information. As Mathews explained it:

When institutions began holding NIF discussions, they shared one central objective: they were decidedly not interested in just making improvements in what they were already doing—providing informative discussions. They wanted to develop a different type of public forum, one that would deal with issues from the public's perspective. That meant going behind technical, ideological, and legislative positions to find out how each issue affects what is most valuable to people. Issues are then re-framed into three or four options that capture these "values" or deeper motivations that are at play.

The issue books spell out the consequences of each alternative approach. Participants in the forums do the difficult work of deliberation—of moving toward a choice on each issue by weighing carefully the pros and cons of every option.

The premise is that the pulls and tugs of having to make choices together will cause people to learn more about policy issues and move from individual opinions toward more shared and reflective judgments.

The objectives of the forums are to help people become a public, to develop the skills needed for public politics, to speak in a public voice, and to contribute to defining the public's interests. Why is "creating a public voice" so important? Mathews explained it this way:

> Democratic governments need broad public support if they are to act consistently over the long term.... Governments can build common highways for us, but not common ground. And governments—even the most powerful—cannot provide the popular will needed for effective political action. Governments can command obedience, but they cannot create will. Finally, it is up to the public to transform private individuals into public citizens, people who are political actors. Citizens can create governments, but governments cannot create citizens. Only citizens can do that.

How do the ideas of representative government and centralized power square with the idea of citizen deliberation? How does the public voice, once organized, get heard through the wall of static thrown up around government and other institutions by special interests, hidden persuaders and money providers? Political scientist Benjamin R. Barber raised the question pointedly in an essay for *The Kettering Review.*

> Deliberation without power is a fraud, and will soon burn out those compelled to talk without being able to make relevant decisions. Just as power without deliberation is despotism, even when it wears the cloak of representative democracy. Too many Americans have given up on voting, in many cases out of frustration, anger, and resentment —a sense that it just doesn't make a difference.
>
> Many more will give up on deliberation if they see it's only talk, venting feelings and opinions that will never touch the conduct of public affairs.... Forums on public issues have always faced this dilemma: fashioning remarkably competent conversation around complex policy issues and getting citizens to reach intelligent consensus on some possible policy solutions, but without being able to move to the action stage.
>
> Yet the challenge of full-blown democratic deliberation is how to turn a conversation that brings us to the edge of the water into a process that allows us to get our feet wet in the deep pool of real power. Although it's true that public deliberation does not often or automatically directly push

the levers of policy, Barber's description of it as a zero-sum game is challenged by those deeply involved in encouraging deliberation and also by history.

Processes such as National Issues Forums help accumulate public judgment, and that public judgment is what, finally, informs, directs and legitimizes governments over the long term. That is surely a form of power, albeit latent. In isolation, deliberative forums can be frustrating and seem futile, as the connection between citizen deliberation and government-institutional power is hard to see in the short term to midterm.

But affecting government action is only one potential result of public deliberation. Another objective, perhaps a more important one, is that public deliberation can identify directions for actions that citizens can take, individually and in association with others, that do not depend on pushing the levers of government for their success. Think back to the earlier idea about journalists positioning themselves in the democratic equation.

If there is a public voice, how can it be heard by those in power and thus transformed into power unless journalists themselves hear it and aid in its transmission? Journalists with both ears directed only to government, journalists who see themselves as one-way conduits from officialdom to the public, cannot help. Journalists with one ear to the sound of public voices are positioned to play a broader role than mere conduit and to help bring alive the latent power of deliberation both on government and outside of it.

Bibliography

Curran, J. (2000) Mass media and democracy: a reappraisal. In J. Curran and M. Gurevitch (eds) Mass Media and Society. London: Edward Arnold.

Curran, J. and Gurevitch, M. (eds) (2001) Mass Media and Society. London: Edward Arnold.

Franklin, B. (2004) Newszak and News Media. London: Edward Arnold.

Franklin, B. (2002) Packaging Politics: Political Communications in Britain's Media Democracy. London: Edward Arnold.

Garnham, N. (2000) Contributions to a Political Economy of Mass Communication, Media, Culture and Society, 1(2): 123-46.

Garnham, N. (2002) The media and the public sphere. In P. Golding and G. Murdock (eds) Communicating Politics. Leicester: Leicester University Press: 37-54.

Hall, S., Critcher, C., Jefferson, T., Clarke, J., and Roberts, B. (eds) (2003) Policing the Crisis: Mugging, the State and Law and Order. London: Macmillan.

Hallin, D. (2000) Commercialism and professionalism in the American news media. In J. Curran and M. Gurevitch (eds) Mass Media and Society. London: Edward Arnold.

Knightley, P. (2001) The Falklands: how Britannia ruled the news. Columbia Journalism Review, September.

Mc Quail, D. (2002) Mass Communication Theory, 3rd edn. London: Sage.

Pilger, J. (2004) Interview with Hugo de Burgh, 29 June 2004.

Smith Anthony, Ethical Journalism. New York: Longman, 2000

Index

M

N

O

P

R

S

T

U

V